Italian Democracy

This textbook, from one of Italy's most eminent scholars, provides broad coverage and critique of Italian politics and society.

Providing the readers with the knowledge necessary to understand the working of the Italian political system, it also offers answers to some of the most important challenges facing the country – and other contemporary democracies – today, such as populism, anti-politics and corruption. Critical but underpinned by thorough data and analysis, it presents alternative views alongside the author's interpretation. Crucially, the book uses a comparative framework to explain Italy's transformation and evaluate its performance. Comparing the rules, institutions, parties and actors at work in the most important European political systems – France, Germany, Great Britain – with those in Italy, the Italian context is better understood and assessed in contrast.

This text will be essential reading for students and scholars of Italian politics and European politics, and more broadly for comparative politics and democracy.

Gianfranco Pasquino is Professor Emeritus of Political Science at the University of Bologna, Italy and Senior Adjunct Lecturer at SAIS-Europe.

Italian Democracy
How It Works

GIANFRANCO PASQUINO

Routledge
Taylor & Francis Group

LONDON AND NEW YORK

First published 2020
by Routledge
2 Park Square, Milton Park, Abingdon, Oxon OX14 4RN

and by Routledge
52 Vanderbilt Avenue, New York, NY 10017

Routledge is an imprint of the Taylor & Francis Group, an informa business

© 2020 Gianfranco Pasquino

British Library Cataloguing-in-Publication Data
A catalogue record for this book is available from the British Library

Library of Congress Cataloging-in-Publication Data
A catalog record has been requested for this book

ISBN: 978-1-138-30185-6 (hbk)
ISBN: 978-1-138-30186-3 (pbk)
ISBN: 978-0-203-73217-5 (ebk)

Typeset in Sabon
by Swales & Willis, Exeter, Devon, UK

Contents

Figures

Tables

Boxes

Acronyms and abbreviations

AN	Alleanza Nazionale / National Alliance
ANPI	Associazione Nazionale Partigiani d'Italia / National Association of Italian Partisans
CCD	Centro Cristiano Democratico / Christian Democratic Centre
CGIL	Confederazione Generale Italiana del Lavoro / Italian General Confederation of Labour
CISL	Confederazione Italiana Sindacati del Lavoro / Italian Confederation of Workers' Trade Unions
CNA	Confederazione Nazionale dell'Artigianato / National Confederation for the Craft Sector
DC	Democrazia Cristiana / Christian Democratic Party
DS	Destra Storica / Historical Right
Ecofin	Economic and Financial Affairs Council
EU	European Union
FdI	Fratelli d'Italia / Brothers of Italy
FI	Forza Italia / Forward Italy
HDI	Human Development Index
ICTWSS	Institutional Characteristics of Trade Unions, Wage Setting, State Intervention and Social Pacts
IdV	Italia dei Valori / Italy of Values
Istat	Istituto Nazionale di Statistica / Italian National Institute of Statistics
LeU	Liberi e Uguali / Free and Equal
LN	Lega Nord / Northern League
M5S	Movimento 5 Stelle / Five Star Movement
MDP	Movimento Democratico e Progressista / Democratic and Progressive Movement
MEP	Member of the European Parliament
MPA	Movimento per le Autonomie/ Movement for the Autonomies
MSI	Movimento Sociale Italiano / Italian Social Movement

NCD	Nuovo Centrodestra / New Centre-Right
NcI	Noi con l'Italia / Us with Italy
PCI	Partito Comunista Italiano / Italian Communist Party
PD	Partito Democratico / Democratic Party
PDL	Il Popolo della Libertà / The People of Freedom
PDS	Partito Democratico della Sinistra / Democratic Party of the Left
PLI	Partito Liberale Italiano / Italian Liberal Party
PPI	Partito Popolare Italiano / Italian People's Party
PR	proportional representation
PRC	Partito della Rifondazione Comunista / Communist Refoundation Party
PRI	Partito Radicale Italiano / Italian Radical Party
PSDI	Partito Socialista Democratico Italiano / Italian Democratic Socialist Party
PSI	Partito Socialista Italiano / Italian Socialist Party
PSIUP	Partito Socialista Italiano di Unità Proletaria / Italian Socialist Party of Proletarian Unity
RC	Rivoluzione Civile / Civil Revolution
RIN	Rinnovamento Italiano / Italian Renewal
SC	Scelta Civica / Civic Choice
SEL	Sinistra Ecologia Libertà / Left Ecology Freedom
UdC	Unione di Centro / Union of the Centre
UDC	Unione dei Democratici Cristiani e Democratici di Centro / Union of Christian and Centre Democrats
UDEUR	Unione Democratici per l'Europa / Union of Democrats for Europe
UGL	Unione Generale del Lavoro / General Labour Union
UIL	Unione Italiana del Lavoro / Italian Labour Union

Preface

It is high time to declare, without any reservation, that when in 1861 he pronounced the famous sentence "Everything needs to change so that everything can stay the same" in Tomasi di Lampedusa's marvellous book *The Leopard*, Tancredi was wrong. Since then, Italy has undergone many significant changes, from a quasi-constitutional monarchy to Fascism, from a difficult democratic Republic to a troubled vacillating post-1994 Republic, and almost nothing has ever remained the same. On the contrary, one ought to recognize that in those same years it was Marquis Massimo D'Azeglio, a major figure of the Historic Right, who presciently pointed to the goal to be pursued: "Fatta l'Italia bisogna fare gli italiani" (We have made Italy, now we have to make Italians). A weak national identity has always been a problem, but a selfish, fragmented, corporatist civil society, never rising above its politics and always responsible for the selection of politicians, has proved to be Italy's perennial drawback.

I was fortunate enough to teach for almost thirty years a course on Contemporary Italian Politics at the Bologna Center of Johns Hopkins University. It was fun and instructive. More than a decade ago, precisely at a time when, once more, Italian politics was transforming itself, the course was suddenly suppressed. Less than knowledgeable comments, articles, blogs and even books on Italian politics have since proliferated, much to my dismay. It took me a while, but then I decided to put into writing what I have learned, what I know, what I think others should come to know. The good scholar has plenty to learn from Italian politics; the good Italian citizen has plenty to complain about. One note of caution: the Italian political system is neither a laboratory nor an anomaly. It is a parliamentary democracy that can be compared with many other parliamentary democracies – this is the best strategy to appreciate what is good (not much) and what is bad (a lot). In fact, dissatisfaction with the functioning of Italian democracy runs very high. My book aims at convincingly explaining why.

I do not want to draw a long list of perfunctory acknowledgements, but I must thank Marco Valbruzzi, a student of mine and a precious collaborator who has always helped me whenever necessary in a variety of ways, not least in finding and drawing the most appropriate tables and figures.

Because I firmly believe that exchanging ideas, receiving criticisms and interacting with all those who have curiosity with regard to the working of their democracy is a civic duty, over a long period of time I have carried out a very intense activity as a lecturer for a variety of political and cultural associations. Indeed, I want to thank the organizers, the activists, the audiences provided by several associations: the National Association of Italian Partisans, the many left-wing splinter groups and dissenting factions, quite a number of students' groups, the General Confederation of Italian Workers, the Association "Cultura e Sviluppo" of Alessandria. I thoroughly enjoyed all those encounters and, not surprisingly, I learned a lot. Hence, I am very grateful to the organizers of those meetings at the same time as I hope that "my political science" has been and will be of some use to them all.

There is no way to, and I have no desire to, hide my profound dissatisfaction with how the Italian political system works and the Italian authorities, politicians, judges, bureaucrats and journalists operate. I am well aware than in the past and even now there are many Italians who abide and work by the rules, who give generously of their time and their energies to construct the conditions for a better politics and a better life. I hope they will eventually succeed. This book is dedicated to them.

Gianfranco Pasquino
Bologna, 1 July 2019

A classic parliamentary Republic

1

Since 1948, the Constitution, institutions and electoral rules have established Italy as a parliamentary Republic. This chapter explains why and how the Italian Constitution matters and briefly suggests how political parties have carved out a role for themselves. It focuses on the many misplaced and failed attempts to introduce modifications to the Constitution and stresses that knowledge of the rules of the political game in Italy is necessary to understand the functioning of the political system, its challenges and its transformations.

Comparing political systems

Stereotypes concerning Italian politics abound. They are frequently formulated by Italian scholars and commentators and then repeated by scholars and commentators outside Italy. The latter are often well-intentioned, but they deliberately underestimate the problems and disadvantages of the Italian political, social, economic and cultural system to some extent (Newell 2010; Emmott 2012). They seem unwilling to criticize the country they are studying and whose politics they are describing (a notable exception is Bufacchi and Burgess 1998). Often, they are embarrassed by certain events and politicians, and only then does their criticism become less muted and more focused. Most of the time, what appears in the media, as well as in scholarly articles, are the myths of Italian politics; of course, this does exist, but it should not be highlighted at the expense of less superficial explorations and better grounded assessments. Unfortunately, once the snowball of folklore and misleading comments becomes an avalanche, all efforts to provide nuanced interpretations are bound to be faced with very many, very high obstacles. Hence, such efforts fail to redress the situation. As a consequence, stereotypes (continue to) prevail and are responsible for the surprise experienced by those who are interested in Italian politics when some apparently unexpected event takes place.

In recent times, the three most unexpected events have occurred at the polls: not the 4 March 2018 elections (discussed in detail later in the chapter), but specifically: (i) the March 1994 electoral (and political) victory of Berlusconi's coalition; (ii) the remarkable number of votes won by the Five Star Movement in their first national appearance at the 24 February 2013 elections; and (iii) Prime Minister Renzi's disastrous defeat at his constitutional referendum held on 4 December 2016. Although there is an element of truth in the statement that all three events were also the products of a significant amount of Italian electoral volatility, none was totally unpredictable. They were all on the cards. All three deserve attention because they substantially changed the course of Italian politics. I do not go as far as to argue that they paved the way for the 2018 victory of the Five Star Movement and the League, but they certainly changed the "feelings" of many Italians about the politics they wanted and thought they needed.

However, the main contention of this book is that Italian politics can be satisfactorily interpreted and understood only through a comparative perspective: that is, by having some knowledge of similar political systems and, whenever possible, by utilizing comparative analyses (here I follow Giovanni Sartori's fundamental lesson that we should use comparative analysis, found in Sartori 1982). Only then will we be in a position to explain and evaluate the similarities and differences between Italy and other contemporary democracies in order convincingly to make sense of the functioning, problems and evolution of Italian politics and to predict changes and their consequences. To begin, therefore, I provide an introduction to the institutional context of the politics of Italy. First, I highlight the features that are absolutely indispensable for understanding and explaining any – and possibly all – political phenomena. I then draw some preliminary conclusions that will guide my analysis in the following chapters.

Parliament, government and the President of the Republic

Since 1948, Italy has been a parliamentary democracy (see Box 1.1). The defining feature of all parliamentary democracies is that their governments are "elected" by Parliament. I use here Walter Bagehot's

Box 1.1 Year of introduction of selected post-1945 West European Constitutions

Italy: 1948
Germany: 1949, revised in 1990
Austria: 1955
France: 1958 – Fifth Republic, revised in 2001 and 2002
Greece: 1975, several revisions
Portugal: 1976, some revisions in the 1980s
Spain: 1978

definition of the verb (Bagehot 2001), where elected means chosen or inaugurated. All parliamentary governments remain in office and continue to function as long as they enjoy the support (the confidence) of Parliament, but they can be replaced at any time by Parliament. In the post-1992 Italian political and institutional turmoil, these basic facts have become the subject of several damaging controversies and clashes. The members of the Constituent Assembly, elected in 1946 to draft the Constitution, had harboured almost no doubt. They decided that the Italian Parliament had to be – and had to remain – bicameral. The bicameral Parliament had to occupy a central role in the political system. The government had to enjoy an explicit vote of confidence from both houses, meaning that an absolute majority of parliamentarians would be asked to visibly commit themselves to supporting the formation and the functioning of the government. Those who drafted the Italian Constitution, being familiar with the instability not only of pre-Fascist Italian governments but of all parliamentary governments in general, approved a recommendation, which has since been quoted frequently, "to look for and to find mechanisms to stabilize the government" (this is discussed further in Chapter 5). That mechanism, the "constructive vote of no confidence", was brilliantly devised by the Germans, who drafted the 1949 Fundamental Law (*Grundgesetz*); together with other factors, this has been responsible for the extraordinarily long tenures of German Chancellors. Since 1949, there have been fewer German Chancellors than British Prime Ministers. The Christian Democrat Helmut Kohl holds the record: sixteen uninterrupted years in office from 1982 to 1998. Drafting their own Constitution, the Spanish promptly imported a slightly revised variant of the constructive vote of no confidence, and this has significantly contributed to the stability of their own Presidents of the government. The Socialist Felipe González remained in office from 1982 to 1996. However, as we will see, the problem of Italian Prime Ministers is less their short tenures than their allegedly limited political and institutional powers. It remains to be seen whether this is the consequence of the so-called "complex of the tyrant"[1] or of the type of Italian bicameralism or of the nature and structure of Italian parties.

The bicameral Parliament, House of Deputies and Senate were the product of long-term factors as well as an evaluation of the situation in 1946–48. Not only had the Italian political system featured a bicameral system after the 1861 formation of the unitary state; bicameralism had already existed in its predecessor, the Kingdom of Piedmont–Sardinia. Thus, a not insignificant tradition played a role. It is not possible to include here the entire discussion on bicameralism held in the Constituent Assembly. However: (i) the Communists were in favour of a unicameral Parliament, arguing that popular sovereignty is indivisible, and therefore it should not be allocated to two different chambers; (ii) those who desired a truly regional state pleaded the case for the Senate to become a chamber of territorial representation (but, in this regard, (too) little was achieved); and (iii) in the end, the case was won by those who argued that a second chamber might be capable of correcting mistakes made under pressure and in emergency situations and would improve the quality of legislation. Hence, Italian bicameralism was the result neither of a plot against the left nor of institutional mistakes. The fact that the government must win a vote of confidence in both chambers has not been a problem – except in a couple of cases – during the entire life of the Republic, as will be argued in Chapter 4, which closely analyses and assesses the political and institutional performance of Parliament. For better or worse, the Italian Republic has been and remains a parliamentary democracy.

Many statements to the contrary notwithstanding, no Second Italian Republic has made its appearance.[2] Only when the most fundamental rules of the game change, as well as the representative and governing institutions, can one legitimately state that a new Republic has come into being. The transition from traditional parliamentarism to semi-presidentialism in France was a qualitative change that allows – indeed obliges – scholars and politicians to distinguish between the Fourth (1946–58) and the Fifth Republic (1958–). Moreover, adopting the label "Second Republic" does not convey any useful information regarding either the political system or Italian democracy, nor does it improve our knowledge of their nature or functioning in any way. Also, the form of the Italian state – that is, a unitary state with some devolution of powers to the regions – though challenged, has not undergone any significant change. The model of government (analysed in Chapter 5), steeped in the very close relationships between the government and Parliament, has remained what was designed and agreed upon in the 1948 Constitution. In terms of rules, it is only the electoral law that has been changed drastically, and often – indeed, too frequently – revised. (I deal extensively with electoral laws in Chapter 2.) Nevertheless, the law drafted by Ettore Rosato, MP of the Democratic Party, that was utilized in the March 2018 elections is widely and rightly criticized and will probably be revised once more or jettisoned. Inevitably, the Rosato law has had an impact on the electoral campaign and its outcome, but it has not ushered in a new "regime".

From the very beginning of the Republic, Italian parties were the backbone of the political system. In a short period of time, they acquired and wielded so much power of all kinds – not only political, but also economic, social and cultural – that they gave birth to what was called *partitocrazia* ("partyocracy", which is discussed later; see especially Hine 1993). All those Italian parties that were dominant systemic actors for almost four decades either disappeared in the 1992–94 period or have been obliged to transform profoundly. New parties have made their appearance since then, but, on the whole, the party system remains quite unstructured (this is dealt with in Chapter 3). Again, although the 2018 party system is totally different from, say, the 1968 party system, the overall transformation cannot be considered sufficient to give birth to a new regime. More importantly, on the whole the functioning of parliamentary and governmental institutions and the institutional circuit have not been affected by any significant reform (see Chapters 4 and 6 on Parliament and the Presidency of the Republic).

The first momentous decision in post-war Italy, after its liberation from Fascism, was the choice to be made between the existing monarchy and a Republic. Through a popular referendum held on 2 June 1946 (this date is celebrated annually as the birth of the Republic), 24,946,878 Italians (89.09 per cent of those eligible to vote) went to the polls. Out of 23,437,143 valid votes, 12,718,641 (54.3 per cent) chose the Republic while 10,718,502 (45.7 per cent) preferred the monarchy.[3] The king, Umberto II, was sent into exile (to Cascais, Portugal). On the same day the voters elected a Constituent Assembly charged with writing a Constitution to replace the previous constitutional document, the *octroyé*, drawn up by the Savoyard King Charles Albert in 1848, which had survived under Fascism.

Drafting the Constitution

The newly born democratic Republic needed its own Constitution. In 1946, very few constitutional democratic charters existed that could be imitated, imported or adapted. Although much appreciated by a number of Italian Constitution makers, the United Kingdom could not serve as an example because of the absence of a written Constitution. The Italians could not learn or import much from the Low Countries or from the little known Nordic democracies, which, incidentally, were all monarchies. At the time, no other European country was a democracy. The model of the Presidential Republic, as exemplified by the USA, made a brief appearance in the constitutional debate, but the popular election of a President was considered too risky, and potentially divisive in a country that had to construct its democracy almost from scratch. Although quite a number of prominent Italian law scholars had studied in Germany during the Weimar Republic (1919–33), obviously that Constitution had been sunk by its tragic history.

Today, positive references are made to the German *Grundgesetz* (the Fundamental Law, so-called in order not to exclude the possibility of reunification with the Eastern Zone) of the Federal Republic of Germany. There is a lot to learn from and to imitate in the Constitution and institutions of contemporary Germany, but the Italian Constitution was approved on 27 December 1947, several months before the enactment in May 1949 of the German *Grundgesetz*. In the end, for many political and cultural reasons, only France could play the unfortunate role of a model. Indeed, the institutional architecture of the Italian Republic resembles very closely what was written in the Constitution of the Fourth French Republic. Interestingly, the French Constitution was challenged by General de Gaulle, who strongly contributed to the defeat in a referendum of the first version, but the second, approved version was always considered by many French authorities and citizens as being largely inadequate in its fundamental structures and it was never fully accepted. It lasted only twelve years: from 1946 to 1958. The Fifth French Republic, which reflects the political and constitutional thinking of de Gaulle and his collaborators, is sometimes mentioned by Italian reformers and, together with the double ballot majority electoral system, considered by some scholars and a few politicians to be the best possible solution to modernize the Italian parliamentary Republic.[4]

The Italian Constitution was the product of long, intense, knowledgeable debates among a significant number of participants who shared a key goal: to endow the new Italian Republic with a document containing truly democratic principles and viable institutions, not giving undue advantages or disadvantages to any specific party. Hence, the overall "spirit" and "vision" of the Constitution are informed by proportionality, not by a winner-takes-all principle (Powell 2000). Of course, several compromises had to be struck, but in the end the document received 458 favourable votes and 62 contrary votes. Only the right-wing and, later, the Neo-Fascists remained adamantly opposed to the 1948 Constitution. In France, the *discipline républicaine* is designed to exclude alliances and voting with the extreme right, and it is invoked in order to do so. In Italy, the so-called "constitutional arc" included all political parties with the exception of the Neo-Fascists. Nonetheless, from May 1947 onwards, the constitutional arc was never translated into governmental coalitions that included the Communists. Some Christian Democrats preferred to refer to the existence of an implicit agreement (*conventio ad excludendum*) to keep them out of government. The truth is that the Communists never won enough votes to make them indispensable for the formation of a government and that, during the Cold War, the Communists were neither accepted nor desired in any Western European government.

In the light of the final vote of approval on the Constitution, all the subsequent statements underlining the reservations held by one or other of the members of the Constituent Assembly should not be taken into serious consideration. Most of these statements are sectarian, aiming to delegitimize the existing Constitution and open the way not just to modifications but to a thorough redrafting of the Constitution, if not its subversion. Some of those who would like to see an entirely new Constitution often quote the famous sentence in a letter sent by Thomas Jefferson, not himself a member of the US Constituent Assembly, to James Madison, stating that "every generation should have the right to write its own Constitution". This was neither the opinion nor the desire of those drafting the Italian Constitution. On the contrary, almost all of them wanted to write a long-lasting document. As expressed by Piero Calamandrei, Professor of Constitutional Law at the University of Florence and one of the most influential members of the Assembly and of the leaders of the small progressive Partito d'Azione (Action Party), the Constitution was meant to be *far-sighted*.

Political cultures and parties

It is impossible to understand the contemporary debate without emphasizing two factors regarding the political cultures that converged in the writing of the Italian Constitution and the method utilized: first, the search for shared formulations; second, the bona fide active involvement of the Communists. The recent accusations by JPMorgan Chase & Co. that the Italian Constitution, written in 1946–47, is a "Socialist" Constitution similar to those of other southern European countries such as Greece, Portugal and Spain, all written in the mid-1970s, and, in fact, quite different (Greece quasi Gaullist; Portugal semi-presidential; Spain a parliamentary monarchy), must be rejected as simply incorrect and ridiculous. The political and institutional culture underpinning the Italian Constitution is a combination of democratic Catholicism, European non-Soviet socialism and classical liberalism. Article 3, emphasizing equality and participation, is a monument to the three major political cultures that significantly contributed to the drafting of the Constitution, and which were justly proud of the results.[5] Unfortunately, the Italian Constitution has never been effectively taught in schools. Moreover, the vicissitudes of the Cold War and the conservative positions taken by the majority of the governing Christian Democrats meant that the more progressive articles of the Italian Constitution were not implemented.

The lack of full implementation combined with the absence of adequate, widespread, deep knowledge of the importance and implications of the Constitution have made it impossible to formulate some variety of "constitutional patriotism". When the first proposals for constitutional changes made their appearance, they were rejected without any serious discussion for fear of undermining a fragile consensus. Then, at all subsequent points, the revisions suggested produced a cleavage between those who always defend the entire Constitution as it is and those who denounce its (alleged) overall obsolescence. For now, it may suffice to say that both the guardians of the Constitution and the self-styled reformers have not been – and are not – part of the solution, but are part of the problem (see later in the chapter for more on this; for an overview, see Bull and Pasquino 2009; Bull 2015).[6] And that problem is how to modernize the Constitution without distorting its fundamental features.

The political cultures that had contributed so significantly to the drafting of the Italian Constitution inevitably changed over time. But, by the mid-1990s, for a variety of reasons, they had all disappeared for good (Pasquino 2015b, 2018). Their disappearance decisively affected the second factor. As I have already hinted, only rarely underlined is the full participation of the Italian Communist Party in the activities of the Constituent Assembly. In spite of the fact that the Communists were ousted for good from the Italian government in May 1947, their full and active collaboration in the writing of the Constitution continued even after the start of the Cold War. The Italian Communists, who were never Stalinist (in contrast to the French Communist Party), were pursuing their domestic legitimization, more out of conviction than convenience, when they contributed to the document that would establish the rules of the democratic game. To a large extent, they succeeded in their overriding goal – so much so that in a variety of difficult moments during the long first phase of the Italian Republic, an appeal was made in the name of national solidarity to the parties included in the so-called "Constitutional arc": that is, those that had approved the Constitution. The Communists always showed themselves to be very proud of the role they had played and they have remained among the staunchest defenders of the Constitution.[7]

When looking at the Communists and their role in Italy, one finds several significant differences with other major European countries. From 1946 to 1989, Italy had both a strong Christian Democratic Party and a strong Communist Party. France had a strong Communist Party, but, technically, no Christian Democratic Party, although the Mouvement Républicain Populaire was imbued with a similar political culture and occupied much of the same political space. West Germany had a strong Christian Democratic Party, but no Communist Party (which was outlawed). Moreover, French Communists were fundamentally Stalinists, while the Italian ones could and did build on the thought and writings of a highly esteemed Italian revisionist Marxist theoretician, Antonio Gramsci, and, from the very beginning, they were committed to governing at the local level, accepted this challenge and fulfilled their role within the limits of the Constitution. Still, up to the very last moment they remained staunch supporters of the foreign policy of the Soviet Union and were identified as such by most Italian voters, 40 per cent of whom repeatedly declared that the PCI (Partito Comunista Italiano) was the party they would never vote for. Hence, the PCI collapsed together with the Berlin Wall in 1989. However, Italian Communists never ceased exhibiting *ante litteram* what in 1979 the German political philosopher Dolf Sternberger called "constitutional patriotism" (later popularized by Jürgen Habermas).

The Italian parliamentary Republic has often been criticized for a variety of good and bad reasons that I will explore and whose validity I will assess throughout the book. As for the Italian Constitution, it has continued to be a shared and generally appreciated framework within which all Italian political actors agree to play the game, to engage in competition, and to represent and govern the Italians (LaPalombara 1987). Little of what has been going on since 1992–94, and especially in the last decade or so, can be understood or explained by those who do not know the Constitution and the struggles surrounding its interpretation, implementation and attempted and failed transformations. Recounting this story is indispensable if one is to illuminate much of the dynamics of Italian politics. From the outset, it must be said that there have always been challenges to the Constitution. In the first ten years or so after its approval, the challenge concerned its implementation (*attuare la Costituzione*), because many of its innovations (namely, regional decentralization and the Constitutional Court) were resisted by the centrist parliamentary majority. Calamandrei denounced this practice, stigmatizing it as "filibustering by the majority".[8] In a second phase, when "partyocracy" had taken over, many political actions were essentially informal violations of the written rules of the Constitution: for instance, on how governments are supposed to come into being (see Chapter 3) and on the relations between government and Parliament. This was so much the case that, in order to define the new situation, the expression "material Constitution" was revived: that is, what is done in practice and is not contrary to the norms of the Constitution, if widely accepted or not openly challenged, is how the Constitution can live and breathe. (The term was originally coined by a famous professor of constitutional law, Costantino Mortati, a former member of the Constituent Assembly and elected as an independent by the Christian Democrats.)

Reforming the Constitution

In some instances, however, the so-called "material Constitution" was denounced for betraying the letter and, perhaps, the spirit of the parliamentary Republic. The catchword then became *tornare alla Costituzione* – go back to the Constitution and behave strictly according to its written articles and rules. When, at the end of the 1970s and in the early 1980s, it became clear that it was too late both to implement successfully some sections and articles of the Constitution and to revert to the correct practices, so long denied and subverted, several politicians and some prominent scholars (see, for instance, Amato 1980; Miglio 1983) launched a request for a reform of the Constitution (*riformare la Costituzione*). This is not the place to recount the long and conflict-ridden story, which has been told repeatedly.[9] Often, fantasy narratives (Bedock 2017 plus most of the Italian sources she quotes) have been produced and spin has proliferated. These versions are all part of the game. Nevertheless, two elements have to be underlined because of their relevance for the reform process. First, some events have taken place and some facts can easily be ascertained. Second, the constitutional reforms proposed by Matteo Renzi's government were explicitly built upon a reconsideration of the past, allegedly, but incorrectly, considered a past of failures that only his new government could overcome. A more precise analysis and a more subtle interpretation are indispensable in order fully to appreciate the proposals, the actual reforms, and their desired and/or unexpected consequences.

First of all, as Table 1.1 clearly shows, the past has witnessed several reforms, some minor, but others major and important (Pasquino 2015a). For instance, in 1993, a wave of referendums was called by a composite alliance of parliamentarians belonging to different parties

Table 1.1   Amendments to the Italian Constitution since 1948

Year	Article(s) amended	Object of the amendment	Final reading percentage approval
1963	56, 57, 60	Composition and length of term of the Chamber of Deputies and Senate	87.6
1963	57, 131	Constitution and institution of the Molise region	92.4
1967	135	Provisions on the Constitutional Court	95.4
1989	96, 134, 135	Crimes of ministers	80.3
1991	88	Dissolution of the houses of Parliament	99.8
1992	79	Amnesty and pardon	99.8
1993	68	Indemnity and immunity of members of Parliament	96.1
1999	121–123, 126	Direct election of the president of the region and regional statutory autonomy	90.1
1999	111	Fair trial principles	96.5
2000	48	Right to vote of Italian citizens living abroad	81.3
2001	56, 57	Number of Deputies and Senators representing Italian citizens abroad	89.2
2001	114–25, 127–30, 132	Powers of regions, provinces and municipalities	50.8
2003	51	Gender equality	97.7
2007	27	Abolition of the death penalty	97.9
2012	81	Introduction of the balanced budget in the Constitution	83.9

Source: Pasquino and Valbruzzi (2017).

and by a number of civil associations. Those referendums abolished three ministries – Agriculture, State Holdings, and Tourism and Cultural Activities – eliminated the controversial law on state financing of political parties, and imposed a reform of the existing electoral laws (see Chapter 2). In 2001, the centre-left completely redefined the relationship between the state and the regions, shifting more powers to regional governments in the hope of undermining the Northern League. Then, creating an unfortunate precedent, the centre-left collected the necessary signatures to hold a popular referendum that was meant to bestow additional, though entirely unnecessary,[10] legitimacy on its reform. It was a pyrrhic victory.

In 2005, Berlusconi's centre-right parliamentary majority proceeded with a major revision of the Italian Constitution. More than a third of the 138 articles were affected, with the aim of strengthening the government, giving it more power vis-à-vis Parliament and getting rid of bicameralism. The centre-right also reformed the 1993 electoral law (see Chapter 2) in a proportional direction. Berlusconi's constitutional reforms were defeated in a referendum (clearly to be defined as "oppositional") called by the centre-left in June 2006. What both the centre-left reforms of 2001 and Berlusconi's reforms in 2005 had in common was that they were fully partisan: that is, formulated and approved by a "governmental" majority against the wishes of the opposition, and fundamentally meant to obtain electoral advantages. Criticisms came especially from former left-wing Christian Democrats and, above all, from former Communists who objected to partisan procedures, claiming that constitutional reforms ought to be shared and approved by the largest possible majority, as had been the case for the Constitution as a whole. This position is certainly reasonable. Indeed, it is likely that the fathers of the Constituent Assembly would have recommended that changes of the Constitution be accepted by a majority larger than the governmental one. However, the Constitution makers' institutional wisdom had also contemplated the likelihood of reforms made by an absolute majority that could be checked and reversed by the majority of those going to the polls.[11]

Changing the Republic

The most ambitious attempt to reform the Italian Constitution – not so much for the significance of the revisions, but for their potential impact on both the functioning of the institutions and the distribution of political power – was probably made by Matteo Renzi, the then secretary of the Democratic Party, especially when he suddenly became Prime Minister on 24 February 2014. In fact, the reformist path had started one month earlier when Renzi decided to involve Berlusconi and his party in the reform process from the very beginning. This was in order to avoid two pitfalls: (i) partisan reforms; and (ii) reforms approved by the governmental majority only. Although I will frequently deal with the nature, content and quality of those reforms in the following chapters, one point should be made immediately. The overall thrust of the reforms was quite similar to what Berlusconi had attempted, and had done, in 2005. Hence, the ageing leader of the centre-right felt somewhat vindicated. Moreover, the electoral law drafted by Renzi and dubbed *Italicum* was to all intents and purposes just a revision of Berlusconi's 2005 electoral law, and therefore fully acceptable to the leader of Forza Italia. In the agreement between Renzi and Berlusconi, which was never made public, it was also decided that the choice of Giorgio Napolitano's successor as President of the Republic would be made jointly. When, at the end of January 2015, Renzi declared that the candidate of the Democratic Party was going to be Sergio Mattarella, Berlusconi felt betrayed (his candidate had been twice Prime Minister Giuliano Amato) and abruptly left the "reformist" table, never to return to it. However, some of the parliamentarians elected from the ranks of Forza Italia followed Berlusconi's right-hand man, the powerful Senator Denis Verdini, and went on casting their votes for the constitutional reforms whenever necessary. Although not fully committing himself to the referendum campaign against Renzi's reforms, Berlusconi announced his negative evaluation, which certainly influenced many centre-right voters.

At the outset of the reform process, Renzi had hurriedly promised that all the modifications would be submitted to the people, through an unnecessary constitutional referendum. Once the reforms had been approved by less than a two-thirds parliamentary majority, Renzi's parliamentarians and the Democratic Party's local leaders activated the procedure to call a referendum. The fragmented opposition followed suit. Renzi launched his electoral campaign immediately, the day after the final vote at the end of April 2016. Later, he and his Minister of Internal Affairs set the date of the vote at the last possible moment (4 December), hoping to recover some of the ground lost to their diversified, but combative, opponents. I will not dwell on the ominous forecast made by Confindustria (the General Confederation of Italian Industry), but its research department devised an algorithm that threateningly predicted major negative economic consequences if the opponents to the reforms won. *Il Sole 24 Ore* and LUISS – the daily business newspaper owned by Confindustria and Libera Università Internazionale degli Studi Sociali Guido Carli, the university it runs – duly followed suit. For some time, the foreign press – *The Financial Times*, *The Economist*, *The Wall Street Journal*, *The Neue Zürcher Zeitung* and *The New York Times* – whose sources all proved to be all highly opinionated, and a couple of rating agencies chose to follow the same line. The European Commission itself set out a bleak forecast. However, by the beginning of November 2016, almost all international economic operators had come to accept the possibility of the victory of the no vote and had already prepared themselves to face the consequences, the disruptive impact of which they had greatly exaggerated.

Accustomed to personalizing his politics and unabashedly convinced of his unique capability to win votes, Renzi started his campaign by stressing that the constitutional reforms were "his" reforms and went on to stress that the referendum was almost a plebiscite on his leadership and his person, so much so that he promised, or threatened, to resign from the office of Prime Minister and even to retire from politics altogether, hinting at much feared governmental and political instability if this were the case. The plebiscitary downturn was gently criticized ("perhaps, an excess of personalization of politics"[12]) even by Giorgio Napolitano, former President of the Republic and a staunch supporter of Renzi and his constitutional reforms. To no avail.

The thrust and content of the constitutional reforms formulated by Matteo Renzi and his collaborators, and initially supported by Silvio Berlusconi, will be covered in detail in the subsequent chapters on electoral law, Parliament, the government and the Presidency. Here, however, two points need to be noted and explained. First, most of Renzi's reforms were neither especially innovative nor, as I have already said, different from the reforms approved by Berlusconi's government in 2005 and rejected by the June 2006 constitutional referendum. Second, Renzi's reforms were a confused package that was not based on any conception of the type of constitutional system Italy should become nor on the model of government to be introduced in the Italian political system. Disjointed and inconsistent, Renzi's reforms would have destabilized the existing institutional equilibrium without creating a new one. The justly revered principle of checks and balances had simply disappeared from the horizon of the self-styled reformers. At this point, I will leave aside any other considerations.

The 4 December 2016 referendum was a turning point in Renzi's governmental career and in the fortunes of his Democratic Party, and it therefore deserves special attention. Following a very long and heated electoral campaign, turnout was unusually high for a referendum: 68.48 per cent. The rejection of the constitutional reforms was crystal-clear. The victory of the no vote was almost overwhelming: 19,420,271 votes (59.12 per cent) versus 13,431,842 (40.88 per cent). Nevertheless, since then, the supporters of the yes vote have incessantly resorted to criticizing their opponents for having kept Italy in the "swamp", derogatorily referring to the so-called First Republic, which, incidentally, had made Italy one of the eight most industrialized and advanced countries in the world – no minor achievement. The crux of the matter is that Renzi's reforms failed to deal with the major issues in a way entrusted by the Constituent Assembly to its successors: how to stabilize (not strengthen) the government; how to streamline the relationships between government and Parliament; and how to improve parliamentary representation. As long as Italian political parties had remained viable and effective organizations, those issues, though significant, had been confronted and solved time after time. The decline of parties also meant that some institutional improvements became absolutely necessary. The referendum vote must be interpreted as the negative answer given by almost 60 per cent of the Italian electorate to the question: "Do you think that the constitutional reforms proposed by the government will improve the functioning of the political system?" The Italian referendum had nothing in common with Brexit, nor should it be considered a populist reaction against a supposedly "liberal" government. If anything, the campaign run by the head of the government himself, Matteo Renzi, was populist (for an excellent overview, see Pritoni, Valbruzzi and Vignati 2017). Whether, in practice, some quite different and necessarily "systemic" constitutional reforms might create a better political system remains to be discussed.

Following what was also a crushing personal defeat, Renzi felt obliged immediately to resign from the office of Prime Minister, but he did not keep his word about abandoning politics altogether. On the contrary, he blatantly steered the course of the governmental crisis, suggesting to the President of the Republic, Sergio Mattarella, that his Minister of Foreign Affairs, Paolo Gentiloni, should replace him as Prime Minister. Since the Democratic Party enjoyed a sizable majority of its own in the House of Deputies, no potential Prime Minister would have been in a position to win a vote of confidence without the support of the Democratic Party. This was yet another instance in which the material Constitution was bound to prevail over the written, formal Constitution that grants the President of the Republic the power to "appoint" the President of the Council of Ministers.

Almost to prove that the existing Italian institutional framework could function swiftly and smoothly, the President of the Republic appointed the new Prime Minister. Quickly, Parliament duly voted its confidence in Gentiloni's government. And the "crisis" was over in less than a week (comparative data can be found in Verzichelli and Cotta 2000). Moreover, the new government, as I will emphasize in Chapter 3, the sixty-fourth in the history of the Republic, composed of the same ministers with only three new entrants, was formed in just one week, coming into existence on 12 December 2016.[13] Although for personal and political reasons Renzi hoped to go to the polls as soon as possible, institutionally the fact that Gentiloni's government was performing reasonably well – certainly on par with his predecessor's – meant that it could not be ousted at the whim of the secretary of the Democratic Party. Not a single one of the negative economic and political consequences resulting from the rejection of the constitutional reforms that had been threatened by their supporters materialized at the time. On the contrary, the Italian economy improved gradually, but constantly and significantly, through the whole of 2017. Growth continued until the fateful March 2018 elections.

The entire 2013–18 parliamentary term was marked by the role played by the Presidents of the Republic. First, Giorgio Napolitano, elected in 2006, was begged by almost all parliamentarians to serve an unprecedented second term. Then he dictated to the parliamentarians their primary task: constitutional and electoral reform. Finally, he "ratified" the outcome of the reform and, many believe, was influential in the choice of his successor, Sergio Mattarella, whose institutional power was satisfactorily tested in the quick solution to the December 2016 governmental crisis, and even more so following the March 2018 elections. In these events, one can see the forceful appearance within the constitutional framework of the Italian parliamentary Republic of a third important actor: the President of the Republic. Here, just a few sentences are needed to suggest that the role and the powers of the Presidency indicate that Italian parliamentary democracy revolves around three institutions: Parliament, the Presidency and the government. In fact, in no other European parliamentary democracy has the Presidency been in a position to affect and, in some circumstances, effectively to steer the course of national politics.

The role of the President of the Republic

Having solved the so-called "institutional question" through the 2 June 1946 referendum, the problem concerning what kind of head of state to create and which political and constitutional powers to entrust to him (or her) confronted the members of the Constituent Assembly. Once more, since practically all West European democracies of the time were monarchies, Italian Constitution makers were left with only two examples to look at: the US Presidential Republic and the Presidency of the Fourth French Republic, which was a traditional parliamentary Republic. Having rejected presidentialism, the choice was more than just ready-made; it was all but inevitable. Since 1948, Italy has had a President of the Republic elected by a joint session of its bicameral Parliament. It is unclear whether the people drafting the Constitution had a precise idea of what kind of presidential figure they were establishing. The best definition was offered in the early 1980s by a highly esteemed Professor of Constitutional Law, then President of the Constitutional Court, Livio Paladin (1988), who wrote of the ambiguity surrounding the powers of the President. With the passing of time and with the transformation of Italian parties and the party systems, the dynamics of Italian politics have led to the growing importance of presidential powers. Especially in the second phase of the Italian Republic, starting after the 1992 general elections, Italian Presidents have played a much more important role than that of Presidents in all the other European parliamentary democracies, for instance the German and Austrian Presidents (Grimaldi 2017).

I devote Chapter 6 to Italian Presidents, but here it is necessary to stress that the Presidency is an institution whose political and constitutional powers, though clearly stated in the Italian Constitution, have been significantly underestimated for a long time. The Presidency is a key institution that fully participates in the triangular relationship between "Parliament–Government–Presidency" (Pasquino 2015a). It is not just a matter of the President exercising his *moral suasion*, which, most of the time, depends on and derives from the prestige of the personality occupying the role and therefore cannot be defined with precision or circumscribed. The Presidency is endowed with autonomous powers whose impact on the functioning of the other institutions and of the political system in general (see Chapter 6) can be and has been remarkable. Here, in the context of describing the defining features of the Italian parliamentary Republic, I want just to highlight the fact that the President has the power to appoint five judges to the Constitutional Court.

The judge of the laws

The Constitutional Court is the most important institutional innovation contained in the 1948 Italian Constitution. Its establishment was opposed by the Communists because they argued that such an institution, endowed with the power to evaluate the constitutionality of the laws approved by Parliament, would expropriate the "sovereignty of the people" as represented by parliamentarians. For their part, because they feared that the court would interfere with laws approved by their government, the Christian Democrats postponed its inauguration until 1956. The Constitutional Court is made up of fifteen judges: five of them are appointed by the President of the Republic; five are elected by Parliament in a joint session of the House of Deputies and the Senate; and five are elected by magistrates. All of them must have a law degree. No Neo-Fascist has ever been appointed or elected to the court, and with good reason, since the Neo-Fascists have never accepted the Republican Constitution. The first Communist was elected in 1977. In order to give representation to all parliamentary parties and their political cultures, no matter how feeble and frail, individuals sponsored by Forza Italia, the Northern League and, finally, in 2015, even by the Five Star Movement have been elected or appointed to the Constitutional Court.

Increasingly, the Constitutional Court has acquired more visibility and more political power, without necessarily becoming "politicized": that is, without supporting any specific political view or political alignment – no mean achievement (see Pederzoli 2008). Its role and the impact of its decisions have grown because, on the one hand, Parliament has been obliged to legislate on several issues affecting the lives and rights of individuals: divorce, abortion, assisted reproduction, end of life and same-sex marriages, for example. Since 1970, the court has also decided on the admissibility of referendums, for instance those concerning electoral laws. On the other hand, since 1994, there has been a significant and deplorable decline in the quality of legislation that has meant that the court has had to become involved to provide for the necessary revisions. Despite a few critical voices, there is widespread agreement that the Italian Constitutional Court has played a progressive role by accompanying, ratifying and even encouraging the transformation of Italian society and politics in the direction of "opening spaces of freedom".

Two criticisms have been addressed to the Constitutional Court. One concerns the possibility for judges to pursue a new career after their nine-year non-renewable term at the court. Quite a few have been recruited by politics and have served as prominent parliamentarians and even ministers. Others have been appointed to chair important authorities (anti-trust, communication, privacy, etc.). The suspicion is that, once they are close to the end of their term, the judges may jockey to position themselves in such a way as to obtain coveted political appointments. The second criticism refers to the decision-making process of the court, where there is a total lack of transparency. Italian judges are not allowed to write either dissenting or concurring opinions on which new jurisprudence might be constructed. In an area that affects more specifically the game of politics, the Constitutional Court has revealed an uncertain approach and an unclear perspective when obliged to deal with the constitutionality of electoral laws. From their early judgment in 1991 to the most recent one in 2017, the Constitutional Court judges have trodden on difficult and shifting ground.[14] Some of their judgments have not provided clear criteria around which to formulate a constitutionally acceptable electoral law. On the whole, however – and especially, but not only, when asked to deal with the many conflicts pitting the regions against the state, the government and its ministers – the Constitutional Court has played a significant political role in creating, protecting and promoting the most satisfactory institutional equilibrium possible in a parliamentary democracy.

The identification of the elements that are essential to any understanding of the institutional and political configuration of the Italian parliamentary democracy would be incomplete without appropriate and considerable attention to both the political parties and the party systems. For a long time, the true backbone of the Italian parliamentary Republic (as well as of all the democratic regimes that have appeared so far) has been represented by the party system. From the very beginning of the Republic, for reasons that have never been fully understood nor explained,[15] Italian political parties proved to be strong, representative, entrenched and even capable of providing competent governmental personnel at all levels. This is, indeed, a point to be stressed, because otherwise it would be impossible to explain the transformation of Italy from a traditional, mostly rural country living off agricultural activities, plagued by a 40 per cent rate of illiteracy among its citizens, into a modern, largely urban country that has almost wiped out illiteracy over a twenty-year period, becoming one of the eight most industrialized nations in the world.[16] Weakened, personalized parties have become the ball and chain of the Italian political system.

A tentative assessment

By the early 1960s, Italy had become a decent parliamentary democracy in which, by all accounts, a lot of political and institutional power was in the hands of party leaders (the Communists included). Through the expansion and enlargement of the state sector of the economy and full control of the radio and television company RAI, Italian parties had created what amounted to a *partitocrazia* ("partyocracy"), to be kept clearly distinct from party government. For example, although Germany was – and still is – defined as a *Parteienstaat*, there the strength of the private sector in the economy and the robustness of civil society and its associations have prevented parties from extending their power from the political arena to the socio-economic and cultural ones.

The exhaustion of the political cultures of Italian parties, which is also due to the lack or impossibility of alternation between parties that has eliminated the need for internal debate, transformation or renewal of ideas, has been significantly responsible for the collapse of parties and the party system between 1992 and 1994. By then, however, too many of the political protagonists had become convinced that the Italian problem had its roots in the country's model of government. An intense, bitter and unilluminating confrontation regarding the reform of political institutions had started more than a decade before. Throughout this book, my contention will be that the Italian problem does not lie with the institutions, that the model of parliamentary government remains viable, and that the culprits behind the not so poor functioning of the political system are Italian parties and leaders, their inability to recruit, train and promote a decent political class, and the party system itself. Hence, what I explore and explain is the relationship between the political class, citizens and their associations.

I have achieved my aim in this introductory chapter if readers can now see more clearly the features and the contours of the institutional framework in which Italian politics takes place and have become fully aware of some of the most important problems to be faced. The chapters that follow will disentangle all the issues and provide, whenever possible, comparative answers and evaluations of the problems and the feasibility of some attempted solutions.

Notes

1 The "tyrant" was the Fascist leader Benito Mussolini, whose power, however, most certainly did not come from the Constitution – which, at the time, was

still the 1848 *Statuto Albertino* – but from his ruthless capacity to resort to violence and to exploit the acquiescence of the King, the armed forces, the bureaucracy, the landowners, the industrialists and, to a lesser extent, the Catholic Church.

2 As I argue in Pasquino (2016), where I clearly state that the existence of a new Republic is entirely dependent on the approval of new rules of the game – rules that are electoral and, above all, institutional. Despite repeated attempts, nothing of the sort has yet made its appearance.

3 There was a clear divide between 66 per cent of Northern voters in favour of the Republic and approximately the same percentage of southern voters in favour of retaining the monarchy.

4 This is also my opinion, for what it is worth, and one that I have argued at length in Pasquino and Ventura (2010). What most politicians fear is the high level of "competitiveness" of both the popular election of the President of the Republic and in the single-member electoral districts.

5 The choice of words prominently visible in Article 3 is revealing: citizens, the key word of liberal bourgeois culture; persona, borrowed by Italian Democratic Catholics from the French Emmanuel Mounier's and Jacques Maritain's personnalisme; and workers, what the Socialists and the Communists preferred.

6 In the vast literature concerning all the attempts to reform the Italian Constitution, there is an implicit bias in favour of any reform at all, as if it did not matter which one were chosen as any reform would improve the functioning of the Italian political system and, to put it in a somewhat rhetorical way, the quality of life of Italian citizens. Hence, those who object to some or all of the reforms are almost automatically labelled "conservatives", although this is not the case. I have extensively argued (Pasquino 2015a) that almost all proposed revisions were poorly drafted, bad and bound to negatively affect the functioning of the political system. They would backfire and therefore they had to be rejected. Better alternatives existed that ought to have been explored.

7 This story deserves to be told, recalled and revived not only because too many actors and citizens seem to have a very short memory, but also because it continues to affect the political debate in a significant way.

8 Interviewing Italian parliamentarians for a book comparing them with British parliamentarians, Robert Putnam (1973) was surprised by the sense of pride expressed by Italian Communists for having collaborated in the drafting of the Constitution and its approval. The role they played made them loyal citizens (not Soviet agents) and also explains why they have always been adamant defenders of the Italian Constitution as it is.

9 Another prominent critic of the violations of the Italian Constitution and of the delays to its implementation was the former secretary of the Italian Socialist Party, Lelio Basso, who had significantly contributed to the writing of several important articles (see Basso 1958).

10 Although I do not always agree with him, I am glad to refer to the writings of Martin Bull (2015, 2016, 2018), who has incessantly and admirably monitored all the most interesting phases of the (non-)reform process.

11 According to Article 138 of the Constitution, the referendums on constitutional revisions can – not must – be requested either by one-fifth of parliamentarians or by 500,000 voters or by five regional councils, not by the government – implicitly not by the parties making up the governmental coalition, especially if they have supported and voted in favour of those revisions. This referendum is an instrument available to those who oppose the revisions approved by a parliamentary majority. Hence, it should not be called "confirmative"; the correct adjective is oppositional. It cannot be requested when a two-thirds parliamentary majority has approved the revisions. The Constitution makers did not want to pit a popular majority against a qualified parliamentary majority for fear of delegitimizing Parliament in a country where anti-parliamentary feelings always run high. Finally, constitutional referendums are valid no matter what percentage of voters go to the polls. The rationale of this clause is that those voters who show their interest, who have probably acquired some information on the revisions and who are willing to spend their time, energy and money to go to the polls must be rewarded. Moreover, obviously, if approved by the electorate, those revisions would acquire more legitimacy and would be more likely to be implemented successfully.

12 Interview, *La Repubblica*, August 2016.

13 Both points must be emphasized: (i) no prolonged absence of the government; and (ii) strong continuity in ministerial offices. Both make it somewhat out of place to speak of political instability. Also, although Prime Minister Gentiloni has exhibited a different style, his policies can be defined as "more of the same" with a few minor adjustments.

14 In fact, through its judgments of 2014 and 2017, the court has fundamentally shaped the debate on the reform of the electoral laws and has clearly influenced the drafting of the Rosato law.

15 Italians are not famous for their associational predispositions nor their interpersonal trust. However, for at least thirty years millions of them joined a political party, especially, of course, the governing Christian Democrats and the Communist Party, a true class-based mass party.

16 A challenging, quite critical, almost compelling evaluation of the overall performance of the Italian socio-economic and political system is offered by Capussela (2018).

References

Amato, G. (1980). *Una Repubblica da riformare*. Bologna: Il Mulino.
Bagehot, W. (2001). *The English Constitution*. Oxford: Oxford University Press.

Basso, L. (1958). *Il Principe senza scettro: Democrazia e sovranità popolare nella Costituzione e nella realtà italiana*. Milan: Feltrinelli.

Bedock, C. (2017). *Reforming Democracy: Institutional Engineering in Western Europe*. Oxford: Oxford University Press.

Bufacchi, V. and Burgess, S. (1998). *Italy since 1989: Events and Interpretations*. London and New York: Macmillan and St Martin's Press.

Bull, M. J. (2015). Institutions and the Political System in Italy: A Story of Failure. In A. Mammone, E. Giap Parini and G. A. Veltri (eds) *The Routledge Handbook of Contemporary Italy: History Politics Society* (pp. 103–114). London: Routledge.

Bull, M. J. (2016). A 'Perfect Storm?': Institutional Reform in Italy after the 2013 National Elections. In R. Kaiser and J. Edelmann (eds) *Crisis as a Permanent Condition? The Italian Political System between Transition and Reform Resistance* (pp. 81–98). Baden-Baden: Nomos.

Bull, M. J. (2018). Renzi Removed: The Italian Constitutional Referendum and its Outcome. In A. Chiaramonte and A. Wilson (eds) *The Great Reform That Never Was* (pp. 131–153). Oxford: Berghahn.

Bull, M. J. and Pasquino, G. (2009). A Long Quest in Vain: Institutional Reforms in Italy. In M. J. Bull and M. Rhodes (eds) *Italy: A Contested Polity* (pp. 14–35). London: Routledge.

Capussela, A. L. (2018). *The Political Economy of Italy's Decline*. Oxford: Oxford University Press.

Emmott, B. (2012). *Good Italy Bad Italy: Why Italy Must Conquer Its Demons to Face the Future*. New Haven and London: Yale University Press.

Grimaldi, S. (2017). The Leadership Capital of Italian Presidents: The Politics of Constraint and Moral Suasion. In M. Bennister, B. Worthy and P. 't Hart (eds) *The Leadership Capital Index: A New Perspective on Political Leadership* (pp. 226–249). Oxford: Oxford University Press.

Hine, D. (1993). *Governing Italy: The Politics of Bargained Pluralism*. Oxford: Clarendon Press.

LaPalombara, J. (1987). *Democracy, Italian Style*. New Haven and London: Yale University Press.

Miglio, G. (1983). *Una Repubblica migliore per gli italiani (verso una nuova Costituzione)*. Milan: Giuffré.

Newell, J. L. (2010). *The Politics of Italy: Governance in a Normal Country*. Cambridge: Cambridge University Press.

Paladin, L. (1988). *Presidente della Repubblica, Enciclopedia del Diritto* (pp. 165–242). Milan: Giuffré.

Pasquino, G. (2015a). *Cittadini senza scettro: Le riforme sbagliate*. Milan: Egea-UniBocconi.

Pasquino, G. (ed.) (2015b). La scomparsa delle culture politiche in Italia. In *Paradoxa* IX, pp. 13–26.

Pasquino, G. (2016). The Second Republic that Never Was. In R. Kaiser and J. Edelmann (eds) *Crisis as a Permanent Condition? The Italian Political*

System between Transition and Reform Resistance (pp. 99–111). Baden-Baden: Nomos.

Pasquino, G. (2018). The Disappearance of Political Cultures in Italy. In *South European Society and Politics* 23 (1), pp. 133–146.

Pasquino, G. and Valbruzzi, M. (2017). Italy Says No: The 2016 Constitutional Referendum and Its Consequences. In *Journal of Modern Italian Studies* 22 (2), pp. 145–162.

Pasquino, G. and Ventura, S. (eds) (2010). *Una splendida cinquantenne: La Quinta Repubblica francese*. Bologna: Il Mulino.

Pederzoli, P. (2008). *La Corte costituzionale*. Bologna: Il Mulino.

Powell, G. B., Jr. (2000). *Elections as Instruments of Democracy: Majoritarian and Proportional Visions*. New Haven and London: Yale University Press.

Pritoni, A., Valbruzzi, M., and Vignati, R. (eds) (2017). *La prova del NO: Il sistema politico italiano dopo il referendum costituzionale*. Soveria Mannelli: Rubbettino.

Putnam, R. D. (1973). *The Beliefs of Politicians: Ideology, Conflict, and Democracy in Britain and Italy*. New Haven: Yale University Press.

Sartori, G. (1982). *Teoria dei partiti e caso italiano*. Milan: SugarCo.

Verzichelli, L. and M. Cotta (2000). Italy: From 'Constrained' Coalitions to Alternating Governments. In W. C. Müller and K. Strøm (eds) *Coalition Governments in Western Europe* (pp. 433–497). Oxford: Oxford University Press.

One, two, many electoral laws   **2**

In 1946, for a variety of reasons, but above all because party leaders and the members of the Constituent Assembly wanted to give fair representation to their fellow citizens, Italy adopted proportional representation (PR) to elect its Parliament. This had no major drawbacks, but, of course, it also softened the impact of any changes in the electoral behaviour of Italians. Out of their dissatisfaction over the slow translation of social and cultural changes into political outcomes, several politicians and a large sector of public opinion supported a momentous choice. In 1993, through a referendum, a mixed-member majority law was introduced. Since then, Italian electoral laws have been changed several times in a partisan way by the governing majorities. This chapter tells a complicated story, describing the different electoral laws and evaluating their consequences for political parties and governments. It is a story that is not yet over.

Overview of electoral laws

There can be no doubt that the electoral system is a very important component of all democratic political systems. It does not simply "translate votes into seats" (in the justly famous words of Stein Rokkan (1970)). The various electoral systems have an impact on the voters, the candidates and the parties well before the vote and produce lasting consequences for all of them, as well as for Parliament and the government after the vote. They shape the form of political competition and often account for the number of parties in a political system and in Parliament. Their impact is felt *before* the vote because their mechanisms affect the way in which parliamentary candidates are selected, how the voters can choose between them – or not choose, through preferential voting – how electoral campaigns are run and, of course, how votes are effectively translated into seats. The different mechanisms of electoral systems also have an impact after the vote on the number of parties obtaining parliamentary representation and on the formation of government coalitions. Although too many Italian electoral "reformers" seem to be unaware of the implications of their proposals and solutions, abundant information – some controversial and some questionable – has long been available on all these aspects (Lijphart 1994; Norris 2004; Herron, Pekkanen and Shugart 2018).

The post-war story of Italian electoral laws began in 1945–46. At the time, the choice of a proportional electoral law for the nascent Republic was expected and went almost unopposed. One of the few dissenting voices was that of Luigi Einaudi, prominent leader of the Italian Liberal Party and later the first President of the Italian Republic (1948–55), who made the case for the British first-past-the-post electoral system. All the other parties preferred PR, which had been the system used in the last free elections before Fascism – in 1919 and 1922 – and promised to offer fair parliamentary representation to all Italian parties, large and small. PR would make it very difficult for large parties to achieve an absolute majority of seats in Parliament, but it would also make devastating electoral defeats highly unlikely. In a situation in which Italian parties were moving in the terra incognita of an atomized society emerging out of twenty years of Fascist rule, proportional representation appeared to be the best of all the possible alternatives. This was so much the case that, in the Constituent Assembly, a young Communist Deputy with a famous name, Antonio Giolitti (his grandfather Giovanni had been Prime Minister several times between 1892 and 1921 and was responsible for introducing PR in Italy), formulated a recommendation to insert the proportional electoral law in the Constitution. Although this was approved, the recommendation was omitted in the final revised text. This omission has proved to be a mixed blessing. On the one hand, thanks to the fact that it is not an article of the Constitution, the electoral law can be (and has been) subject to popular referendum.[1] On the other hand, the possibility of revising, changing or totally transforming the electoral law has opened up a sort of Pandora's box overflowing with highly partisan and poorly drafted alternatives.

In fact, the proportional electoral law, which many in Italy, especially the Communists, long considered the electoral system par excellence of modern democracies,[2] faced an early attempt to introduce a major modification just few years after its first implementation and following only one national election. In order not to fall prey to the increasing influence of the Neo-Fascist party, but rather to consolidate and enlarge the centrist governing coalition (DC, PSDI, PRI, PLI), in 1953 the Christian Democrats masterminded parliamentary approval of a new electoral law that was immediately dubbed by the opposition the "swindle law" (detailed analyses published on the fiftieth anniversary of its parliamentary approval can be found in Piretti (2003) and Quagliariello (2003)). The structure of the new law remained proportional; the innovative and highly controversial feature was the majority bonus. This bonus would have been given to the parties that had declared themselves partners in a coalition and whose total votes amounted to 50 per cent plus one of the national vote. The coalition parties would then receive two-thirds of the parliamentary seats, while the remaining seats would be allocated proportionally to the other parties. Leaving aside the fact that the new law would produce significant disproportionality, and deliberately so, in order to strengthen the governing coalition (allegedly providing and assuring, in today's catchword, "governability"), some of its sponsors and admirers, then and later, also argued that it might encourage a transformation of the left, conceivably obliging the Italian Communists to de-Sovietize themselves, and give rise to a neat bipolar competition. However, there was also a very dark side to this proposed system.

Thanks to the majority bonus, the winning coalition would have had enough parliamentary votes to elect the President of the Republic by itself, and, later (when the Constitutional Court came into existence in 1956), to elect all five constitutional judges. Finally, the winning coalition would even have been in a position to reform or rewrite the Constitution, preventing any attempt to call a referendum: it is possible to submit to voters only those reforms approved by fewer than two-thirds of parliamentarians. From this point of view, the new electoral law was more than just a swindle. Giving an exaggerated amount of power to the victorious coalition, it would have derailed the Constitution, which, at the time, was taking its early difficult steps. Somewhat surprisingly, at the end of an extraordinarily bitter electoral campaign, the four-party coalition missed the 50 per cent plus one target by 54,000 votes. It was not just a matter of numbers; it was a political defeat. It meant that Italian voters had rejected a request to give too much parliamentary and governing power to an artificially created majority. Later, the law was repealed.

For decades, the Italian proportional law went unchallenged (see Table 2.1). Its existence did not increase the number of parliamentary parties, which oscillated between seven and nine. It was rare for more than a couple of small parties to obtain parliamentary representation. Seen from a systemic perspective, probably the most important

Table 2.1 Electoral systems used in Italy at the national level since 1946

Period	Type	Preference voting	Majority bonus	Multiple candidacies	Legal threshold
1946–93	Proportional	Yes	No	Yes	1 seat and 300,000 votes
1994–2005	Mixed-member majoritarian (Mattarella law)	No	No	Yes	4%
2006–17	Proportional (Calderoli law)	No	Yes	Yes	4% (2% party in coalition; 10% coalition)
2018–	Mixed-member proportional (Rosato law)	No	No	Yes	3%

inconvenience of the proportional electoral law was that it did not discourage party splits. The left was especially vulnerable to splits. In 1947, the Social Democrats left the Socialist Party; in 1964, the PSIUP abandoned the Socialist Party. Crowning this history of splits, in 1991, when the Italian Communists gave birth to the Partito Democratico della Sinistra (Democratic Party of the Left), a left-wing faction regrouped to form a new party called Communist Refoundation. By then, however, proportional representation was being challenged for other reasons: that is, not because it allowed – and perhaps encouraged – party splits, but because it was considered largely responsible for preventing governmental alternation. In fact, whatever its merits, PR Italian-style always had two significant consequences. First, it regularly softened the impact of any changes, never huge, in the distribution of votes among the various parties, especially those within the governing coalitions (see Chapter 5 for more on the government). Second, it gave too much power to the political parties and their leaders to choose what kind of coalition to form after the vote, according to their pleasure and their convenience; this occurred both at the national level and at the too often neglected local level,[3] where it created all sorts of distortions of the popular vote.[4]

Reasons for dissatisfaction

At the end of the 1980s, a Committee for Electoral Reform was formed, made up of parliamentarians, entrepreneurs, trade unionists, professors and leaders of civic associations – all of them dissatisfied with the working of PR. The Committee argued for reform of the proportional law. A constellation of factors led to the Committee's formation and sustained its activity. First, there were two major electoral and political scandals, followed by a significant change in the political landscape.

As regards the scandals, throughout the 1980s the ruling *pentapartito* (five-party) coalition (PLI, DC, PSDI, PRI, PSI) was working towards its own version of *Gleichschaltung*. Their attempt was to make all local governments similar in composition to the national government: that is, not only should five-party coalitions be formed and rule towns and cities whenever numerically possible, but the mayor would be chosen with reference to intraparty bargaining processes at the national level and not according to votes obtained by his or her party in each municipality.

In practice, the allocation of local roles and offices was decided by the national secretaries of the five parties. Thus, for instance, the mayor of Rome had to be a Socialist even though the Christian Democrats polled three times more votes. The mayor of Genoa had to be a Republican, although the party had received only about 2 per cent of the votes, because this was the outcome of the overall agreements previously reached among the leaders of the five-party national coalition. The logic of power relationships collided with the preferences of the voters and created dissatisfaction and disenchantment. Then, something took place in the Naples-Caserta electoral constituency in the 1987 national elections that proved damaging in the eyes of public opinion and highlighted the fact that some features of PR (or, more precisely, preferential voting) could be – and were – manipulated to a significant extent by party and faction leaders, without, however, affecting the outcome (the Naples-Caserta example is discussed in more detail later in the chapter).

Generally speaking, Italian elections have been free, fair and competitive. This also means that turnout has been quite high during the entire electoral history of the Republic. Up until 1993, voting was compulsory, but the sanctions for not voting were practically irrelevant and the overall turnout was not influenced by a fear of being punished. A moderate decline in turnout started at the end of the twentieth century (see Figure 2.1), but, on the whole, a higher percentage of Italian voters still goes to the polls than in other European democracies. As can be expected, the North votes more than the South, those with a job and a decent income vote more than the unemployed and the less affluent,

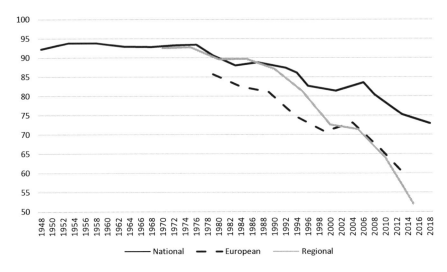

Figure 2.1 Turnout in Italy at national, European and regional elections, 1948–2018 (percentage)

and middle-aged people vote more than seniors and young voters. Men vote slightly more than women, but the turnout of young women approximates and is often higher than that of men in the same age cohorts. So far, non-voting has not been considered a major problem; however, Italian journalists lump all non-voters together, despite the different reasons for not voting (social isolation, lack of will, physical or legal obstacles), and call them "the party of non-voters". Heterogeneous, disorganized, with different motivations and lacking social ties, non-voters have never affected the dynamics of Italian politics and have never been taken into consideration by Italian electoral reformers who have not searched for remedies to any obstacles (early voting, postal votes, and so on).

Minor episodes of corruption and of the selling and buying of votes have taken place, but no large-scale fraud has ever been discovered or denounced. It is likely that in some areas, especially in the South, what has been called "vote of exchange" (Parisi and Pasquino 1979) has often been practised – to the advantage, of course, of those parties and candidates who could credibly offer something in exchange for votes (the case of Naples, analysed by Allum (1973), is emblematic), and therefore, generally speaking, not by the Communists or the Neo-Fascists, who had practically no access to state or local government funds and resources. One instrument through which certain corrupt practices were made possible was preferential voting (see Figure 2.2). Those who drafted the proportional electoral law intended for preferential voting to give voters the power to choose up to three or four candidates from the lists put forward by the various parties. In a way, preferential voting was considered necessary in order to counterbalance the power of the parties and their leaders in selecting candidates. To some extent it was meant to provide an opportunity that, in practice, not many voters have proved willing to exploit.

There were always five actors capable of orienting and channelling preference votes: the party apparatus, especially, but not only, of the Communist Party; faction leaders and their collaborators; the wide network of Catholic organizations; professional associations (particularly trade unions) and interest groups; and organized crime, although its influence should not be exaggerated and, of course, it applied only in selected southern areas. While some candidates and parliamentarians, especially Christian Democrats, could claim to "own" large numbers of preference votes, in practice any such votes came via their relations with associations – and this was a rare occurrence. To give a few examples,

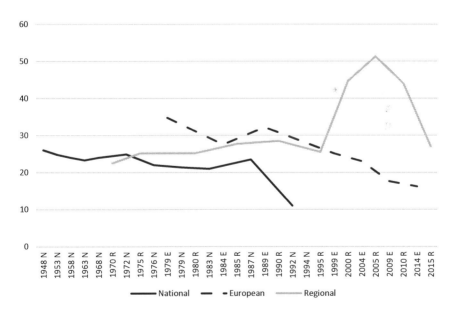

Figure 2.2 Preferential voting in national, European and regional elections in Italy, 1948–2015 (percentage)

Note: Percentages are of preferential votes cast for all regional, national and European elections.

Source: Passarelli (2017: 10).

in the case of Giulio Andreotti, several thousand preference votes regularly came from Catholic confessional associations in Latium; the powerful DC leader Antonio Bisaglia in Veneto received votes from Coldiretti, the Small Farmers' Association; and, in Turin, Carlo Donat-Cattin, a member of the DC and a minister several times, obtained votes from the Catholic trade union CISL. To be precise, most of the time it was not the candidate who "won" preference votes; rather, those votes were channelled by associations to specific candidates for a variety of reasons, of which the fact that he – or, very rarely, she – would represent, protect and promote the interests of those associations was far from being a minor one.

Preference votes could be expressed by writing either the name of the candidate(s) on the ballot or the ranking number they had on the party's electoral list. Hence, minor frauds were always possible, for instance by manipulating the numbers or adding numbers to blank ballots. All this required some coordination and acquiescence on the part of poll officials appointed by municipal electoral authorities and by the party representatives who had the right to be present when the ballots were opened and the votes counted. There may have been cases of collusion, but only a few, not very dramatic ones were ever denounced until it was discovered that, in the 1987 national elections in the constituency of Naples-Caserta, many preference votes were "cast" – or, more precisely, polling officers had added the names or numbers of candidates where voters hadn't used all their preferences – in favour of selected candidates belonging to the five-party government coalition and to the disadvantage of dissenting candidates within those same parties.[5] This was also done because, in some parties, the number of preference votes won by the elected candidates was considered to be a measure of his (or very rarely her) political clout, and this was rewarded with offices in Parliament (such as committee chairs) and government. Thus, vicious circles were inaugurated and reinforced: more preference votes meant more chances to obtain powerful positions from which to reward voters and increase the number of preference votes, and, as a consequence, the power deriving from them.

Leaving aside the specific consequences of the Naples-Caserta scandal, what is important is that this story played out among parliamentarians and associations who were asking for and acting in the interests of a reform of the proportional law. Launched by a conservative Christian Democratic parliamentarian, Mario Segni (his father, Antonio, had been a minister several times, Prime Minister, and finally President of the Republic from 1962 to 1964), the Committee for Electoral Reform submitted a request for three popular referendums on features of the existing electoral law. When the Constitutional Court confirmed its view that no elective body could be entirely deprived of its electoral law, the sponsors of the referendum had to proceed to the complex work of cutting words and sentences in order to obtain the desired result: that is, to move away from proportionality to majoritarianism. In 1990, the Court struck out two referendum requests and allowed only the one that appeared to be less threatening to the various parties, but especially to the Socialists and the Christian Democrats, who, at the time, were adamantly and vehemently opposed to any reform of PR.

What became the "Referendum on the Single Preference" asked voters whether they were in favour of deleting certain words from the House of Deputies' electoral law, thus leading to a situation in which only one preference vote could be cast by writing the name of the candidate (and thereby making scandals such as the one in Naples-Caserta almost impossible). Technically, this modification was of minor importance, even though, for instance, it meant that candidates on a party list were deprived of the possibility of creating networks – something that faction leaders had always done. Hence, the candidates found themselves obliged to compete against each other by campaigning for preference votes among and beyond faithful party workers and voters. The single preference referendum acquired an unexpected salience for two reasons. First, by relying on a very appealing slogan – "Choose your parliamentarian" – the sponsors of the referendum were also indicating to voters the likelihood of transforming PR into a plurality electoral system in single-member districts. Second, because practically all the party leaders except the Communists – who were uncertain, and also were enmeshed in a difficult transition from the PCI to the PDS – decided to defend PR, the referendum also appeared as a challenge launched against the pervasive and highly criticized power of the parties and their reciprocal collusion (*partitocrazia* or partyocracy).

Electoral referendums

It was therefore no surprise that the referendum, an instrument of effective citizen participation, quickly acquired a larger, much more significant political meaning: that is, voters mobilized to express their support for an electoral reform that would give them more power against all the political parties, and especially against the parties of the incumbent government coalition. Party leaders from the Christian Democrats to the Socialists, from the Neo-Fascists to the Northern League and the other minor centrist parties used a variety of suggestions ("Go to the seaside", "Take a walk in the woods of the Padania", "Stay home with your friends", "Play cards") to encourage voters not to go to the polls in the hope that the quorum needed for the referendum to be valid (a turnout of 50 per cent plus one) would not be reached, thus nullifying the outcome. On a clear and mild Sunday, 9 June 1991, 62.5 per cent of Italians went to the polls and 95 per cent of them approved the proposal. The long story of subsequent electoral reforms in Italy began that day. The next step was for the Committee for Electoral Reform to rephrase the question, deleting words and phrases in the Senate's electoral law in order to overcome the objections of the Constitutional Court. In the meantime, in order to prevent a referendum that might lead to a truly majoritarian law for local governments at the expense of all the minor parties, Parliament hurriedly approved a new law concerning the popular election of the mayor. This momentous shift of political power from the party secretaries to the voters has produced truly positive consequences for the stability of local governments and for the responsiveness and accountability of mayors. Since its first utilization in 1993, this law has gone unchallenged.

The April 1993 electoral referendum marks a watershed in the evolution of electoral laws in Italy. The absolute numbers and the percentages tell the story more than any elaborate analysis: turnout 77 per cent (36,992,390 voters); "Yes" 82.74 per cent (28,936,747); "No" 17.26 per cent (6,034,640). The vote was, I believe, correctly interpreted as the desire by an overwhelming majority of Italian voters to move substantially away from proportional representation and to introduce a different electoral system based on a majority formula. The outcome of the referendum was what remained after the shrewd and ingenious deleting of various words in the text of the existing proportional law that had been utilized for the election of the Senate. Those new clauses and mechanisms could be applied immediately to the Senate elections. Three-quarters of the Senators were going to be elected in single-member constituencies using a first-past-the-post formula and the remaining quarter according to a proportional formula. The referendum did not directly affect the electoral law for the House of Deputies, but there followed a consensus that the House electoral law should also be changed according to the voters' opinions expressed in the referendum. The modifications introduced for the House elections by the rapporteur, Christian Democrat Sergio Mattarella, gave the voters two ballots: one for the candidate in the single-member constituency and one for party lists. Only those parties receiving at least 4 per cent of the national vote were allowed to take part in the allocation of proportional seats. Multiple candidacies were permitted in one single-member constituency and in up to three lists. Interestingly, both the President of the Committee for Electoral Reform, Mario Segni, and the rapporteur (who was jokingly dubbed

Mattarellum by Giovanni Sartori, the play on words suggesting that the law contained some "crazy" – *matto* – elements) were defeated in their single-member constituencies. Both won the proportional seat. Indeed, there are many very good reasons to believe that the method of allocating proportional seats in the House was engineered so as not to jeopardize the electoral chances of prominent party politicians, the ones who held enough power to be candidates in single-member constituencies as well as appearing in up to three party lists (an explanation of the technicalities can be found in Katz (2001)).

The Mattarella law transformed the electoral and political game for all the players in a very substantial way. Voters certainly acquired more power in single-member constituencies, even though the lack of a residency requirement meant that too many carpetbaggers – that is, candidates parachuted in to supposedly safe seats – made their appearance. As for the parties, first they were forced to adjust; second, they gave birth to a new unstable party system, although with some difficulties (see Chapter 3 on parties and party systems); and third, they had to build pre-electoral coalitions behind their candidates in single-member constituencies. The leader of these pre-electoral coalitions would come to be considered as the candidate for the office of Prime Minister; in any case, he was supposed to add value to the electoral appeal of his coalition.[6] Finally, a political system based on multipolar competition and deprived of government alternation was catapulted into the era of bipolar competition and possible alternations. In fact, the Mattarella law, which was used in three national elections, saw the victory of Berlusconi's two-pronged coalition in 1994, the ascent to governmental office of an unprecedented centre-left coalition in 1996, and Berlusconi's return to government in 2001, leading a more cohesive coalition. From many points of view, the functioning of the Mattarella law, though not perfect, was certainly more than satisfactory. However, no satisfaction was felt by Berlusconi because the combined total of the votes obtained by the parties in his coalition(s) was always greater than the overall number of votes won by the coalition candidates in single-member constituencies. Briefly, Berlusconi's candidates rarely enjoyed the same visibility and name recognition of those of the centre-left.

Berlusconi's (and Renzi's) partisan reform

The justification offered several times by Berlusconi was that, being professional politicians, centre-left candidates enjoyed an initial advantage because they were naturally and automatically better known in those single-member constituencies. The majority of Forza Italia's candidates, who were selected not with reference to their previous political roles but because of their professional biographies and their work experiences, were less well known and therefore at a disadvantage. From time to time Berlusconi also added that it was his name, his personal appeal and his charisma that attracted votes for Forza Italia and for the coalition of which he was the undisputed leader. A less local and more national competition was much better for Forza Italia and the centre-right. These were the main "structural" considerations that led Berlusconi to reform the electoral law in the way that he did (discussed later in the chapter). The reason why his reform was hastily approved in December 2005 was that it was meant to make the centre-left's victory in the forthcoming national elections of April 2006 – a victory that was predicted by all the surveys – more difficult and with a smaller than expected number of seats. A similar attempt had been made in 1985 by the French President, the Socialist François Mitterrand, when his parliamentary majority replaced the two-ballot majority system with proportional representation in order to scale down the size of the predictable victory of the centre-right led by the Gaullist Jacques Chirac. Neither Mitterrand nor Berlusconi succeeded in escaping defeat, but Romano Prodi's 2006 electoral victory, especially at the Senate, was by a razor-thin margin, which meant that in less than two years his second government collapsed, also because it was undermined by the extreme heterogeneity of the coalition ironically called "Unione".

The 2005 electoral law officially carries the name of its rapporteur, Senator Roberto Calderoli, but it is better known as Porcellum ("Big Pig"), a nickname again devised by Sartori and intended to critique the new law's prominent feature – that of being an intentional dirty trick (*porcata* in Italian). In Calderoli's law, parliamentary seats were allocated proportionally in large constituencies for the House and in regional constituencies for the Senate. However, only parties that had passed the threshold of 4 per cent on a national scale and 8 per cent by region could take part in the proportional allocation of seats for the House of Deputies and the Senate respectively. The party or coalition receiving the highest number of votes nationally was rewarded with a majority bonus that would take the number of its seats in the House up to 340 (the absolute majority being 316). For the Senate majority, bonuses of different sizes, depending on the population of each region, had to be allocated region by region. For a variety of reasons – the most important one being that the centre-right was traditionally very strong in some of the most populated regions (Lombardy, Sicily, Campania and Veneto) that had a large number of seats and thus conspicuous majority bonuses – these bonuses were highly likely to lead to the appearance of opposing majorities in the House and in the Senate, especially in the case of a centre-left victory in the House (Pasquino 2007).

Two other features of the Calderoli law deserve a mention. First, all party lists were closed and, second, multiple candidacies were allowed. Hence, all Italian voters could do was to put a cross against the party symbol of their choice and nothing more. In practice, all parliamentarians were "appointed" by party and faction leaders who had the power to decide the ranking order in the party lists. Moreover, party and faction leaders could be candidates in *all* constituencies and, if elected in more than one, which was often the case, they could choose which constituency to represent at the expense of the candidates they thought to be less reliable. For instance, in 2013, Berlusconi decided to become the Senator for Molise out of all the possible constituencies. Once he was ousted following his conviction for tax evasion, his successor did not join the Forza Italia parliamentary group in the Senate, but the group led by Angelino Alfano, who had split from Forza Italia in October 2013. What is highly questionable is the fact that, at the end of the day, no Italian voter was in a position to know at the time of voting who was going to be his or her representative.

Although widely criticized, there is no denying the fact that the Calderoli law was quite liked by party and faction leaders, of the centre-right as much as of the centre-left. It was used in three elections: 2006, which saw a slim centre-left victory; 2008, a major victory for the centre-right; and 2013, when the centre-left won the majority bonus for the House of Deputies but had no majority in the Senate. As a consequence of the results, the issue of reforming the electoral law became salient, also because its constitutionality was challenged by a committee of progressive lawyers. Following negotiations relating to the wider framework of constitutional reforms between Matteo Renzi, the secretary of the Democratic Party and soon to become Prime Minister, and Silvio Berlusconi, yet another electoral law was drafted. This was called Italicum, supposedly to emphasize its unique Italian features. In fact, there was no other electoral law in the world resembling the Italian one. Repeatedly, Renzi boasted that all of Europe would envy the Italian electoral law and half of the European states would soon imitate it. The Italicum was drafted in order to satisfy three criteria. First, the law pursued the goal of making it known to voters, thanks to the majority bonus, who was the winner on the night of the vote. Second, the winner had to be either a party or a list, not a coalition. Third, the winner was entitled to obtain a sizable bonus in seats so that it would be in a position to govern alone.

Governability assured by a one-party parliamentary majority was the uppermost goal of Renzi's electoral law (all these elements are discussed by D'Alimonte (2015), who allegedly contributed to the drafting of the law).

Some features of the Italicum were quite similar to the previous electoral law, but they were slightly redefined during the parliamentary debate (my early assessment can be found in Pasquino 2015). All the details that I present and discuss here are meant to suggest how the new electoral law was drafted to satisfy purely partisan appetites. Multiple candidacies were still allowed, but in no more than ten constituencies. Instead of the full list of candidates being closed, only the head of the list would automatically be elected (on the condition that his or her party had overcome the 3 per cent national threshold). All the other candidates would be elected according to the number of preference votes they obtained. Voters were allowed to cast one or two preference votes, provided that in the second case they chose both a male and a female candidate (or vice versa). The majority bonus would still reward the victorious party or list with 340 seats in the House of Deputies, but the requirements in order to obtain it were significantly different. The bonus would not go automatically to the party or list winning the highest number of votes, but a 40 per cent threshold was introduced. If no party or list obtained 40 per cent of the national vote, a run-off had to take place between the two highest placed parties or lists. At the beginning of the debate, Renzi had proposed a 37.5 per cent threshold, which was very close to the percentage of votes most surveys were suggesting that only the Democratic Party might be capable of winning. The barely disguised reason why Renzi wanted the bonus to be given to a single party and not to a coalition was quite simple. At the time, none of the three centre-right parties (Fratelli d'Italia, Northern League and Forza Italia) was close to even 15 per cent of the vote. Hence, the projected run-off would take place between the PD and the Five Star Movement, and Renzi felt confident that enough centre-right voters would converge on his party. This confidence suffered a brutal blow in June 2016 when, out of 20 run-offs in municipal elections, Five Star mayoral candidates won 19, including the two most important ones in Turin and Rome, where the duel pitted a PD candidate (in Turin a national figure who was the incumbent mayor) against a Five Star candidate. The Italicum was treading a dangerous electoral and political path.

In a way it was the Constitutional Court that removed the chestnuts from the electoral fire. Invested with a request to evaluate the constitutionality of several features of the Italicum, the Court stated that a party could indeed be given the majority bonus if it won at least 40 per cent of the votes. But the Court struck down the run-off because it might entail a major distortion of proportionality if the bonus were to go to a party that had received a rather low percentage of votes, for instance 25–28 per cent – this was more or less the threshold reachable by the PD and the Five Star Movement, and almost certainly by the centre-right if it reorganized itself. Finally, the Court stated that multiple candidacies were acceptable, but that the victorious candidates could not choose which constituency to represent. A lottery would decide that. With regard to the electoral law for the Senate – which Renzi had not bothered to draft, being confident that he would win the referendum on his constitutional reforms involving significant changes in the composition and formation of the Senate – the Court cancelled the majority bonus, automatically instigating a proportional law.

It is impossible to provide a complete account of the debate, the proposals and the clashes that followed. I would add that it is also useless. But some points need to be made for future clarification. First, understandably but not commendably, all parties and party leaders have continued incessantly to advocate for and to assess the reform proposals through their highly partisan eyes. To remain with this metaphor, all those eyes are short-sighted. Second, Italian party leaders have consistently refused to take into consideration the idea of importing one of the European electoral systems that works: for instance, the German electoral system or the French one.[7] Contrary to the hard lessons of history, they all seem to believe that Italian party leaders, parliamentarians and politicians are more capable of devising an electoral system that will provide simultaneously the coveted political goods of representation and governability. Most of them, especially those who are confident of winning, add that, were it necessary to sacrifice one goal or the other, they would opt for more governability at the expense of representation. However, nobody has been able to quote or refer to any article or book within the literature confirming that there is indeed a trade-off between representation and governability, nor to indicate which specific situations and circumstances will allow us convincingly to evaluate the advantages and costs of any such trade-off. Unfortunately, the alleged necessity to choose between representation and governability continues to pollute Italian public discussion. Third, criss-crossing vetoes have made it impossible to formulate a decent electoral law behind a veil of ignorance: that is, providing fair competition at the expense of and despite vested interests.

Electoral law in 2018

After several months of idleness and an aborted attempt at drafting a distorted version of the German electoral system, in autumn 2017 an agreement was reached once more between Renzi's Democratic Party and Berlusconi's centre-right partners. Carrying the name of the head of the House parliamentary group of the Democratic Party, Ettore Rosato, the new law maintained what Berlusconi and, to a slightly lesser extent, Renzi consider an extremely important feature: closed lists, so that they can, to a (un)reasonable approximation, fundamentally select practically all the candidates who will then be elected.[8] The second partisan goal on which both the Democratic Party and the parties of the centre-right converged was to allow the formation of composite coalitions – despite the fact that the acceptance of coalitions was going head-on against the prohibition of coalitions inserted by Renzi in his much vaunted Italicum. The possibility of forming coalitions – indeed, the encouragement to do so – was meant as a strong blow to the Five Star Movement, whose founding principle is "purity": that is, the rejection of any coalition with those responsible for the poor performance of the past and for the wide web of corruption, never mind that running alone would automatically mean the impossibility of governing alone. Indeed, the excellent outcome of the 2018 elections obliged the Five Star Movement to look for governmental coalition partners. The rules of the parliamentary game proved capable of bending the Five Star's political commitment.

The Rosato law is a mix of plurality and PR,[9] technically a mixed-member proportional system. Slightly more than one-third of parliamentarians are elected in single-member constituencies according to a plurality formula. The remaining two-thirds are elected in relatively small constituencies: no more than six seats to be allocated through a proportional formula in those constituencies to the parties winning at least 3 per cent of the votes nationally.[10] In principle, the relatively low threshold was, of course, not meant to prevent the fragmentation of parties, but it has encouraged small parties to reach a deal with large parties (obviously, the PD and Forza Italia) in order to take advantage of their participation in the coalition. Voters have just one vote: that is, they cannot, as in Germany, choose a candidate in the single-member district and a different party in the "proportional" constituency. Their vote either for a candidate or for a party list will be considered validly cast for both.

Another feature on which both Renzi and Berlusconi, but also other party and faction leaders, were and remained in agreement is the possibility of being a candidate in more than one constituency.[11] The Calderoli law had been extremely generous: a candidate was allowed to be present in all constituencies. The Italicum had reduced to ten the number of constituencies available to each candidate. Finally, in the Rosato law, the number is down to five: that is, a candidate may run in one single-member district and in five PR constituencies. As Table 2.2 clearly shows, all parties have taken advantage of the possibility of putting up some of their candidates in more than one constituency. It is easy to understand that the system is designed, on the one hand, to assure a parliamentary seat to all party and faction leaders as well as to their most loyal, disciplined, subservient followers; on the other, it offers the opportunity to party leaders and to some prominent candidates to test their electoral appeal. Closed lists combined with the high likelihood of carpetbagger candidates mean that, on the one hand, the great majority of Italian voters cannot possibly know who "their" parliamentarian(s) were and/or are going to be; and, on the other – and worse – that there is no possibility and no need for parliamentarians to create and maintain any tie or relationship with the voters. Their re-election is never in the hands of those who have voted for them, also because powerful parliamentarians are always in a position to decide in which constituency they want to run next time.[12] (There is a very easy solution to the problem of carpetbaggers – a residence requirement – but this has never been taken into consideration.)

Table 2.2   Percentage of multiple candidacies in multi-member and single-member districts, by party

	FI	FdI	League	LeU	M5S	PD
1+0	77.0	84.2	76.8	65.6	77.2	75.6
1+1	10.3	3.9	8.9	24.1	22.8	19.1
2+0	6.1	4.9	6.4	4.7	0.0	1.8
2+1	2.8	2.0	3.4	1.4	0.0	0.9
3+0	0.9	0.0	0.5	0.5	0.0	0.9
3+1	2.3	1.0	0.5	0.9	0.0	0.0
4+0	0.0	1.0	1.0	0.5	0.0	0.0
4+1	0.0	0.5	1.5	1.9	0.0	0.4
5+0	0.0	0.5	0.0	0.0	0.0	0.0
5+1	0.5	2.0	1.0	0.5	0.0	1.3
Total	100.0	100.0	100.0	100.0	100.0	100.0

Notes: The first figure refers to the candidacies in multi-member districts; the second to the candidacy in single-member districts. For instance, 2+1 indicates the frequency of candidates in two multi-member districts and in one single-member district.
Source: Pedrazzani, Pinto and Baldini (2018: 115).

Exploring all the technicalities of the different electoral laws used in Italy is not a productive political or intellectual exercise. The risk is high of looking at many different trees without ever seeing the forest: that is, the combination of the motivations and the goals of party leaders and their impact on the parties, the party system, Parliament and the government – in sum, how the political system works in practice.

Italy's political problems in terms of disaffection, electoral apathy, anti-political beliefs and behaviour have their deep roots in what is correct to define as a crisis of representation. "Unchained" parliamentarians are part of the problem. The Rosato law does not (and did not want to) provide a political remedy to the problem of political representation or, above all, of political accountability.[13] On the contrary, it was fundamentally meant to give power to party leaders. In most areas of the country, Italian political parties are no longer territorially organized. Only in very few areas do some of them seem to be entrenched. Personalization has supplanted the organization at the expense of any representation of local interests and preferences except those put forward through clientelistic networks. The Rosato electoral law contains no incentive to encourage the reorganization of the parties or the competitiveness of the party system (issues that will be analysed in Chapter 4). Curiously, the prospect of having to write yet another electoral law, after all the negative components of the Rosato law were tested in the March 2018 elections, began to be taken into serious consideration immediately after the approval of the law. Practically all the protagonists were sending a message that the Italian transition will go on for a while longer until an electoral law can be drafted that is deemed by all – or almost all – the protagonists to be the only game in town. For the time being, drafting another electoral law does not seem to be a priority of the yellow–green governing coalition (yellow being the colour of the Five Star Movement and green that of the League). Waiting for the forthcoming approval of a constitutional bill to cut the number of parliamentarians by a third, the debate to change the electoral system (and to return to PR) has made its reappearance. In any case, the solution to the many political problems of Italy will never come exclusively from the electoral law, no matter how good it is.

Nonetheless, a poor electoral law such as the Rosato law is responsible for the deterioration of Italian politics. It does not encourage the selection of candidates of good quality. It concentrates political power in the hands of the party leader and his or her collaborators, usually a small group. It makes it well-nigh impossible, and in any case unnecessary, for parliamentarians to exercise the virtue of accountability. It does not provide for meaningful competition among political parties. It does not offer any political incentive for the revitalization of the existing obsolescent party structures nor for the restructuring of the Italian party system (Regalia 2019).

This chapter has told the story of the vicissitudes of the Italian electoral law (Regalia 2015; Chiaramonte 2015). It is also the story of the many misguided and misfired attempts by rather incompetent politicians to obtain advantages for their organizations and careers. In comparative perspective, Italy is the post-war democracy that has significantly redrafted its electoral laws more often than any other country. The Italian electoral law remains an important part of the problem – that is, the functioning of the political system – but at best it can be only a minor part of the solution.

Notes

1 The articles of the Constitution cannot be repealed by a popular referendum. They can be revised and/or fully eliminated only by Parliament through a special procedure. Then a constitutional referendum called by 500,000 citizens or five regional councils or one-fifth of parliamentarians can reject the revisions and reinstate the article.

2 By saying this they were absurdly excluding all Anglo-Saxon majoritarian political systems from the category of democracies.

3 Due to the decreased and declining prestige of Italian parties and their leaders, it is understandable that Italian voters wanted to tie the hands of those party leaders to some extent. But, first, what the voters wanted is practically impossible in parliamentary democracies where all governments are born (and usually die) in Parliament; and, second, in a relatively fragmented party system, it is always quite difficult to interpret the preferences and the "messages" of the voters. Nevertheless, all surveys regularly and constantly revealed that there was no majority favourable to including the Communist Party in a governmental coalition.

4 "Distortion" means that, especially during the *pentapartito* period (1980–92), the five parties in the national government (from right to left: PLI, DC, PRI, PSDI, PSI) went a very long way to ensure that, especially in the major cities, local governments reflected the composition of the national coalition.

5 It was an easy game to play. Very often, the scrutineers, who are mostly suggested by the parties themselves, had the opportunity to write the names of candidates or their numbers on paper ballots left unmarked by the voters, or even to alter the numbers. Thus, 4 could be transformed into 14 or 41, and so on.

6 The story is much more complicated than this, as we will see in Chapters 5 and 6, also because of its impact on the formal/material Constitution. It was a somewhat clumsy and misguided attempt to tie the hands of the President of the Republic in relation to his constitutional power to appoint the Prime Minister.

7 Of course, both the German and the French electoral laws fit into a specific model of government and, to some extent, would also require further institutional modifications.

8 Another important motivation is that Berlusconi wanted to obtain the power to "nominate" all his parliamentarians. Goal achieved.

9 A detailed analysis of the Rosato law is provided by Chiaramonte and D'Alimonte (2018) and Baldini, Pedrazzani and Pinto (2018).

10 For comparison purposes, the threshold of access to parliamentary representation is 3 per cent in Spain, whose electorate is about 34 million; 4 per cent in Sweden, with an electorate of about 8 millions; and 5 per cent in Germany, with an electorate of about 66 millions.

11 For both Berlusconi and Renzi, the weight of the (recent) past has played a decisive role. In 2013, Forza Italia suffered a parliamentary split that allowed the government led by Democrat Enrico Letta (see Chapter 5) to survive a vote of no confidence. Moreover, the group formed by the "rebels" went on supporting the successor government led by Renzi. The secretary of the Democratic Party suffered a similar fate when, at the beginning of 2017, slightly more than a handful of Senators and Deputies left the parliamentary groups of the PD and went on to establish a new party to the left of the PD. As a consequence, both leaders wanted to acquire full control over the nomination process. In any case, one should not forget that closed lists were the foremost feature of the Calderoli law (Porcellum), that they were unable to prevent the slow haemorrhage of the 2008–11 period, and that they were largely retained in the Italicum.

12 As expected, the candidates who were given, or simply "grabbed", many constituencies were national leaders: for instance, Giorgia Meloni, Ignazio La Russa and Daniela Santanché (all Fratelli d'Italia), Maria Elena Boschi and Marianna Madia (PD) were present in all five constituencies and in one single-member district; Matteo Salvini and Giulia Bongiorno (League), Laura Boldrini and Roberto Speranza (Liberi e Eguali) in five constituencies. Interestingly, all sixteen candidates present in five proportional constituencies and in one single-member district were females, as well as twelve out of fourteen candidates in four proportional constituencies and one single-member district, and nine out of thirteen in three PR constituencies and one single-member district. It is not too farfetched to hypothesize that those candidacies were used as mirrors for larks (i.e. to attract ill-informed voters) whose subsequent mandatory standing down opened the way to Parliament to male candidates.

13 All the cherished goals flamboyantly stressed by Renzi when he launched the Italicum – that is, (i) the name of the winner to be known on the night of the elections; (ii) the government to be elected by the voters; (iii) governability to be assured by a majority bonus – no matter how feasible or unfeasible they might be, have been shamelessly dropped by the same Renzi and his closest collaborators, Rosato being unabashedly one of them, and by friendly journalists and political pundits.

References

Allum, P. A. (1973). *Politics and Society in Post-war Naples*. Cambridge: Cambridge University Press.

Baldini, G., Pedrazzani, A. and Pinto, L. (2018). *How Italy Experienced (Yet) Another Electoral System and Why It May Soon Change It Again*, Posted on 8 May by The Constitution Unit.

Chiaramonte, A. (2015). The Unfinished Story of Electoral Reforms in Italy. In *Contemporary Italian Politics* 7 (1), April, pp. 10–26.

Chiaramonte, A. and D'Alimonte, R. (2018). The New Italian Electoral System and Its Effects on Strategic Coordination and Disproportionality. In *Italian Political Science* 13 (1), pp. 1–11.

D'Alimonte, R. (2015). The New Italian Electoral-system: Majority-assuring but Minority-friendly. In *Contemporary Italian Politics* 7 (3), December, pp. 286–292.

Herron, E. S., Pekkanen, R. J. and Shugart, M. S. (eds) (2018). *The Oxford Handbook of Electoral Systems*. Oxford: Oxford University Press.

Katz, R. S. (2001). Reforming the Electoral Law 1993. In M. S. Shugart and M. P. Wattenberg (eds) *Mixed-member Electoral Systems: The Best of Both Worlds?* (pp. 96–122). Oxford: Oxford University Press.

Lijphart, A. (1994). *Electoral Systems and Party Systems: A Study of Twenty-Seven Democracies, 1945–1990*. Oxford: Oxford University Press.

Norris, P. (2004). *Electoral Engineering: Voting Rules and Political Behavior*. Cambridge: Cambridge University Press.

Parisi, A. and Pasquino, G. (1979). Changes in Italian Electoral Behavior: The Relationships between Parties and Voters. In *West European Politics* 2 (3), pp. 6–30.

Pasquino, G. (2007). Tricks and Treats: The 2005 Italian Electoral Law and Its Consequences. In *South European Society and Politics* 12 (1), March, pp. 79–93.

Pasquino, G. (2015). Italy Has Yet Another Electoral Law. In *Contemporary Italian Politics* 7 (3), December, pp. 293–300.

Passarelli, G. (2017). Determinants of Preferential Voting in Italy: General Lessons from a Crucial Case. In *Representation* 53 (2), pp. 167–183.

Pedrazzani, A., Pinto, L., and Baldini, G. (2018). Nuovo sistema elettorale e scelta dei candidati: cosa è cambiato? In M. Valbruzzi and R. Vignati (eds) *Il vicolo cieco: Le elezioni politiche del 4 marzo* (pp. 99–125). Bologna: Il Mulino.

Piretti, M. S. (2003). *La legge truffa: il fallimento dell'ingegneria politica*. Bologna: Il Mulino.

Quagliariello, G. (2003). *La legge elettorale del 1953*. Bologna: Il Mulino.

Regalia, M. (2015). Electoral Systems. In E. Jones and G. Pasquino (eds) *The Oxford Handbook of Italian Politics* (pp. 132–143). Oxford: Oxford University Press.

Regalia, M. (2019). Electoral Reform as an Engine of Party System Change in Italy. In M. J. Bull and G. Pasquino (eds) *Italy Transformed: Politics, Society and Institutions at the End of the Great Recession* (pp. 80–95). London: Routledge.

Rokkan, S. (1970). *Citizens, Elections, Parties*. Oslo: Universitetsforlaget.

Political parties, party government and partyocracy

3

Starting in 1946, Italian parties performed an indispensable and positive task in organizing democracy, offering participation to Italian citizens, structuring the political system and making it work satisfactorily. However, the lack of alternation in government facilitated the emergence of what has rightly been called *partyocracy*: an excessive amount of power held by the parties that control too many economic and social resources. The degeneration of Italian parties led to the collapse of the party system in the 1992–94 period. No party system has followed; rather, personalist and quasi-populist parties have appeared whose performance has been poor and deplorable. This chapter aims to explore the overall trajectory of Italian parties and the party system(s), explaining all the negative transformations and highlighting the difficulties of a democratic regime whose parties are sadly unable to (re)acquire a decent role.

"The parties created democracy and modern democracy is unthinkable save in terms of parties." This short, dense but important sentence by American political scientist Elmer E. Schattschneider (1942: 1) indicates the existence of a strong relationship between parties and democracy, most certainly in his time, but in all likelihood in our time as well. Schattschneider attributes to political parties a very significant role, and his definition suggests that problems will arise in situations in which parties do not function satisfactorily, have become weak or are on the verge of disappearing. For several years, the Italian political system has been a place where some of these phenomena have taken place, negatively affecting the quality of democracy. There is no doubt that the contribution of Italian political parties to the (re-)establishment and consolidation of post-World War Two Italian democracy has been considerable, and probably decisive. The role they have played since then, how and why they all collapsed between 1992 and 1994, whether, how and in what shape they have reappeared and what is their contemporary condition are all subjects of this chapter (a useful overview of the evolution and transformation of Italian parties can be found in Ignazi (2018)).

The way things were

Italian society had never been densely organized, robust nor vibrant – adjectives used by US political scientists for their pre-Trump, supposedly Tocquevillian society – but between 1922 and 1943 it was further and deliberately atomized by Fascist rule. Only the Catholic Church successfully opposed the Fascists in their hegemonic drive, preserving some functional autonomy for its many diversified associations at the price of abstaining from any political activity. All the other associations, especially those created and supported by the left, were declared illegal and disbanded by Fascism. Hence, in the immediate post-1945 period, many religious, social, cultural and, to some extent, professional Catholic associations "heard the call" and quickly translated their significant social, economic and cultural power into the formation of a political party. The left – that is, the Socialists and the Communists – had a more difficult time in reviving the trade unions, the cooperatives and those cultural associations that had existed before the advent of Fascism. Most of the energies of the left were devoted to the restructuring of their party organizations. While the Christian Democrats became the political arm of Catholic associations and the Vatican to a large extent, leftist parties were often the sponsors and promoters of a network of civic associations. Therefore, on the whole, as I noted in Chapter 1, Italian political parties appeared strong mainly because, on the one hand, civil society was weak and, on the other, because representative institutions at all levels, from local governments to Parliament, had to be staffed by party personnel.

Not unlike all the other European parliamentary democracies, Italy quickly became an example of a *party government*. As defined by Katz, the main features of party government are as follows:

> Firstly, all major governmental decisions must be taken by people chosen in elections conducted along party lines, or by individuals appointed by and responsible to such people. Secondly, policy must be decided within the governing party, when there is a "monocolour" government, or by negotiations among parties when there is a coalition ... Thirdly, the highest officials (e.g. cabinet ministers and especially the prime minister) must be selected

within their parties and be responsible to the people through their parties. Positions in government must flow from support within the party rather than party positions flowing from electoral success.

(Katz 1986: 43)

There is no doubt that all these features applied neatly, regularly and consistently, with very few and only minor exceptions (that is, the recruitment of some non-party ministers), to all Italian governments from 1946 until 1992. Then, quite a different story began, with the parties obliged to hide their inadequacies and their decline by recruiting outsiders of all kinds – professionals, and anyone but those with a political biography – to fill even top ministerial offices.

Throughout the forty years of its golden age, slowly but inexorably party government degenerated into *partyocracy*, which I would define as a situation in which all parties collude in sharing available state resources ("spoils") and take hold of them for the benefit of their organizations, leaders, followers and voters.[1] In such situations, parties create, promote, infiltrate, fund, control and steer civil associations, extract resources from them, and recruit and demote members, making life difficult, if not impossible, for those associations that strive to maintain their autonomy. Although it was criticized right from the very beginning,[2] partyocracy was largely accepted, thrived and became a major feature of the Italian political system, almost the keystone of its parliamentary democracy. As long as economic development continued and resources remained abundant, partyocracy was considered a way of life by the very large number of those who, one way or another, participated in political activities, and especially by all the Italian parties, with the exception of the Neo-Fascist Movimento Sociale Italiano (Italian Social Movement), which was adamantly opposed to the "regime of parties" and, in any case, was almost always kept away from access to the distribution of "political" resources.

Some citizens' resentment surfaced as early as 1974, when, in the wake of a scandal concerning funds going from oil companies to many parties, a law on state financing of political parties was hastily approved. The referendum called to repeal the law failed, but almost 14 million Italians (43.59 per cent) voted yes, revealing their widespread discontent. No surprise, then, that twenty years later not only partyocracy but the entire Italian party system collapsed in the wake of yet another referendum called to repeal state financing. In 1993, the system could no longer be "saved": more than 31 million Italians (90.25 per cent) voted to totally repeal the law. Together with the elimination of three ministries (Agriculture, State Holdings, and Tourism and Cultural Activities, all sources of patronage), Italian voters also repealed several articles of the existing electoral law for the Senate, putting an end to proportional representation and opening up the way to a plurality formula (see Chapter 2), though by no means to a majoritarian democracy. The 1993 wave of referendums was meant to be a major blow to the Italian partyocracy. In fact, in combination with other factors,[3] the entire party system and all its components were practically swept away. In a nutshell, the Italian party system was completely de-structured, never to be restructured – so far. The March 1994 national elections proved to be a watershed in the history of the Italy. The "Republic of the parties" (Scoppola 1997), whose apparently powerful organizations had shaped the political system and decisively influenced its evolution, was wiped out in one stroke. It was not the beginning of a Second Republic, but those elections most certainly inaugurated a second phase of the Italian Republic, a transition towards an as yet unknown destination.

The beginning of a new phase

The entire post-1994 phase up until the time of writing can be analysed by looking at its most important protagonist, Silvio Berlusconi, and his political vehicle, Forza Italia. The national elections were preceded by mayoral elections in the four most important Italian cities: Milan and Turin (June), Rome and Naples (November). All of them provided a very clear lesson. In no case did the candidates of the once dominant Christian Democratic Party succeed in getting to the run-off. The centre of the Italian political alignment had foundered, not to be revived. It became easy to predict that, on the national level, the disappearance of all centrist parties was bound to leave several million voters without political representation. There existed a large available electorate that could not be reached by the left: that is, by the "former Communists, Communists, post-Communists", as Berlusconi would repeatedly put it. That electorate was available and in search of political representation. While, of course, there are those who believe that Berlusconi entered the field essentially in order to protect his many entrepreneurial activities, especially his TV empire, what counts is that he founded and launched a new political movement, Forza Italia (Poli 2001; Raniolo 2006). It immediately became the most important new party in post-war Europe, almost as successful[4] as the Gaullist party in all its changing guises and durability. It also proved to be a game-changer.

A look at the party alignment in the 1994 Parliament provides the necessary information to understand and assess the monumental changes that had taken place in less than two years (see Table 3.1 and Box 3.1). The format, to use Sartori's (1976) definition, of the Italian party system

Table 3.1 Electoral results of the 1994 general election (Chamber of Deputies)

	Votes (proportional tier)	Votes (proportional tier) (%)	Number of seats		
			Proportional	Majoritarian	Total
Centre-left coalition					
PDS	7,855,610	20.4	38	86	124
PRC	2,334,029	6.0	11	27	38
Greens	1,075,311	2.7	–	11	11
PSI	841,739	2.2	–	14	14
Democratic Alliance	452,396	1.2	–	18	18
La Rete	718,403	1.9	–	8	8
Pact for Italy					
PPI	4,268,940	11,1	29	4	33
Segni List	1,795,270	4,6	13	–	13
Centre-right coalition				4	
Forza Italia	8,119,287	21,0	30	79	109
Northern League	3,237,026	8.4	11	105	116
National Alliance	5,202,698	13.5	23	85	108
CCD	2,646	0.1	–	27	27
Pannella List	1,355,739	3.5	–	6	6
Others	1,368,198	3.5	–	5	5
Totals					
Voters	41,359,464	85.9			
Valid votes	38,358,646	92.7			
Total electorate	48,135,041	100.0	155	475	630

Box 3.1 Parties and leaders

(Northern) League (founded 1987)	Forza Italia (founded 1994)	Democratic Party (founded 2007)	Five Star Movement (founded 2008)
Bossi 1987–2013	Berlusconi 1994	Veltroni 2007–09	Grillo 2008–17
Salvini 2013–		Franceschini 2009	Di Maio 2017–
		Bersani 2009–13	
		Epifani 2013	
		Renzi 2013–16	
		Renzi 2017–18	
		Martina 2018–19	
		Zingaretti 2019–	

was multiparty. From right to left there were the substantially "reconstructed" Neo-Fascists, who had transformed themselves into a new organization called Alleanza Nazionale. Then, the Northern League, officially founded in 1991 (although its leader, Umberto Bossi, had been elected to the Senate in 1987). Forza Italia occupied a central position close to some former Christian Democrats called Popolari in a coalition with other Christian Democrats, already on the verge of a split, who had followed the leader of the electoral referendum movement to form the Patto Segni. The Greens had won barely more than a handful of seats thanks to being in coalition with the former Communists. The largest parliamentary group was made up of representatives of the Partito Democratico della Sinistra (PDS, or Democratic Party of the Left). Those who believed that the future of Communism was still to come had given birth in 1991 to Rifondazione Comunista (Communist Refoundation), comprised largely of former members, activists and leaders of the Partito Comunista Italiano (PCI). (Most of the confusing overall complexity and the changes in individual parties and the party system are convincingly described and analysed by Newell (2000)).

More than twenty years and five national elections later, only two of those parties have survived: the Northern League and Forza Italia (see Table 3.2). Even though one can loosely trace some of their roots to the past, all the other parties are fundamentally new. The Partito Democratico is the product of a 2007 "cold" merger between the Left

Table 3.2   Comparison between the results of Italian general elections (Chamber of Deputies) in 2013 and 2018

	2018	2013	Difference 2018–13	2018 (%)	2013 (%)	Difference 2018–13 (percentage points)
Radical left	521,564	860,028	−338,464	1.6	2.5	−0.9
SEL/LeU	1,114,298	1,089,231	25,067	3.4	3.2	0.2
PD	6,153,081	8,646,034	−2,492,953	18.7	25.4	−6.7
Other centre-left	1,380,905	332,319	1,048,586	4.2	1.0	3.2
FI/PDL	4,957,738	7,332,134	−2,374,396	13.9	21.5	−7.6
League	5,717,513	1,411,510	4,306,003	17.3	4.1	13.2
FdI + La Destra	1,440,107	889,401	550,706	4.4	2.6	1.8
Ncl–UdC	431,042	476,020	−44,978	1.3	1.4	−0.1
M5S	10,764,371	8,704,809	2,059,562	32.6	25.5	7.1
Scelta Civica and allies	–	3,591,541	−3,591,541	–	11.3	−11.3
Radical right	441,921	184,575	257,346	1.3	0.5	0.8
Others	410,255	286,499	123,756	1.2	0.8	0.4
Valid votes	32,972,803	34,078,191	−1,150,388	100.0	100.0	

Source: Author's own compilation. Data from: Italian Ministry of Internal Affairs (http://ele zioni.interno.gov.it/).

Democrats and La Margherita (former Democratic Catholics, Popolari, who had not joined Berlusconi). Fratelli d'Italia (Brothers of Italy) is essentially the successor party of Alleanza Nazionale, which has been defunct since 2008. The Five Star Movement, born in Milan in 2009, entered Parliament for the first time in February 2013. There were other minor parliamentary groups, the consequences of the typically Italian phenomenon called *trasformismo* (see Chapter 4) or of party splits, as was the case of Articolo 1 – Movimento Democratico e Progressista (MDP, or Article 1 – Democratic and Progressive Movement). Produced by a split from the Democratic Party, MDP joined with other splinter groups and gave birth in 2018 to the electoral coalition called Liberi e Uguali (LeU, or Free and Equal).

As can also be seen from the fact that practically all these parties are very often, if not always, identified with reference to the names of their leaders,[5] the contemporary landscape offered by the Italian party system is made up of personalist parties. In Table 3.3 I have classified them according to the most important features of "personalism"

Table 3.3 Strength of parties' organizations and their leaders

	Organization		
	Entrenchment and pervasiveness	Internal democracy	Members' loyalty
Democratic Party	75	80	60
Forza Italia	60	0	99
Five Star Movement	70	2	95
Northern League	60	80	90
Fratelli d'Italia	50	80	80
Liberi e Uguali	25	80	60

	Leader				
	Power	Charisma	Electoral value	Communication	Nomination
Democratic Party	85	70	75	75	90
Forza Italia	90	100	95	90	100
Five Star Movement	90	80	80	80	50
Northern League	90	70	75	85	60
Fratelli d'Italia	70	70	70	85	60
Liberi e Uguali	40	50	30	50	20

(Kostadinova and Levitt 2014). Instead of utilizing adjectives that have little power to differentiate between leaders and organizations, I am resorting to an admittedly very subjective score: 0 means that a specific trait or quality does not exist; 100 that it has blossomed fully.

I am aware that all my scores need a thorough explanation capable of throwing light on the Italian parties, their present and, to some extent, their future. Even though, by all accounts, the Democratic Party is the only party with an organization and that deserves the "party" label, my scores are meant to stress that there areas of the country – for instance, Veneto, Sicily, and Trentino–Alto Adige – where the party is organizationally quite weak and exposed to internal and external challenges. As far as the always controversial topic of internal democracy is concerned, overall the PD works according to the rules. Its representative bodies at the various levels are elected. The party especially emphasizes its openness to outside supporters and sympathizers for the election of the party leader and for the nomination of candidates to elective offices, including that of Prime Minister. The PD has held quite a number of primaries, at the time of writing more than 1,000 (Venturino 2017). As in several other parties, one can detect within the PD strong pressure coming from the top not to dissent, often enforcing a high level of conformism and culminating in a tendency to discount and dismiss opposing views. The relatively low score for members' loyalty highlights the fact that almost from the very beginning Renzi's leadership was not fully accepted or respected. Later, his way of leading the party was openly disobeyed, and, finally, it was challenged in the April 2017 electoral contest for the office of secretary of the PD. Together, the two challengers obtained slightly more than 30 per cent of the votes. They did not gracefully accept defeat, nor, on his part, did the secretary try his best to reshape a welcoming organization. From many points of view, the Democratic Party has proved to be what Floridia (2019) has aptly called "a wrong party" (see Ventura 2019 and more later in this chapter).

Electorally, for more than ten years after 1994, Forza Italia often achieved important electoral results. It has been a highly successful personalist party from its very beginning. Founded practically from scratch by Berlusconi in 1994, it was led by him to three national electoral victories, often obtaining a high percentage of the votes. At its height it was both bigger than the PD and spread throughout the Italian territory in a more balanced way than the PD was. But, in the 2018 general elections, following a period of relative decline due to its leader's personal liabilities, Forza Italia lost the status of the party with the best polling results within the centre-right to Matteo Salvini's League, and, although its leader is still credited with some of the qualities indispensable to building victorious electoral coalitions, it has entered a twilight zone. Forza Italia has never held party conventions and has no identifiable power structure, except, of course, for the dominant position of its leaders. Internal democracy is not even an issue. Forza Italia's strength has consisted in the unwavering loyalty of almost all parliamentarians and local power holders to Berlusconi. For better or for worse, there have never existed personalized factions within Forza Italia and no challengers to Berlusconi, who remains in full control of all communications and all nominations. However, a succession crisis looms in the near future and the viability of Forza Italia without Berlusconi is highly questionable.

The Five Star Movement is yet another product of the dissatisfaction of Italians with ongoing politics and "professional" politicians. The importance of the role played by its founder, the comedian Beppe Grillo, is undeniable, which made it, certainly at the beginning, a personalist party to some extent comparable with Forza Italia, although it was more bottom-up than top-down. From election to election, the Five Star Movement is in the process of building and strengthening its territorial presence. Hence, to speak of its "organization" would be somewhat misleading. It rotates around local activists, especially when there are electoral contests and it is necessary to put forward candidates. It is enhancing its pervasiveness and, apparently, all areas of Italy have shown a rather high degree of receptivity. The Five Star Movement prides itself on its constant practice of electronic democracy and on full equality among participants. There is no way to check whether internal democracy is really the outcome of this or whether, as many critics argue, subtle manipulations of all kinds take place and are simply accepted as a matter of fact. But expulsions and resignations suggest that within the Movement not everything runs smoothly and that tensions and conflict surface with some frequency. My score of 2 is meant to indicate that, in the end, Five Star's internal democracy is what two individuals decide it should be. It is almost a defining precept that the members of the Movement must be loyal to Beppe Grillo (some would add that Grillo is dependent to an extent on his techno-guru Davide Casaleggio) and that Grillo himself fundamentally decides, whenever necessary, who is in and who is out. Since there have been several cases of voluntary exits as well as of expulsions (are they instances of breaches of internal democracy?), my score for the loyalty of members cannot reach the maximum point (the best overall analysis of the Five Star Movement is to be found in the original essays collected by Tronconi (2015)). In the government since May 2018, the Movement is confronting difficult political challenges: to implement some (or most) of its cherished policies without losing electoral support and to compete with the League, a more experienced and more solid governmental partner.

When analysing the League, one must, of course, keep in mind that its original label "Northern" was indicative of pre-eminent attention to just one specific area of Italy. The new leader, Matteo Salvini, has successfully attempted to go beyond the North and to expand its appeal to the rest of Italy. There is no doubt that in the area called Padania, the Northern League is well-entrenched and pervasive. It has repeatedly won the presidencies of three regions: the two wealthiest ones, Lombardy and Veneto, plus Friuli-Venezia Giulia. My not very high score regarding its entrenchment is meant to emphasize that the League only made inroads in much of the country outside Padania in the 2018 elections, and it is difficult to evaluate whether and for how long the breakthrough is going to last. Internal democracy became an issue in the last period of its founder Umberto Bossi's rule. Now, it is no longer a problem. There have been very few instances, none of them spectacular, in which confrontations on this subject have taken place and Salvini seems willing to listen and to adjust his policies. Membership loyalty towards the organization and the leader is very high. So far, in only one, though highly publicized, case has there been a defection; this was essentially motivated by thwarted personal ambitions.[6] Populist (Passarelli 2015) and "sovereignist", Salvini's League is thriving in Italian politics.

In terms of entrenchment, Fratelli d'Italia (Brothers of Italy, and the first line of the national anthem) enjoys what has been left by Alleanza Nazionale, a true, though relatively small, party that suffered a sudden decline and the haemorrhage of some of its leaders when its founder and President Gianfranco Fini challenged Berlusconi and lost. Subsequently ostracized by Berlusconi, Fini proved unable to survive out in the cold. Nobody in Fratelli d'Italia has so far raised the issue of internal democracy. Apparently, the party is cohesive and united behind its leader, a capable female politician and former minister, Giorgia Meloni, determined but not antagonistic and an excellent communicator. Members are aware that only as long as they remain united will it be possible for Fratelli d'Italia to retain a political role.

Liberi e Uguali has fundamentally been an electoral cartel. It should not be considered a party and it is unlikely to survive for long. It is noteworthy as yet another instance of the inclination of the left to fragment itself. It has put together parliamentarians who have left the Democratic Party, supporters of a minor left-wing party called Left and Liberty, and a small group called Possibile. Both the former Speakers of the House and the Senate have counted among its leaders; indeed, the name of the latter, Piero Grasso, a former anti-Mafia judge, was added to Liberi e Uguali's electoral logo. Its composition suggests that it will be quite difficult for Liberi e Uguali to acquire a stable presence in the landscape of the changing Italian party system. Its role and its future are bound to be (re)defined with reference to what the Democratic Party and its leaders are capable of doing and are willing to offer, plus, of course, to the mechanisms of electoral law. Reconstructing and restructuring the Italian left remains a Sisyphean task (and there is no Italian Mitterrand in sight).

The roots of personalist or personalized parties

In personalist parties, the state of organizations, their internal dynamics and the relationships among the members are, of course, significantly – and in some cases decisively – influenced by the leader of the party. Indeed, personalist parties put much of their political capital and their energies behind the leader. Therefore, in order to learn what personalist parties are and how they work, not only in the Italian context, it is imperative to look at and possibly measure the characteristics of their respective leaders. This exercise illuminates much of Italian (party) politics as well and its potential transformations.

The Partito Democratico has gone through a large number of changes in its leadership, all reflecting events that have had a negative impact on the life of the party. Since its birth in 2007, the PD has had seven secretaries, four of whom were chosen through elections open to all of those who, accepting the party programme, decided to cast their vote: Walter Veltroni (2007–09), Pier Luigi Bersani (2009–13), Matteo Renzi (2013–16; 2017–18) and Nicola Zingaretti (elected in March 2019). Three secretaries – Dario Franceschini (2009), Guglielmo Epifani (2013) and Maurizio Martina (2018) – served as caretakers following the resignation of the secretary. It is not easy to evaluate the consequences of the leadership instability on the PD's policies or on the political consensus, but, obviously, they have been less than positive. There is no doubt that Matteo Renzi, elected as secretary in December 2013 and re-elected in April 2017, acquired a lot of power within the party and in the Italian political system, by far more than all – and I stress *all* – his predecessors. At the beginning of his lightning career, he could also be credited with a fair amount of political and personal charisma, and with the ability to produce stunning results such as obtaining the highest percentage ever for the PD in the 2014 European elections. Reliable researchers at the Istituto Cattaneo have evaluated his own contribution to the very positive outcome: close to 5 per cent of the votes. Moreover, Renzi has always had a lot of confidence in his own communication capabilities and is definitely more flamboyant than all his competitors and predecessors, past (Veltroni and Bersani) and present (Zingaretti), within and outside the PD, with the exception of Berlusconi and, recently, but to a lesser extent, Salvini. He has also made full, and often callously unscrupulous, use of the power to nominate his faithful collaborators to important positions. Having duly underlined these points, however, the way in which he personalized the campaign on the 2016 constitutional referendum and his devastating defeat seem to have squandered much of his power and negatively affected his fragile charisma. Retaining his power to nominate not only those who occupy important political and institutional offices available to the PD, but especially candidates to Parliament, he has decimated any internal opposition and recruited a parliamentary group made up of faithful and reliable party members.[7] When his party's votes plummeted in the March 2018 general elections to their lowest percentage ever, Renzi was obliged to resign. Elected to the Italian Senate, it is unclear how much political (and blackmailing) power he still retains, and how, when for what purposes he will wield it.

This kind of individual recruitment of all his collaborators and parliamentarians is what Berlusconi has always done, but he enjoyed an initial advantage. Apart from a few exceptions, all those recruited for Parliament by Berlusconi, coming from a variety of professional backgrounds, had no political power base of their own. All of them were perfectly aware that only by supporting the leader completely would they be rewarded with re-selection and a return to Parliament. The few counterexamples of those who disagreed with Berlusconi, fell out of favour with him and have completely disappeared, not only from the political scene, continue to serve as unforgettable lessons. As founder and owner of Forza Italia, Berlusconi has always been in full control not only of the nominations but of the process of TV communication as well, also because of his unusual capabilities and qualities in this field.[8] Forza Italia electoral campaigns have constantly been run stressing the name and the personality of the leader, who most certainly adds value. More importantly, Berlusconi has been a truly charismatic leader of the Weberian type, something that has largely been underestimated by domestic and foreign commentators. He took the field of Italian politics in 1994 when there was widespread socio-political anxiety in several sectors of Italian society. The so-called "First" Republic, together with its flexible rules and reassuring rituals, was considered worn out, perhaps defunct. The disappearance of the five parties that had governed Italy from 1980 to 1992 had left millions of Italian voters potentially without political representation, very much afraid of an electoral victory by the former Communists and of a government formed by them. Berlusconi offered an important practical alternative, grounded in his representational qualities, persuasively claiming that he was one of those artisans, small entrepreneurs, employees in the private sector or professionals who had made it: an example to follow, to imitate, to reward with one's vote. He accomplished the miracle of winning against all the odds, and then of surviving politically in opposition from 1996 to 2001 and winning again, and by a sizable margin, in 2001, after his *traversée du désert* (to quote de Gaulle's famous words)[9] and once more in 2008 (Newell 2018).

No collective anxiety can explain the rise of the Five Star Movement, but there are two factors that have been at the root of most populist phenomena: anti-establishment resentment and anti-political sentiments, both of which are widespread in Italy. The Five Star Movement is the product of Beppe Grillo's relentless and successful effort to mobilize the dissatisfied and to channel their discontent. The sudden rise and electoral surge of the Five Star Movement have been the most important events in Italian politics since Berlusconi's victory in March 1994. Indeed, when one compares their first appearances on the national scene, only Forza Italia has obtained more votes in the Chamber of Deputies than the Five Star Movement (10,076,653 compared with 8,688,231), but turnout was considerably higher in 1994 than in 2013. No other "novice" European party has ever come close to the number of votes won by the Five Star Movement. Defining itself a non-party with a non-charter/statute, the Five Star Movement is not just another example of a populist party. Of course, there is more than a hint of populism in what the Five Stars say and do, but their electoral and political fortunes must be explained with reference to something very familiar to the political culture (or lack of it) of the Italians: anti-politics. The criticism and rejection of politicians and politics – or, at least, as they are, and, in truth, as they have been for quite some time in Italy – represent the bedrock of their electoral strength and political sympathies. Anti-politics strikes a familiar chord in the hearts and minds of many an Italian and it is here to stay. Effectively combining conviction and convenience, the Five Star Movement has formulated positions against the EU, going as far as promising a referendum on Italy's permanence in the Eurozone (which, however, is not possible to call according to the Italian Constitution), only to backtrack during the 2018 electoral campaign. Finally, although it challenges Italian representative democracy in the name of a supposedly superior digital democracy, in practice the Five Star Movement remains dominated by two personalities: the founder, comedian Beppe Grillo, and Davide Casaleggio, the son of the late Gianroberto Casaleggio, Grillo's closest collaborator, who is in charge of the online platform called "Rousseau". Faced with the test of forming an Italian government and of occupying important ministerial offices, after one year of activity, the Five Star Movement can claim mixed results. The best and the worst are yet to come.

Grillo's power can be compared with Berlusconi's with reference to their respective communication capabilities. More precisely, Berlusconi is a master of television communication whereas Grillo is at his best in the squares of Italy, enjoying physical contact with his followers, something Berlusconi too would love, but for reasons of personal security cannot afford. Grillo, who runs a highly successful blog, and Casaleggio are in full control of all internal and external communication flows. As for nominations, on the one hand, the Five Star Movement's online consultations seem to be channels for democratic outcomes, but, on the other hand, so far only a very small number have taken part in these processes (20,000–30,000 at most, and in many instances just a few hundred). In any case, in the final instance, Grillo has been the trump (pun intended), just saying "Fidatevi di me" ("Trust me")[10] – he decides who and what. Democracy certainly doesn't exist in the Five Star Movement.

Within the limits that inevitably arise from the very origins and nature of the Northern League (Cento Bull 2015), in the past three or four years Matteo Salvini has acquired full control of the party and has shown remarkable leadership qualities. Salvini enjoys and exercises unfettered political power. In his case, one cannot speak of charisma, especially because the charismatic leader of the League was its founder Umberto Bossi. Being leader for almost thirty years exhausted Bossi. As a communicator capable of appealing well beyond his potential voters, Salvini has repeatedly shown himself to be an electoral advantage for the League. For his power in nominating the League's candidates to elective offices, the relatively low score I have given him reflects not his weakness but the fact that a large number of those candidates come from the geographical area and are deliberately chosen not just to please the leader but essentially because they are in a position to offer convincing political or parliamentary representation to those specific territories.

The political story of Fratelli d'Italia, the successor to an ideological party, at the time small but pervasive, is, of course, quite different from the Northern League's. Interestingly, however, when it comes to the assets of its leadership, there exist many similarities together with one important peculiarity that has not been emphasized as much as it should be. Fratelli d'Italia is the only Italian party ever led by a woman. In her early forties, Giorgia Meloni is a relatively young woman with a long political career. She does not boast of having political power or charisma, although she revitalized a dying organization. She is an excellent debater and TV communicator. As to nominations, she is shrewd enough to impose her views exclusively when it is necessary and so far she has not been challenged within the party. At the same time, she has made a significant contribution to keeping the party afloat in difficult times.

Having said all this, two elements are really important to an understanding of Italian parties and the party system. The first is the rather strong identification of all parties with their leaders, which means that a decline, for whatever reason, in the personal qualities of the leader (a process we have already witnessed in the cases of Bossi and the Northern League; Berlusconi and Forza Italia; and, most recently, and hence even more convincingly, Renzi and the Democratic Party) is bound to negatively affect the party itself from a political and electoral perspective. The second element has to do with the party system, its format and its mechanics. In a way, the format is easy to define. The number of parties presenting lists of candidates and electing some of them at the March 2018 elections amounted to just six. In fact, all six possess the two features, according to Sartori, that are indispensable: coalition potential and blackmailing power. In itself, the existence of six parties is not sufficient to argue for the existence of an extreme multiparty system, to be interpreted as a situation that makes government coalitions difficult to build and sustain. Stressing that the government that followed the 2018 elections is a coalition made up of two parties only (see Chapter 5), it would be wrong to define the format of the Italian party system as tripolar, as many Italian commentators are doing. The format is multiparty, with all parties having the possibility to vie for and obtain an opportunity to participate in the government coalition. All parties have a coalitional potential and none of them enjoys the power of blackmail. This is a positive development not to be discounted or underestimated.

The multiparty format of the Italian party system leads to inevitable consequences for the mechanics of the party system. Although somewhat fuzzily, the second phase of the Republic has been characterized by a bipolar confrontation: centre-right versus centre-left. This is largely the product of a combination of the Mattarella electoral law, utilized in 1994, 1996 and 2001, and Berlusconi's willingness and ability to "polarize" all political competitions. Leaving aside the fact that bipolar competition was taking place in a party system unable to reach a stage of structural stability – that is, in which several small parties came and went and centre-left coalitions never found an acceptable shape or unity of purpose[11] – the emergence of the Five Star Movement has definitely created a new situation. By itself, the Movement represents one pole and, in more than one way, it affects the coalition game, both because it is indispensable for most governing coalitions and because it can play the role of a powerful (anti-system) opposition. Moreover, the Rosato electoral law, which was designed to protect the position of a few individual parties and their short-term interests, as I argued in Chapter 2, is bound to freeze any attempts to make changes to the existing format of the party system.

The "new" Italian party system will not become what Sartori called "polarized pluralism", because the Five Star Movement has been obliged by its very electoral success to drop its rejection of coalition agreements and to establish a government with the League. At this point, there is one overriding consideration to be noted: the Italian party system is in a situation of flux that is not conducive to a satisfactory consolidation. Both former major parties – the Democratic Party and Forza Italy – are, for different reasons, undergoing a visible phase of decline. As far as Forza Italia is concerned, as a more personalist party than all its competitors, its existence and survival largely depend on the leadership and the energies of its eighty-two-year-old founder Silvio Berlusconi. In the case of the PD, the very nature and structure of the party are being challenged while no new transformative leadership appears on the horizon.

Clay-footed parties

So far, the emphasis has been on personalist parties and, as a consequence, on their leaders, few of them stable or durable, many challenged, and many quite transient. But the picture would not be complete and would not be capable of illuminating the future if one were not to take into consideration three, or possibly four, elements: class, religion, political culture and the EU. In fact, those familiar with voting behaviour in the first phase of the Italian Republic know that the two most important cleavages were represented by religion and class, in that order (see Dogan 1967). Neither cleavage still figures in the second phase of the Republic and no party can rely on either of the two traditional divisions in order to get votes.[12] Indeed, the two parties that have formed and led the governments in the 1994–2018 period – Forza Italia and the Partito Democratico – were not the product of old cleavages and are now on the wane.

Berlusconi promised a "liberal revolution" in a country where not only the Christian Democrats and the Communists had always been rather distant from liberal ideas (and practices), but the Liberals themselves had remained no more than a tiny minority of Italian voters ("*quattro gatti*" – four cats – in their own jargon). How could the "bourgeois" mass media believe for a moment that a TV tycoon, a duopolist in the industry, drenched in a major conflict of interest and believing that the electoral consensus would put him above the law, could lead such a liberal revolution? The answer is still to be explained.[13] In any case, Forza Italia did not devote time or energy to drafting a political manifesto containing anything about "liberal" political culture, or anything else. Its affiliation with the European People's Party is, perhaps, sufficient to give it the kind of political coat of paint it needs. The political ideas, principles and goals of Forza Italia are what Berlusconi says they are and wants them to be. As for the former Communists and the former Christian Democrats, no organization and no leader seemed to be able to offer a new identity or to shape a new political culture. Despite repeated attempts to idealize it (the most recent being Colasio (2018)), the Olive Tree (L'Ulivo) coalition, led by the Professor of Industrial Economics and state manager Romano Prodi to electoral victory in 1996, was little more than an umbrella electoral cartel. Despite claiming to represent the best of all Italian reformist cultures (with the incomprehensible exclusion of the Socialist one), the Democratic Party has been unable to formulate any kind of document that would give substance to its claim, either at its creation in October 2007 or since then. As former Prime Minister Massimo D'Alema has scathingly declared, the PD was and remains a "botched amalgam" (Pasquino and Valbruzzi 2010). In fact, the Democratic Party has been a failure first and foremost in its declared uppermost goal: to blend all Italian reformist cultures – that is, progressive, Democratic Catholicism and environmentalist. Instead, it has become just a political vehicle for its leaders: first, Walter Veltroni, then Matteo Renzi. In fact, the disappearance of any political culture in the PD is a major part of the problems faced by the party.[14]

On the other hand, the Northern League has contributed to the "discovery" of a primordial "territorial" political culture and has nourished it and given representation to those territories. Building on some success and having learned that it could, in fact, move from "Padania first" (Padania comprising the most productive and wealthy regions of northern Italy) to "Italians first", Salvini goes well beyond any territorial cleavage, stressing instead "change versus conservatism". Also, the Five Star Movement has surpassed any type of social cleavage and, for that matter, any reference to political culture of even the most vague populist brand.[15] Obviously, it is not enough to live in the same area in order to learn and share the same political culture. In the recent past, having geographically defined its territory as the Padania, the Northern League proceeded to imbue its supporters and potential voters with autonomist, independentist, secessionist ideas under the veil of an alleged federalist culture. The soil was fertile because many voters who could no longer look to the vanished Communist Party or, especially, to the evanescent Christian Democrats and to the fading minor centrist parties were obliged to redefine their political or electoral identity. It was not too difficult for them to discover that they could be and were northerners, an identity that the Northern League was more than ready to recognize and nourish, with success. The change in name – they have dropped the adjective to become just the League – has been accompanied by a nationwide appeal, strengthened by sharp criticisms addressed to the bureaucrats and the technocrats allegedly dictating EU policies.

Unstoppable decline

When, in August 1941, Altiero Spinelli together with Ernesto Rossi wrote the Manifesto of Ventotene, envisaging a United States of Europe, he prophesied that the most important forthcoming political distinction would no longer be between left and right, but between those in favour of a federal united Europe and those defending the national state. No realignment of this kind has yet taken place in Italian politics. The potential split between those supporting and those opposing the EU has finally become visible, but it is not yet decisive nor capable of redefining the party system. Generally speaking, the centre-left, hence the PD and some groups to its left, is in favour of a federal Europe while the right is clearly and adamantly opposed to it, with Berlusconi taking an ambiguous position. The Five Star Movement, though often critical of the EU, has jettisoned its "exit" option, arguing the case for staying and reforming the EU. On the whole, in Italy the so-called populists characterize themselves as *sovereignists* who want to reacquire their national sovereignty which has supposedly been expropriated by the EU. So far, they have been unable to formulate a political culture that is more than mere nostalgia, while federalism is a recognized, though not widely shared, political culture. In any case, attitudes towards the EU seem unlikely to produce a significant realignment of Italian parties.

Personalist parties without political culture cannot be anything but weak and transient organizations. There is no way that their competition will lead to a restructuring of the Italian party system. *Partitocrazia* has gone forever, but a stable party system has not made its appearance. Party government remains what Italy relies on, but it has only a pale and fragile resemblance to the cluster of parties that served Italy from 1946 to 1992. The fact is that no new party system has made its appearance. Unstructured political vehicles inevitably lead to a situation of electoral volatility and the instability of the parties themselves, of their coalitions, and of the party system. All this negatively affects the already poor quality of Italian democracy.

The widespread lack of political ideas, principles and values whose combination may give life to a political culture is responsible for two important political phenomena: electoral volatility and parliamentary *trasformismo*. If no perceivable differences exist between the various parties with reference to their political culture, few voters will retain enough attachment to a specific party and most voters will feel free to evaluate time after time, election by election, the offer of platforms and leaders made by a variety of competing parties, or will prefer to withdraw themselves from the political arena altogether. By resorting to massive doses of *trasformismo* (Valbruzzi 2015) – that is, by demonstrating that they feel free to move from one parliamentary group to another – many parliamentarians clearly indicate that the distinctive line between different parliamentary groups is, to say the least, blurred, that there is no obstacle to their mobility deriving from political cultural principles, and finally that the disappearance of political cultures has increased electoral volatility and office-seeking urgency and expediency.

In this chapter we have seen how important, for better or for worse, Italian parties have been for the establishment, consolidation and evolution of the political system and of democracy itself. I have argued that their degeneration, when they were too strong and too voracious, created problems for the overall political system. Their inability to renew their politics, to recruit more competent personnel and to provide better representation and leadership to a changing society is responsible for their visible decline – far more significant qualitatively and quantitatively than of most European parties and party systems. Since parties have occupied a central role in the Italian political and socio-economic system, their decline has already affected all the major institutions, especially the government and Parliament. To learn more, it is time to turn to an analysis of Parliament.

Notes

1 Understandably, on the Italian partyocracy there is an extremely abundant literature of all kinds, from political science, history and journalism to literature. Unfortunately, there is no work of synthesis. Good material can be found in Di Mascio (2012) and in Cotta (2015).

2 Some of the criticisms, especially those by liberal scholars and intellectuals, for instance by Giuseppe Maranini (1983 [1967]), were easily rejected because too often they went so far as to question the role itself, and not just the behaviour, of the political parties, in a way even challenging the existence of Italian parliamentary democracy. Other journalists have played the game of criticizing all party politicians; the most successful in recent times have been G. Stella and S. Rizzo (2007), who most certainly bear some responsibility for reigniting a powerful anti-politics and anti-parliamentary fire.

3 The factors that undermined the remaining power of already declining Italian political parties were, chronologically: (i) the fall of the Berlin Wall, 8–9 November 1989; (ii) the Maastricht Treaty, February 1992, which obliged Italian politicians to put the Italian public finance system in order; (iii) the assassination by the Mafia of the judges Giovanni Falcone (22 May 1992) and Paolo Borsellino (19 July 1992).

4 For a variety of reasons, not least a fair amount of political expediency, Berlusconi proved not to be an institution builder. It is necessary to add that both the former Christian Democrats and the former Communists strenuously objected to (partisan) constitutional reforms.

5 So far, only the Democratic Party has somewhat resisted the trend, partly because it has undergone frequent leadership changes, but for some time many believed that the party had been significantly transformed and should have been called Renzi's party (Pasquino and Valbruzzi 2017). No doubt the actions of the then secretary have given substance to this perspective.

6 The mayor of Verona, exploiting the national and international visibility of his city, aimed for higher office. Running against the League, his performance has been disappointing and he has since almost disappeared from politics.

7 This intention is translated into the insistence on retaining closed lists for the election of all parliamentarians. As stated in Chapter 2, the electoral law that carries the name of Rosato is based on closed lists.

8 His March 1994 TV duel with the leader of the Progressives, former Communist and seasoned politician Achille Occhetto, was memorable. Berlusconi won fundamentally thanks to his superior ability to communicate to a television audience. This is a quality he has retained notwithstanding the passing of time.

9 From many points of view, the comparison between General de Gaulle and Silvio Berlusconi is by no means out of place (see Campus 2010).

10 This was an unfortunate, though revealing, phrase when, in June 2017, overturning the results of the primaries in Genova, he chose a candidate who went down in a scathing defeat.

11 In 1994, the centre-left was unable to build a coalition and suffered a major defeat. In 1996, L'Ulivo (Olive Tree) was a broad coalition that won thanks to an agreement to stand down with Communist Refoundation. In 2001, the centre-left was indeed a coalition, mainly between the Left Democrats and former left-wing Christian Democrats.

12 Both the subtitle of an important book devoted to electoral behaviour, "From belonging to choice" (Bellucci and Segatti 2010), and the rather brief chapter on class, religion and territory are revealing on the subject of the disappearance of the old cleavages.

13 Two explanations are possible. The media believed, first, that Berlusconi was necessary and helpful in eradicating what remained of the Communist Party and of former major Communist political personalities, and, second, that they could then significantly influence and orient Berlusconi's behaviour and his largely inchoate public policies. I surmise that the most important Italian newspaper, the *Corriere della Sera*, entertained both expectations.

14 There is no analysis of a political culture whose elaboration has not even been attempted, but some reflections can be found in Pasquino and Valbruzzi (2017).

15 Not even the most detailed study of the Five Star Movement (Ceri and Veltri 2017) has succeeded in unearthing something one might reasonably define "political culture".

References

Bellucci, P. and Segatti, P. (2010). *Votare in Italia: 1968–2008. Dall'apparte-nenza alla scelta*. Bologna: Il Mulino.

Campus, D. (2010). *Anti-Politics in Power: Populist Language as a Tool for Government*. Cresskill: Hampton Press.

Cento Bull, A. (2015). The Fluctuating Fortunes of the *Lega Nord*. In A. Mammone, E. Giap Parini and G. A. Veltri (eds) *The Routledge Handbook of Contemporary Italy* (pp. 204–214). London: Routledge.

Ceri, P. and Veltri, F. (2017). *Il Movimento nella Rete: Storia e struttura del Movimento 5 Stelle*. Turin: Rosenberg & Sellier.

Colasio, A. (2018). *Il tempo dell'Ulivo*. Bologna: Il Mulino.

Cotta, M. (2015). Partitocracy: Parties and their Critics in Italian Political Life. In E. Jones and G. Pasquino (eds) *The Oxford Handbook of Italian Politics* (pp. 41–520). Oxford: Oxford University Press.

Di Mascio, F. (2012). *Partiti e Stato in Italia: Le nomine pubbliche tra cliente-lismo e spoils system*. Bologna: Il Mulino.

Dogan, M. (1967). Political Cleavage and Social Stratification in France and Italy. In S. M. Lipset and S. Rokkan (eds) *Party Systems and Voter Alignments* (pp. 129–195). New York: The Free Press.

Floridia, A. (2019). *Un partito sbagliato: Democrazia e organizzazione nel Partito Democratico*. Rome: Castelvecchi.

Ignazi, P. (2018). *I partiti in Italia dal 1945 al 2018*. Bologna: Il Mulino.

Katz, R. S. (1986). Party Government a Rationalistic Conception. In F. G. Castles and R. Wildenmann (eds) *Visions and Realities of Party Government* (pp. 31–71). Berlin and New York: de Gruyter.

Kostadinova, T. and Levitt, B. (2014). Towards a Theory of Personalist Parties: Concept Formation and Theory Building. In *Politics & Policy* 24 (4), pp. 490–512.

Maranini, G. (1983 [1967]). *Storia del potere in Italia: 1848–1967*. Florence: Guaraldi [Vallecchi].

Newell, J. L. (2000). *Parties and Democracy in Italy*. Aldershot: Ashgate.

Newell, J. L. (2018). *Silvio Berlusconi: A Study in Failure*. Manchester: Manchester University Press.

Pasquino, G. and Valbruzzi, M. (2017). The Italian Democratic Party, its Nature and its Secretary. In *Revista Española de Ciencia Politica* 44, July, pp. 275–299.

Pasquino, G. and Valbruzzi, M. (2010). A che punto è il PD? Analisi organizzativa di un amalgama mal riuscito. In G. Pasquino and F. Venturino (eds) *Il Partito Democratico di Bersani: Persone, profilo e prospettive* (pp. 13–33). Bologna: Bononia University Press.

Passarelli, G. (2015). Populism and the Lega Nord. In E. Jones and G. Pasquino (eds) *The Oxford Handbook of Italian Politics* (pp. 224–239). Oxford: Oxford University Press.

Poli, E. (2001). *Forza Italia: Strutture, leadership e radicamento territoriale*. Bologna: Il Mulino.

Raniolo, F. (2006). Forza Italia: A leader with a party. In *South European Society and Politics* 11 (3–4), pp. 439–455.

Sartori, G. (1976). *Parties and Party Systems: A Framework for Analysis*. Cambridge: Cambridge University Press.

Schattschneider, E. E. (1942). *Party Government*. New York: Holt, Rinehart, and Winston.

Scoppola, P. (1997). *La Repubblica dei partiti: Evoluzione e crisi di un sistema politico: 1945–1996*. Bologna: Il Mulino.

Stella, G. A. and Rizzo, S. (2007). *La casta: Così i politici italiani sono diventati intoccabili*. Milan: Rizzoli.

Tronconi, F. (ed.) (2015). *Beppe Grillo's Five Star Movement: Organisation, Communication, and Ideology*. Farnham: Ashgate.

Valbruzzi, M. (2015). *Trasformismo*. In E. Jones and G. Pasquino (eds) *The Oxford Handbook of Italian Politics* (pp. 26–40). Oxford: Oxford University Press.

Ventura, S. (2019). The Italian Democratic Party from Merger to Personalism. In M. J. Bull and G. Pasquino (eds) *Italy Transformed: Politics, Society and Institutions at the End of the Great Recession* (pp. 180–195). London: Routledge.

Venturino, F. (2017). *Primarie e sindaci in Italia: Politica locale e democrazia intrapartitica, 2004–2015*. Sant'Arcangelo di Romagna: Maggioli.

A Parliament of parties 4

In a parliamentary democracy, Parliament understandably occupies a central role. But from the very beginning in Italy a strong anti-parliamentary sentiment has manifested itself, accompanied by several, often misplaced, criticisms. This chapter explores what the Italian Parliament does and how satisfactorily it performs. It assesses its transformations through time and, especially, its relationships with the government. It also evaluates the proposals for additional changes. Although parliamentary representation remains the most important and irreplaceable task to be fulfilled by Parliament, it is negatively affected by *trasformismo*, an Italian political disease with deep roots in the past.

Structure and composition

When deciding which kind of Parliament the new Italian democratic Republic should have, the members of the Constituent Assembly (1946–48) were confronted with three options. The most radical was the one formulated, but not defended all the way, tooth and nail, by the Communists: a unicameral system. Their reasoning was crystal clear: popular sovereignty cannot be divided into two chambers. It can most appropriately be located and represented in a single house. Already aware of the numerical strength and the party discipline of the Communists, the Christian Democrats and others were quick to see the political risk of this kind of solution. In one chamber the Communists could have won frequently on important issues. The second option was the easiest one: it simply pointed to the fact that both the Kingdom of Sardinia and Piedmont and the political system of unified Italy since 1861 had been a bicameral Parliament, with a House of Deputies and a Senate of the Kingdom (which had been left untouched by Mussolini). The most difficult option argued the case for a differentiated (asymmetrical) bicameralism, largely still to be shaped. Some wanted a second chamber to represent the (yet to be established) regions. Others thought that two chambers were likely to provide for better political representation. Others wanted to obtain and give more specific representation to a variety of socio-economic interests, but this goal resembled too closely the Fascist Chamber of Corporations. In the end, the winning option was the product of a combination of institutional inertia (changing the Senate of the Kingdom, Senato del Regno, to the Senate of the Republic, Senato della Repubblica – the official name since 1948) with comparative lessons drawn from the existing European democracies of the time, all of them bicameral.[1]

The most convincing justification, hinted at by some members of the Constituent Assembly, was that bicameralism would produce better legislation since "mistakes" made in one chamber could be corrected in the other, and additional useful information could be acquired during the legislative process. At the time, nobody expressed any preoccupation with the speed of the legislative process. Nor did anybody think that the existence of two chambers might be a (mixed) blessing for the government. Due to the absence of some parliamentarians – those, for instance, with governmental responsibilities – from one chamber, the government might lose some votes. The second chamber would then get the bill on track again, returning it to the first chamber for the final vote when all the parliamentarians belonging to the majority could attend. In any case, the *navette* (back and forth process) could be stopped at any time just by enforcing party discipline. No surprise then that Italian bicameralism has served the interests of diversified governmental majorities well, not only between 1948 and 1992, and, I would stress, of the political system itself as well.

In order for bicameralism to carry the day, its many sponsors had to find differentiating criteria they could agree on. Two of them appeared reasonable to the members of the Constituent Assembly: territoriality and age. In anticipation of the regional decentralization that took twenty-two years to be implemented, it was established that the Senate had to be elected on a regional basis (Article 57). An attempt was also made to have Senators directly elected by the voters provided they received 66 per cent of the votes in their constituency, a threshold that was attained only a few times and exclusively by

Christian Democratic candidates in one or two of their strongholds in the Veneto region.[2] There were two age criteria: (i) voters for the Senate had to be at least twenty-five years old; and (ii) candidates had to be at least forty. The reasoning behind this was that senior parliamentarians would be less inclined to emotional and "irrational" behaviour. In practice, the average age of Senators has always been only slightly higher than the average age of Deputies (see Table 4.1). Powerful politicians, the secretaries of the political parties and all Prime Ministers, with only two exceptions so far, have always been members of the House of Deputies.

Since 1963, the House of Deputies has had 630 members and the Senate 315 elected members plus a number of life Senators. There are two types of life Senators: (i) de jure – that is, all former Presidents of the Republic (at the time of writing, there is only one: Giorgio Napolitano (2006–15)); and (ii) up to five Senators appointed by the President of the Republic (Article 59) because they have "brought prestige to the Motherland for their outstanding merits in the social, scientific, artistic and literary fields". There should be a total of five life Senators of this category; there is no prerogative for each President to appoint five life Senators, which is how President Sandro Pertini (1978–85) wilfully interpreted the Constitution (hence creating an infelicitous precedent).[3] In the past, some Presidents of the Republic have misinterpreted or manipulated the Constitution and have appointed career politicians to the office of life Senator. President Giovanni Leone gave a consolation prize to Christian Democrat Amintore Fanfani, the Prime Minister several times as well as a repeatedly defeated candidate to the Presidency, making him a life Senator in 1972. Fanfani continued his active political career, serving as President of the Senate in 1979–82 and 1985–87, and for a short time as Prime Minister as well. And, in a decision that was not especially appreciated, in 1991 President Francesco Cossiga (1985–92) appointed as a life Senator the longest-serving Italian parliamentarian, seven-times Prime Minister Giulio Andreotti, soon to be accused of close ties with the Sicilian Mafia and put on trial.

Life Senators enjoy all the political prerogatives and have all the socio-economic privileges of elected Senators. Indeed, some of them – namely, Francesco Cossiga in the past and more recently Giorgio Napolitano – have continued to participate actively in Italian political life. Strong criticisms were provoked by the repeated votes of life Senators in the 2006–08 parliamentary term that decisively helped the very fragile centre-left government led by Romano Prodi to survive, although, in the end, they could not save it.

Table 4.1 Changes in the socio-demographic characteristics of Italian Deputies and those related to political experience

Legislature	Gender (percentage of women)	Mean age of MPs (years)	Tenure (average number of legislatures in Parliament)	Professional politicians (percentage)	MPs without experience in local government (percentage)	MPs without experience in party organizations (percentage)
XV (2006–08)	17	52	1.2	21	32	18
XVI (2008–13)	21	51	1.3	19	35	21
XVII (2013–18)	30	46	0.9	5	44	29
XVIII (2018–)	35	43	0.7	5	53	39

Source: Adapted from Marino, Martocchia Diodati and Verzichelli (2019).

What the Italian Parliament does

In all parliamentary democracies, parliaments have important political tasks and carry out many activities that cannot be left to any other institution. Although there are different ways to identify what a Parliament does and ought to do, I believe that Walter Bagehot's perspective[4] still provides the best analytical framework. Moreover, Bagehot's categories can be used as an appropriate yardstick to evaluate the performance of different parliamentary assemblies. According to Bagehot, the most important function of a Parliament in a parliamentary democracy is to "elect a ministry well" – that is, to give the power to govern to a cabinet made up of the Prime Minister and his or her party representatives who enjoy the support of a parliamentary majority – and to remain willing and capable of keeping the cabinet alive, sustaining its activities. From this point of view, the Italian Parliament has a mixed record. Yes, it has always been capable of giving birth to a government: indeed, to more than one government in all parliamentary terms (see Table 4.2). How "well" it has done this is debatable, but when those governments were not good, was it the fault of Parliament as such or of the Italian parties?

Table 4.2   Number of cabinets and Prime Ministers in Italy, by parliamentary term

Legislature	Cabinets	Prime Ministers
I (1948–53)	3	1
II (1953–58)	6	6
III (1958–63)	5	3
IV (1963–68)	4	2
V (1968–72)	6	4
VI (1972–76)	5	3
VII (1976–79)	3	1
VIII (1979–83)	6	4
IX (1983–87)	3	2
X (1987–92)	4	3
XI (1992–94)	2	2
XII (1994–96)	2	2
XIII (1996–2001)	4	3
XIV (2001–06)	2	1
XV (2006–08)	1	1
XVI (2008–13)	2	2
XVII (2013–18)	3	3
XVIII (2018–)	2	1

The kind of relationship to be established between Parliament and government did not receive great attention during the working of the Constituent Assembly. It was given an apparently easy solution in Article 94: "the government must receive the confidence of both houses of parliament". As a consequence, any and all governments can be defeated by a motion of no confidence. At the time, the paramount issue was not, as has often been said, how much power the government (and its head) should have, but the stability of governments. Again, it was not simply the Italian experience from 1861 to 1922 that suggested that governmental instability could become a systemic problem; rather, the tragic trajectory of the Weimar Republic (1919–33), very well known to the majority of the members of the Constituent Assembly, was even more influential. I will not deal with this issue here, as it will be analysed more appropriately in Chapter 5. Here, suffice it to say that it is not just a matter of inter-institutional relationships. For better or for worse, political parties are the intervening actors that carry much of the responsibility and the blame for how Parliament and government interact.[5]

To start with, well aware that in their lifetime they could not aspire to have a say in the formation and functioning of Italian governments, the Communists worked very hard to have their view accepted: Parliament had to be considered "central" in the institutional network. The meaning of the "centrality of Parliament" was subject to different interpretations, but there was sufficient agreement that it implied the need and will to take into account not only policy contributions and suggestions coming from the opposition, especially from the Communists, but to accept negotiations with them on several issues. What I would consider the myth of Italy being a consociational democracy was constructed on the alleged *centrality of Parliament* and on the inevitable exchanges that took place in multiparty representative assemblies (see Box 4.1).[6] Indeed, what is often neglected, even totally forgotten, is that the Italian Parliament, whatever its shortcomings (and merits), and also thanks to the PR electoral law, was a truly representative assembly accommodating a variety of parties, reflecting the voters' preferences and interests and translating them into public policies.

The sociological representativeness of the Italian Parliament (see Table 4.3) was not sufficient to exempt it from being criticized, but for a long time, at least until the late 1980s, anti-parliamentarism was less than virulent. It was not very widespread and it did not show any populist stigmata. Much to the merit of the Communists, who, obviously, had their own advantage in using Parliament as a political tribune, the Italian Parliament as such was not delegitimized. Nor were

---

Box 4.1 The centrality of Parliament

In 1971, through a reform of the parliamentary rules, more power was given to Parliament on several issues, uppermost among them the power to set the agenda. This meant that the governments led by the Christian Democrats always had to bargain with other parties, and especially with the Communist opposition.

Table 4.3   Professional origin of Italian Deputies, 2006–18 (percentage)

Occupation	2006	2008	2013	2018
Fully paid politician	24.4	22.1	7.9	8.8
Journalist, writer, media sector	7.7	8.2	10.5	11.8
Private employee	3.2	3.2	15.8	8.8
Public sector	23.9	22.6	26.3	23.5
Entrepreneur, manager	15.2	18.3	15.8	14.7
Law-related profession	11.1	12.0	2.6	2.9
Other private occupation	14.4	13.6	21.1	29.4

Source: Adapted from Tronconi and Verzichelli (2010) for the XV and XVI parliamentary term.

parliamentarians, whose job was considered important and even prestigious. Generally speaking, the blame was put on political parties and, of course, on the government(s). In 1983, the secretary of the Socialist Party, Bettino Craxi, was the first important political leader to launch a vicious criticism of the Italian Parliament, which he accused of being an "cattle pen". Berlusconi, too, has generally considered Parliament mainly as a hindrance to his activities as Prime Minister, an obstacle to a swift decision-making process, a trap in which "snipers" could make an attempt on the life of "his" government. He went so far as to ask that parliamentary votes be cast only by the heads of parliamentary groups.[7] The fact is that, like most parliaments in the world, the Italian Parliament has been and still is a Parliament of parties – even more so because, as was the case in 2006, 2008, 2013 and 2018, all parliamentarians have been chosen by their party and faction leaders.[8] The question Sartori (1963) asked at the end of a major research project on the Italian Parliament still stands. Which sanction for their behaviour do Italian parliamentarians fear the most: the one coming from the electorate, from interest groups, or from party leaders?

The limited amount of empirical research on Italian interest groups reveals (Mattina 2010; Pritoni 2018) that they may attempt to influence the behaviour of elected parliamentarians by providing technical support, financing some of their political activities or offering "structured" advice. But, since 2006, the electoral law has not allowed them any opportunity to elect their own parliamentarian(s), even though, of course, powerful interest groups make a strong and largely successful case for some of their "people" to be accommodated on the parties' lists. In practice, in the past, and even more so today, some parties have been more than willing to recruit representatives of specific interest groups and have widely publicized their presence on their party lists in order to obtain some kind of support and, in some cases, the votes of members of certain interest groups. However, the trade unions and all the Catholic associations would reject the very idea of being defined as "interest groups". This is not the case for the already quoted Small Farmers' Association, the General Confederation of Italian Industry (Confindustria) and its many regional and city branches, the teachers' associations, the Association of Real Estate Builders, and so on – they were all very happy to have one or more people elected to Parliament and appointed to the relevant committees. In any case, the most powerful of the interest groups rely only in a very limited way on individual parliamentarians. Either they seek to influence entire parliamentary groups and therefore the party leaders or they try to obtain access to the staff of ministers and undersecretaries in the departments where the bills are drafted. On the whole, it is likely that several parliamentarians have divided loyalties: to the leader of the party who has "nominated" them and to the association or organization to which they owe their visibility and to which they may return after their parliamentary experience (see Figure 4.1).

Leaving aside the always present instances of conflict of interests and of corruption, but recognizing their existence and occurrence, there appears to be one important activity that the Italian Parliament has most certainly performed in a satisfactory way: the reconciliation of interests. Too much reconciliation of too many interests, critics would claim. However, in a situation in which, for a long time, the Italian Communist Party could not even hope for some kind of presence in the government, the fact that some of the interests the party represented could be heard in Parliament and have a bearing on the parliamentary decision-making process has to be evaluated positively. This kind of reconciliation of interests certainly contributed to the functioning of the Italian political and socio-economic system. It also encouraged the Communist Party to devote some – and frequently

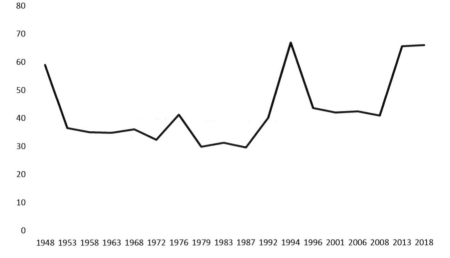

Figure 4.1 Parliamentary turnover in the Chamber of Deputies, 1948–2018 (percentage)

a lot – of its political time and human energy to parliamentary activities through the training of capable representatives as an outlet for ambitious cadres and a resource for Parliament. Incidentally, the French Communist Party constantly remained well below the Italian one from the perspective of its contribution to the working of Parliament and to the training and promotion of good parliamentarians.

Bagehot often states that a body of great men[9] put in the middle of a society has the opportunity to exert a great (and positive) influence, educating that society. Also, all decent parliaments can indeed be places for great debates. While collecting data on these activities is a very difficult enterprise, what we know about the Italian Parliament offers a lot of food for thought. Throughout much of the first phase of the Italian Republic, Parliament was rarely considered the most important subject to be reported on by the mass media. The media's attention was much more focused on parties and party leaders, their statements, their proposals, their reactions to each other and, most recently, their insults. After all, this is what one would expect from a situation of partyocracy: parties *über alles* monopolizing political communication (and the parties belonging to the governing coalition being put in control of RAI, the Italian radio and TV broadcasting company). Unparadoxically, the newsworthiness of the Italian Parliament started to increase hand in hand with the slow, gradual, almost inevitable decline of Italian parties. In the past twenty-five years, the Italian Parliament has been at the centre of all political reportage, widely narrated as well as criticized.

Recently, the very idea that the Italian Parliament is (or ought to be) made up of honourable men and women pursuing a political career has been challenged by the parliamentarians of the Five Star Movement. It is too early to provide an evaluation of the parliamentary performance of the Five Star representatives, but their impact on the status of parliamentarians and on the "popular" image of the Italian Parliament has been remarkable, for better or for worse, and has largely contributed to the decrease of its prestige. From the very beginning, the Five Star parliamentarians claimed to be just "citizens", no different from those who had voted them in. They therefore miss the crucial fact that parliamentarians perform the function of representing "the nation" – that is, more than all the voters, and, in any case, not just their own voters, who are not identifiable anyway[10] – and that they have a duty to learn how to do this effectively. Many of the Five Star parliamentarians also thought that there was not too much to be learned in order to play the role of "citizens" in Parliament among professional, seasoned parliamentarians: that is, parliamentarians who had already served one or more terms. Their own non-statute contains a rigid clause concerning term limits: two terms for all offices at all levels.[11] There is more than a hint of populism in all the requests to impose term limits on representative[12] offices and strictly implement them. The Five Star Movement has accompanied this request with an obsessive anti-parliamentary campaign – which, in fact, was initiated and sustained by the daily *Corriere della Sera* and some of its journalists – not fully aware of its implications and consequences for the privileges, as if they were a *Casta*, enjoyed by parliamentarians, starting with their allowances and continuing to their retirement indemnities (see Chapter 3, footnote 2).

If parliamentarians are just citizens among citizens, they should be treated as citizens, but which group of citizens? The entire story cannot be told here because there is no end in sight, but if parliamentarians are treated as citizens, then their legitimacy as representatives who make difficult decisions in complex circumstances, who are obliged to negotiate in order to reach agreements and who attempt to acquire the best available information and interpret it for their fellow citizens suffers a precipitous decline. Similarly, credibility could be denied to parliamentarians when they decide on European issues, when they pass a bill making a certain number and type of vaccines compulsory, when they try to solve the thorny issue of whether and how to grant Italian citizenship to migrants' sons and daughters born on Italian territory (*jus soli*), and so on. If parliamentarians are not considered a body of civilized and competent persons, there is no way they can "educate" their voters. Having said this, however, Figure 4.2 shows that, although parliamentarians enjoy low prestige, Italians retain a fair amount of trust in their Parliament.

If and when Parliament is considered just an assembly of citizens, then all other citizens may feel justified in not paying attention to parliamentary debates, in not listening to parliamentary pronouncements, in rejecting the decisions Parliament has arrived at, even if they are approved by a majority vote cast by representatives belonging to a variety of groups. This is what has occurred in the Italian Parliament elected in 2013, making most parliamentary debates not "educational" events for public opinion but rhetorical battles for forthcoming electoral contests. The damage has already been done to the reputation of the Italian Parliament and its parliamentarians, no matter who they are or will be, thanks to the Five Star Movement, but also with the contribution of many parliamentarians of the Democratic Party and their former secretary Matteo Renzi (who was not a member of the 2013–18 Parliament). Of course, many of the Five Star Movement's criticisms have become somewhat muted following their 2018 electoral victory and their acquisition of powerful offices on many parliamentary committees.

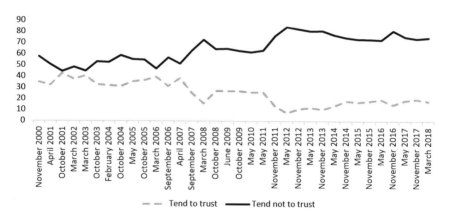

Figure 4.2 Trust in the Italian Parliament, 2000–18 (percentage)

Note: The question was "Please tell me if you tend to trust or tend not to trust the national parliament".

Source: Author's own compilation on data provided by Eurobarometer (2018).

In more than one way, Parliament ought to accomplish the task of overseeing what the government does, what it does not do and what it does poorly (for a comparative perspective on this and much more, see Pasquino and Pelizzo (2006)). More precisely, Parliament is an arena where the government and the opposition encounter each other and play a complex game to their own advantage and to that of public opinion. The Italian Parliament has generally worked positively in this way, providing an arena and a meeting ground, but critics have stressed two, not minor, drawbacks. For a long period, the dissenters, called *franchi tiratori* (snipers), could hide themselves behind secret voting, occasionally "killing" the government (which would soon be resurrected, as we will see in Chapter 5) and some of its bills. In the 1980s, the Socialist secretary Bettino Craxi fought a long, obstinate and acrimonious battle in order to abolish secret voting altogether. If successful, he would have acquired full control of all Socialist parliamentarians, but he would also have obliged all shades of Christian Democratic parliamentarians to come out into the open, something that the majority of DC parliamentarians was opposed to. In any case, secret voting in the Italian Parliament is now very rare and any "control" over parliamentarians is acquired at the time of their selection and with those parliamentarians' full knowledge that their re-selection will depend very much on their voting discipline.

The process of law-making

The second drawback derives from the internal arrangement of the Italian Parliament. All legislation and other activities have to start their journey in specialized parliamentary committees before being sent to the floor. Daily transcripts of all committee meetings are available, but it is not always possible to find out who has voted for what. In the past, the Christian Democrats and the Communists were accused of reaching a variety of backroom deals at the expense of the state budget.[13] In addition, only in exceptional circumstances (such as, for instance, the first Gulf War) can individual parliamentarians be held responsible for their votes. Personal accountability is not a staple of Italian parliamentary customs and procedures. John McCain was not born in Italy.

Most Italians would have no hesitation in stating that the most important task of Parliament is to make laws. As is well known, Bagehot would strongly disagree, in principle and in practice. So do I, but what counts is that the data tell a story in which the Italian Parliament is not *technically* the "author" of laws. It is a participant – more precisely a junior partner – in the legislative process. First, it is important to clarify what one means by making a law. The process starts with the drafting of a bill. The correct question to ask, then, is who has and uses their power to sponsor a bill. Figure 4.3 contains the answer: about 70 per cent of the bills come from the government. Still, at the beginning of every new legislature, quite a number of Italian parliamentarians reintroduce bills they have already presented in previous parliamentary terms and that have probably never been discussed. Usually less than 10 per cent, at most 15 per cent, of those bills make it to a specialist committee. They will be briefly taken into consideration, in one quick session, and then sidelined – "pigeonholed", as the US legislative jargon has it. Nevertheless, those bills serve some purpose, above all that they send a message: to the voters that "their" parliamentarian is indeed quite hardworking; to the interest groups that he is indeed working for them; to party leaders and possibly to the government that there is an issue in search of a solution and that the solution, or at least part of it, can be found in the parliamentarian's bill.

Once a bill, of whatever origin, is sent to a parliamentary committee, parliamentarians have the right to submit amendments. The representative of the government has the opportunity to make clear the government position in favour or against any amendment, but the members of the committee are in principle free to vote according to their preferences and judgements. Obviously, most of them follow their party's line. At all

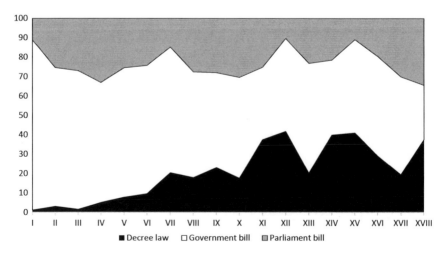

Figure 4.3 Sources of Italian bills by sponsor and parliamentary term (percentage)

times, the government may exercise its prerogative to withdraw its bill. Subsequently, amendments can be introduced on the floor, including by the government. At any point in time, the government may also decide to ask for a confidence vote on any bill. All amendments will be "killed" at the request of a confidence vote and the government will get what it wants, provided, of course, that Parliament – that is, the chamber concerned – votes for the confidence vote. The data depict a situation in which all Italian governments, with a few exceptions, have regularly been capable of seeing their bills duly approved on one condition: that those governments knew what they wanted and that their parliamentary majorities were willing to support their choices, which, I think it is important to stress, has almost always been the case. Thus, Figure 4.3[14] tells us a lot about the government and its parliamentary majority and also about (the working of) Parliament.

Factually, from a purely descriptive point of view, it is ascertainable that the laws originate from the government. They are drafted by the Prime Minister and his ministers, they are introduced into Parliament by the government, and accompanied and sustained by ministers and undersecretaries. Parliament examines, may amend and even improve them, but they must approve them. In the end, most of the time all the governmental majorities have been in the position of being able to translate their policy promises into public policies whose quality and suitability to their purpose are, of course, questionable. But no government has been obliged to swallow bills contrary to its agreed-upon platform. It is remarkable that, no matter how weak the government (that is, supported by a conflict-ridden political and parliamentary majority) or how strong (supported by a cohesive and disciplined majority), whether it is non-partisan or comprises a more or less cohesive coalition, the percentage of bills initiated and duly approved has remained significantly high (see Tables 4.4 and 4.5; Pedrazzani 2017).

From a normative point of view, once more siding with Bagehot, I would stress that the government has received a mandate from the voters. By electing parliamentarians who have run their campaign on the respective party platforms, voters have given their approval to those platforms, as far as possible, and are expecting to see those proposals translated into public policies. No matter how much the voters may like the parliamentarian they have elected, there is no way that individual parliamentarians might be able to translate their own special preferences and/or those of selected groups into public policies. *La République des députés*, well-known to the French citizens of the Third Republic (1871–1940), where Deputies successfully exchanged votes on their own petty bills, has never received an enthusiastic appraisal. For a long time, and for most of

Table 4.4 Law-making in Italy, by sponsor and rate of approval

Legislature	Bills presented by the government		Bills presented by parliamentarians		Total bills
	No.	Approved (%)	No.	Approved (%)	
I (1948–53)	2,547	80.6	1,375	18.9	3,922
II (1953–58)	1,667	84.8	2,514	19.1	4,181
III (1958–63)	1,569	82.8	3,688	13.0	5,257
IV (1963–68)	1,569	75.4	4,414	17.5	5,983
V (1968–72)	977	64.2	4,189	5.1	5,166
VI (1972–76)	1,255	67.7	4,597	5.9	5,852
VII (1976–79)	1,022	55.5	2,646	3.7	3,668
VIII (1979–83)	1,358	55.6	3,980	7.2	5,338
IX (1983–87)	1,287	44.1	4,642	4.7	5,929
X (1987–92)	1,471	50.3	6,920	4.6	8,391
XI (1992–94)	862	27.9	4,269	5.3	5,131
XII (1994–96)	1,143	23.0	5,020	0.9	6,163
XIII (1996–2001)	1,453	49.1	10,479	2.3	11,932
XIV (2001–06)	707	77.2	8,637	1.7	9,344
XV (2006–08)	284	35.0	5,062	0.3	5,346
XVI (2008–13)	482	63.1	8,399	1.1	8,881
XVII (2013–18)	412	68.7	6,896	1.4	7,308
XVIII (2018–)*	173	32.5	2,972	1.5	3,145

Source: Adapted from De Micheli and Verzichelli (2004: 221), with author's update.
Note: * = period of analysis 23 March 2018–1 June 2019.

Table 4.5 Number of laws approved in five European countries, 2009–15

	2009	2010	2011	2012	2013	2014	2015	Yearly average
France	82	114	111	82	84	91	97	94.4
Germany	147	89	153	128	178	90	129	130.6
United Kingdom	28	46	25	25	40	32	37	33.3
Spain	32	53	50	25	36	44	64	43.4
Italy	87	73	70	110	38	72	87	76.7

Source: www.camera.it/application/xmanager/projects/leg18/file/VOLUME_I_Nota_di_sintesi_14_marzo_2017.pdf.

the time, the existence of organized and rather cohesive Italian parties has made it impossible for Italian parliamentarians to exchange favours and to independently pass legislation opposed by the parties and, above all, by the government. Also, from a normative point of view, in a parliamentary democracy, the government has not only the right but also the political duty to attempt to have as much as possible of its platform enacted. Voters then enjoy the opportunity to consider the government responsible for what it has done, has not done, or has done badly. A decent electoral system would allow the accountability loop to exist for the benefit of the democratic regime, of interested, well-informed, participant voters, and, of course, of ambitious and capable parliamentarians. Unfortunately, from 2006 onwards, most Italian parliamentarians have been obliged to be totally subservient to their party or parliamentary leaders, never claiming any personal credit for their representational capabilities or legislative initiatives.

Reforming Italian bicameralism?

In a way, it is impossible to fully understand the working of the Italian Parliament, its contributions to Italian democracy and its weaknesses if one does not analyse it in relation to the government. While in parliamentary democracies the government may well be the "executive committee of parliament", it is also true that the government almost always is in a position of command vis-à-vis its parliamentary majority. Therefore, without offering too many details concerning, for instance, the highly controversial legislation by decree practised by Italian governments of all types (see Table 4.6), the important question is: how correct is it to criticize the Italian Parliament for not performing satisfactorily some of its functions without taking into account the role of the government when it comes to those functions? Although responsibility for the less than satisfactory functioning of the Parliament–government relationship should not be put entirely on the Italian Parliament, its structure and its functioning, Parliament has inevitably become the target of severe criticisms and the object of several reform attempts.

One of the most frequent motivations in favour of a reform of Italian bicameralism, as well as other bicameral systems (Russell 2000), is that the existence of two houses slows down the legislative process in a manner that is unacceptable when quick decisions have become absolutely imperative; this is even more the case when the two houses have the same legislative powers. The data convincingly indicate that those who criticize the Italian bicameral Parliament for slowing down

Table 4.6 Decree laws, legislative decrees and laws in Italy, 1987–2018 (number and percentage)

Legislature	Decree laws		Legislative decrees		Laws	
	No.	%	No.	%	No.	%
X (1987–92)	213	15.0	129	4.9	1,076	42.7
XI (1992–94)	192	31.8	97	9.5	314	32.9
XII (1994–96)	163	32.0	52	5.6	295	32.7
XIII (1996–2001)	204	13.7	378	12.8	906	35.0
XIV (2001–06)	216	22.0	288	13.8	476	26.1
XV (2006–08)	48	17.5	114	20.1	112	23.9
XVI (2008–13)	118	16.0	230	16.0	391	31.8
XVII (2013–18)	100	13.5	260	18.4	379	32.5

Source: Author's own compilation based on data provided by the Chamber of Deputies (www.camera.it) and the Senate (www.senate.it).

Table 4.7 Length of the law-making process in the Italian Parliament, by origin of the bill (average number of days)

	1996–2-001	2001–06	2006–08	2008–13	2013–18	2018–
Government	271	158	120	116	222	47
Parliament	494	505	183	442	628	38
Region	–	–	–	400	547	–
Citizen	709	–	–	–	420	–
Average	321	232	127	193	324	45

Source: Author's own compilation based on data provided by the Chamber of Deputies (www.camera.it) and the Senate (www.senate.it).

governmental legislation or for not approving it largely miss the point (see Table 4.7) The length of the legislative process depends essentially on two factors: the cohesion of the governmental majorities and their capabilities in defining their priorities and "accompanying" their favourite bills. The table clearly indicates that when the centre-left governed for the entire parliamentary term (1996–2001 and 2013–18), its composite and litigious coalitions meant that it took them almost a year to enact a law. Centre-right coalitions (2001–06 and, in part, 2008–13) proved more efficient. One may also want to ask a different question: that is, how much either house "interferes" with government legislation, or whether parliamentarians are successful in their attempts to introduce amendments representing purely partisan positions or catering to the preferences of specific interest groups.[15] Going against the flow in Italy, but most certainly with Bagehot's support and approval, I would re-emphasize that the parliamentary majority has the political duty – even the obligation – to approve all government bills that translate into public policies that fulfil the promises contained in the platform submitted to the voters and on which the parliamentarians belonging to the majority have been elected (and, thanks to their enactment, may win the opportunity of being re-elected).[16] As a logical and political consequence, the government has the right to oppose all the amendments that might twist its bills out of shape. Italian governments have done this whenever it has been necessary.

In the Italian context, the second motivation to reform the bicameral system was to eliminate the possibility of the government being exposed to the frequent risk of losing votes of confidence. In the available data there is absolutely no support for the arguments that either bicameralism or, more specifically, the Senate has been responsible for the frequent demise of Italian governments.[17] The third motivation for reform had a populist flavour: downsizing the number of parliamentarians. As expected, the Five Star populist instincts have easily been translated into the proposal to reduce the number of Deputies from 630 to 400 and of Senators from 315 to 200. As for the then Prime Minister Renzi, the solution he offered in order to successfully achieve all his constitutional goals was sought via a major transformation – not abolition, as many of the supporters of the reform wrongly argued during the referendum campaign – of the Italian Senate. Renzi's sloppily drafted reforms were resoundingly defeated on 4 December 2016 (more on this later).

Renzi's resoundingly defeated vocal and clandestine supporters still complain that their reforms might have simplified the "system" and made it more capable of facing any new (unspecified) challenges promptly. A brief discussion of the failed reform may serve as a reminder of the poor institutional knowledge of the would-be reformers and of what should not be done in the future. According to the text of the reform, the Senate would have lost the power to vote to show its confidence or withdraw it. The legislative power of the Senate was drastically reduced so that very few bills would have to be approved by both chambers. In the few cases in which a bill had to be approved by both chambers, it was up to the House of Deputies to cast the decisive vote (remember that, because of a conspicuous bonus of seats, the electoral law of the time would have created a large majority in the House for the victorious party). The number of Senators was set at 100 and they were going to be chosen from regional councillors (74) plus one mayor for each region (21). It was never clarified how this would happen: that is, whether voters could indicate which of the regional councillors should also serve as a Senator or if it was up to the Regional Council, and therefore to the parties, to designate or appoint Senators, "taking into account the results of the elections" (which means in proportion to the strength of the different groups in each region: hence, they would not represent their region, but the parties that nominated them). The decision to retain five Senators appointed by the President of the Republic (plus former Presidents becoming de jure life Senators themselves) was inexplicable. Had the reform been approved, there would have followed a remarkable concentration of legislative power in the House of Deputies and a probable confusing overlap of spheres of activities, plus many conflicts between the House of Deputies and the Senate concerning their respective legislative prerogatives and powers.

There might have been different solutions to the transformation of the Italian Senate. Some would have gone so far as to advocate its full elimination. Perhaps it might have been a good idea to look at the experience of the German Bundesrat, arguably the second chamber that is the least expensive, most restricted (sixty-nine members), most truly representative of territorial differences and most powerful in contemporary parliamentary democracies. No foreign model was ever taken into serious consideration by Italian reformers. In the end, the new Senate would have had 100 Senators chosen within and by the Regional Councils, therefore representing the parties and not regional communities, with limited legislative powers extended to fields such as EU politics and the evaluation of public policies – areas in which there was a legitimate doubt about the amount of knowledge these regional councillors appointed as Senators could bring to bear. Nor was the possibility of conflicts between the House of Deputies and the Senate significantly curtailed, and the length of time needed to pass the remaining pieces of bicameral legislation – of which there were several, and they were not minor – was not convincingly reduced. Finally, the reform was not even met with unconditional approval by the regions. Their "territorial" representation was bought at the exorbitant price of a supremacy clause allowing the central state – that is, the government of the day – to block practically all regional decisions in the name of a superior national interest.

The electoral campaign for the constitutional referendum, a true political watershed, was largely focused on the issue of governability: that is, how to give more powers to a government made more stable by the electoral law. The paradox was that, in practice, there was nothing in the constitutional reforms specifically concerning the government, its prerogatives or its activities. Moreover, the most frequent complaint of Italian citizens is not that they feel they are not "governed",[18] but that nobody cares about them, about what they think or what they need, and nobody represents their interests or preferences. Unfortunately, acceptable measures of the "representativeness" of a Parliament do not seem to exist. From a purely numerical point of view, one can, of course, point to the way votes are translated into seats. Of course, a proportional formula may be the first step on the road to improved representativeness. However, too much proportionality may encourage and sustain party and parliamentary fragmentation at the expense of representativeness. The combination of mass parties interested in recruiting and promoting to Parliament their members, often endowed with previous experience in local government, and a proportional elect-oral law made the Italian Parliament from 1946 to 1992 truly represen-tative of the preferences and the interests of Italian voters. For several good reasons, most of the time Italian parties selected candidates who were emerging from the "territory" (ground) and could and would pro-vide representation to those voters and strived to have them elected. On the whole, this was done quite successfully.

The link between candidates or parliamentarians and their voters was first weakened by the electoral law drafted by Mattarella in 1993.[19] Then, to all intents and purposes, since 2006 the link has been destroyed by the law dubbed Porcellum because the existence of closed lists meant that all parliamentarians owed their election to the designa-tion of their party leaders and nothing else. Hence, none of the parlia-mentarians elected with the 2005 law have had anything to gain by accepting, showing or striving for accountability to their voters. The "games" played with the electoral laws that have followed and have accompanied a dramatic decline and transformation of what remains of Italian parties have produced a situation in which it is highly justified to speak of a "crisis of representation". The question asked more than fifty years ago by Giovanni Sartori (1963) – "Which sanction do the parliamentarians fear the most: that of the voters, that of party leaders or that of interest groups?" – has had one and only one categorical answer since the 2006 national elections. The sanction that has been feared the most by Italian parliamentarians of all parties is the one that can be imposed on them by their party and faction leaders. Either they behave in a highly disciplined way or they will simply not be re-selected. It is interesting to stress that the threat of de-selection has been repeatedly used since 2014 by the secretary turned Prime Minister of the most powerful political party, the Partito Democratico, and by his closest collaborators against those parliamentarians who dared formulate and express their dissent.[20] Finally, it was uncompromisingly implemented in the selection of candidates for the 2018 general elections.

Trasformismo

Non-democratic parties and "irresponsible" parliamentarians without ties to unknown voters have resuscitated an ancient Italian phenomenon: *trasformismo* (Valbruzzi 2015). Since time immemorial (a slight exaggeration, since 1876 would be more exact), quite a number of Italian parliamentarians, left and right, have protected and promoted their political careers by resorting to a not so modest dose of *trasformismo*. Elected as representatives of a specific party (or coalition), usually a party that is bound to stay in opposition, some have been willing to "help" the government (the parties in the government coalition) in exchange of something, perhaps a ministerial office, useful political resources, opportunities outside Parliament, or, above all, the promise to be put forward as candidates in the next election. Between 1876 and 1919, *trasformismo* was a frequent practice involving more than a quarter of parliamentarians. After 1946, when Italian parties acquired a rather stable organizational structure and the political competition had a clearly drawn axis between "pro-West" and "pro-Communism", until 1994, when the party system collapsed, the number of parliamentarians moving from the ranks of the opposition into the parliamentary or governmental majority tended to be no more than a handful. Of course, there were party splits and new parliamentary groups were created, but this is a different story. *Trasformismo* resurfaced again in massive doses after 1994. New unorganized or disorganized parties, weak identities, the absence of political cultures capable of keeping together the newly elected parliamentarians, and, finally, governments relying on precarious majorities – all this produced an abundant stream of *trasformisti*. Two additional facilitating conditions have made their appearance. First, all-encompassing coalitions, on both the left and the right, took on board personalities with no party affiliation – a sort of "mirror for larks" – who felt no attachment and had no obligation towards those who had recruited them. Second, the persistent state of de-structuring of the party system means that, if and when the party that has elected them disappears, all those incumbent parliamentarians are obliged to look for alternative future generous "selectors".[21] Thus, in the 2013–18 Parliament, more

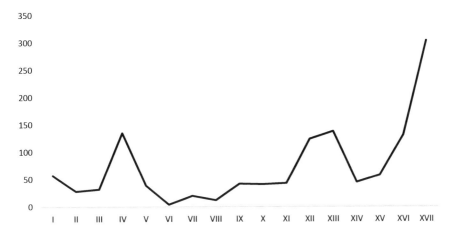

Figure 4.4 Number of party switches in the Chamber of Deputies, by parliamentary term

Source: Author's own compilation based on data provided by Valbruzzi (2015).

than a third of the 945 parliamentarians made the transition from one parliamentary group to another (see Figure 4.4).

Trasformismo affects both representation and accountability. The link between the voters who have chosen a parliamentarian, also because he or she has been put up by a specific party, is broken the very moment when that parliamentarian abandons the party's parliamentary group, never to be revived. When quite a number of parliamentarians behave in a similar way, the crisis of representation explodes. Since it is highly unlikely, often even impossible, for the *trasformisti* parliamentarians to return to "their" voters to explain what they have done, not done, or done poorly, and why, the circuit of accountability cannot come into being. Voters will be deprived of the power to re-elect their parliamentarian(s) and of the possibility of defeating and ousting him or her. *Trasformismo* constitutes a *vulnus*, a wound in the body of parliamentary democracies. Two remedies are being discussed. The first is a reform of the rules of the House and the Senate concerning the parliamentary groups (caucus). Any and all parliamentarians who leave their parliamentary group will not be allowed to join another parliamentary group, but will go into the so-called Mixed Group; this has a limited amount of resources available and a limited access to offices. The second remedy has been proposed by the Five Star Movement: *binding mandates*. All parliamentarians will be obliged to vote strictly following the indications of their parliamentary group, working to implement the party platform submitted to the voters. The sanction for contrary behaviour will be expulsion from the group, something the Five Stars have resorted to already in more than thirty instances, and even perhaps the loss of the seat. Leaving aside any discussion concerning the applicability and impact of binding mandates in parliamentary democracies, a (difficult) reform of the Italian Constitution would be required. In the Italian case, where coalitions change, platforms are not precisely designed and political actors are accustomed to reaching all sorts of compromises, binding mandates would make the necessary flexibility impossible and cause all parliamentary activities to come to a standstill.

Renzi's ill-conceived reform of the Senate had nothing to say with regard to *trasformismo*. It was not going to simplify or streamline the relationships between Parliament and government. It did not tackle the issues not just of accelerating the legislative process, but of improving the quality of legislation. It had a visible personalistic goal: to show that the Prime Minister was more determined than all his predecessors and better able to succeed where they had failed. This wasn't true, but the question concerning how to reform the Italian bicameral Parliament remains alive. It will be more effectively tackled within a larger framework that must include the reform of the government. Neither institution and their reforms can stand alone.

This chapter has tried to provide the amount of information necessary to understand the importance of the Italian Parliament in the network of institutions. It has hopefully made clear that the working of Parliament, its contributions and its shortcomings have a lot to do with the role played by Italian parties. I have also argued that what the Italian Parliament does and how it performs depend significantly on its relationships with the government. The next chapter will further explore the connection between Parliament and the government, but the main focus will be on the role played by Italian governments and how their functioning could be improved.

Notes

1 An excellent overview of the structure of all parliaments in the world can be found in Tsebelis and Money (1997). Definitely worth reading is Crick (1964).

2 Interestingly, the formulation of this article made it possible in 1993 through the cutting of some words to submit the proposal of an electoral referendum meant to move away from proportional representation towards a plurality system.

3 Today's Senators for life are: Professor of Economics, former Prime Minister Mario Monti; researcher in the field of stem cells Elena Cattaneo; star architect Renzo Piano; winner of the Nobel Prize in Physics Carlo Rubbia (all appointed by Giorgio Napolitano during his long presidential tenure); and Liliana Segre, Auschwitz survivor (appointed by President Mattarella).

4 First published in 1867, Bagehot's book (2001) still provides the best framework to analyse the activities of parliaments in a parliamentary democracy.

5 The entire issue is dealt with in depth in Pasquino (2015), where I also criticize the (non-)solutions offered in Renzi's constitutional reforms.

6 The myth was given some substance by Di Palma (1977), but on all major decisions the convergence, if any, on governmental positions was made fundamentally by the Communists.

7 Berlusconi's less than perfect knowledge of Parliament and party politics prevented him from realizing that, due to the fragmentation of the centre-left, there were more heads of parliamentary groups in the ranks of the opposition than those supporting his government.

8 This is because, as we have already seen, the 2006 and the 2018 electoral laws did not give the voters any possibility of choosing their parliamentarians or of rewarding them.

9 I strongly doubt that even today Bagehot would like to be "politically correct" and write "personalities". In any case, the composition of many contemporary parliaments is still not coming close to a fifty–fifty situation. In Italy in 2016 there were 198 female Deputies (31.4 per cent) and 92 female Senators (28.8 per cent), more than in any previous Parliament fundamentally because of the irruption of the parliamentary delegation of the Five Star Movement. The 2018 Parliament has witnessed the election of 307 women and 643 men, respectively 32.3 and 67.7 per cent.

10 Article 67 of the Italian Constitution states that "each member of Parliament represents the Nation and carries out his duties without a binding mandate" (more on this later).

11 The existence of term limits has already produced counterproductive consequences such as a popular Five Star mayor not running for a second term in his town in order to be able to run for at least one term in Parliament and the Five Stars losing the local election.

12 A not too dissimilar manifestation of populism can be found in the catchword launched by Matteo Renzi announcing the need for the scrapping (*rottamazione*) of long-standing PD parliamentarians, as if they were old, outdated cars.

13 Nevertheless, public debt remained about 60 per cent of the gross national product until the mid-1980s. It started to grow considerably when the Communists had become anything but influential.

14 Because of the existence of different political and quantitative governmental majorities, the evaluation of parliamentary productivity in terms of

law-making when Prodi, Berlusconi, Monti, Letta, Renzi and Gentiloni served as Prime Ministers is especially revealing.

15 That this may be the case was stated by Giuliano Amato, Professor of Constitutional Law, several times a minister (for instance of the Treasury) and twice Prime Minister. He compared the government to a castaway who puts their message (or bill) in a bottle and throws it into the sea (of Parliament). Eventually, the bottle reaches the beach, but the message is almost unreadable and bears no resemblance to the original (governmental) text. There may be more than a grain of truth in Amato's parable. However, the castaway's vicissitudes tell us something not just about Parliament, but about the government and its coalition. The more diversified the coalition, the weaker the Prime Minister and the more likely that all the partners will strive to get something out of a governmental bill and that the Prime Minister (and the ministers) will feel obliged to yield in order to survive.

16 The fact is that Italian governments are rarely in a position to claim that they are, indeed, translating their programme into public policies and that often those governments are supported by parliamentarians elected as candidates of parties that are not governmental partners. The reader may have noticed how difficult it is when discussing Parliament to keep the government out of the picture. This is one of the "secrets" of the English Constitution according to Bagehot: the fusion between the government and its parliamentary majority. It is no longer a secret and, with variations, it can be found in all parliamentary democracies, Italy, of course, included.

17 In the past twenty years, only two governments have been defeated by a vote of no confidence and had to resign: Prodi I (October 1998) and Prodi II (January 2008). The first lost a vote of confidence unnecessarily requested in the House of Deputies. The second was ousted in the Senate where it had a razor-thin majority when one of its coalition partners withdrew its support. Any indictment of the bicameral Parliament seems very out of place.

18 In different times and in different circumstances, both Samuel Huntington ("The most important political distinction among countries concerns *not their form* of government *but their degree* of government" (1968: 1, emphasis added)) and Richard Rose (1984) have stressed that the question is not "whether" we are, can and will be governed, but "how" and "how much" we are governed. Perhaps of great interest to democratic citizens is also by "whom" they are governed.

19 Since there is no residency requirement in the Italian electoral laws, too many single-member constituencies witnessed candidates having no connection with the voters – carpetbaggers in the American political jargon, "parachuted" being the Italian version. If they are powerful within the party organization, these candidates do not feel obliged to establish ties with the voters and the various associations. When the time comes for

another election, if necessary, they will migrate to another safe seat. Mershon and Shetsova (2018) provide an excellent analysis of the motivations, policies, offices and timings of re-elections entertained by the "switchers".

20 In the end, it is quite likely that several of these parliamentarians left the Partito Democratico for two good reasons. First, their dissenting opinions were never taken into consideration; rather, they were often ridiculed and always quashed. Second, they received the not so subliminal message that they had no chance of being re-selected by the PD. Hence, they decided that it was time to go and look for alternatives

21 In the 2013–18 Parliament, this was the case of the group founded by Mario Monti called "Scelta Civica" (note the emphasis on "civic" as opposed to political), which after less than one year was in full disarray.

References

Bagehot, W. (2001). *The English Constitution*. Oxford: Oxford University Press.

Crick, B. R. (1964). *The Reform of Parliament*. London: Weidenfeld and Nicolson.

De Micheli, C. and Verzichelli, L. (2004). *Il Parlamento*. Bologna: Il Mulino.

Di Palma, G. (1977). *Surviving without Governing: The Italian Parties in Parliament*. Berkeley: University of California Press.

Huntington, S. P. (1968). *Political Order in Changing Societies*. New Haven and London: Yale University Press.

Marino, B., Martocchia Diodati, N., and Verzichelli, L. (2019). Members of the Chamber of Deputies Following the 2018 Election. In L. Ceccarini and J. L. Newell (eds) *Italy in Uncharted Territory: The General Election of 2018* (pp. 271–295). London: Palgrave.

Mattina, L. (2010). *I gruppi di interesse*. Bologna: Il Mulino.

Mershon, C. and Shetsova, O. (2018). *Party System Change in Legislatures Worldwide: Moving Outside the Electoral Arena*. Cambridge: Cambridge University Press.

Pasquino, G. (2015). *Cittadini senza scettro: Le riforme sbagliate*. Milan: Egea-UniBocconi.

Pasquino, G. and Pelizzo, R. (2006). *Parlamenti democratici*. Bologna: Il Mulino.

Pedrazzani, A. (2017). *Fare le leggi nella Seconda Repubblica: Come cambia il Parlamento*. Milan: Egea.

Pritoni, A. (2018). *Lobby d'Italia: Il sistema degli interessi tra Prima e Seconda Repubblica*. Rome: Carocci.

Rose, R. (1984). *Understanding Big Government: The Programme Approach*. Beverly Hills: Sage.

Russell, M. (2000). *Reforming the House of Lords: Lessons from Overseas.* Oxford: Oxford University Press.

Sartori, G. (ed.) (1963). *Il Parlamento italiano, 1946–1963.* Naples: Edizioni Scientifiche Italiane.

Tronconi, F. and Verzichelli, L. (2010). Verso il ceto politico della 'Terza Repubblica'? La rappresentanza parlamentare nella XVI legislatura. In ITANES (ed.) *Proporzionale se vi pare: Le elezioni politiche del 2008* (pp. 173–202). Bologna: Il Mulino.

Tsebelis, G. and Money, J. (1997). *Bicameralism.* Cambridge: Cambridge University Press.

Valbruzzi, M. (2015). Trasformismo. In E. Jones and G. Pasquino (eds) *The Oxford Handbook of Italian Politics* (pp. 26–40). Oxford: Oxford University Press.

Governments   5

Instability has been the hallmark of Italian governments. But governmental instability is made up of many factors and hides several specific elements of Italian politics, bad and good. This chapter will explore the reasons why Italian governments have been (and continue to be) unstable. It will also stress that quite a number of Prime Ministers have led several cabinets and served long periods in office. In any case, one mistake should be avoided: equating the instability of Italian governments with the instability of Italian democracy. This is not the case. Still, governmental instability has negatively affected the performance of the political system.

Of many party governments

"Italy has a new government. Don't expect it to last long." This was the title of an article by Silvia Marchetti published in *Time* on 14 December 2016. The opening sentence of the article stated: "The newly-appointed government of Paolo Gentiloni is the 64th in the barely 70-year-old history of the Italian republic – and it is also set to have one of the shortest lifespans." These few words contain and convey the usual stereotypes regarding Italian governments. They are unstable ("don't expect it to last long") and usually short-lived ("set to have one of the shortest lifespans"). Some of the stereotypes catch and reflect, though only in a partial way, the political reality. Others are simply incorrect and misleading. All require an explanation.

To begin with, the average tenure of Italian governments is slightly more than one year, about 14–15 months. Hence, since

Gentiloni's government lasted until the natural end of the parliamentary term (12 December 2016–23 March 2017), its tenure was 15 months and 11 days.[1] It did not have "one of the shortest lifespans", but was fully in line with most previous Italian governments in "normal" times. The second point is, I grant, somewhat difficult to explain to the average journalist and reader. In more ways than one, Gentiloni's government was fundamentally a continuation and an offshoot of Renzi's government (which had lasted 1,024 days – that is, 2 years, 9 months and 20 days – the fourth longest government in the history of the Italian Republic). Following Renzi's disastrous defeat in the constitutional referendum, Gentiloni was upgraded from his office as Minister of Foreign Affairs to Prime Minister. Only three new ministers were appointed, one of them being promoted from his previous position as undersecretary. One minister was shifted from Internal to Foreign Affairs. Would this, on the whole, quite limited reshuffle justify the reference to "instability"? Certainly, those few and minor changes cannot be taken to indicate political discontinuity, nor, even less, political confusion and disarray. A different, better substantiated, interpretation of Italian governments and their dynamics is sorely needed.

The questions this chapter will try to answer are many, but all, I believe, are legitimate, difficult and important. Why has Italy had so many governments, many more than all other contemporary parliamentary democracies? Only the Fourth French Republic had more governments in its short life (1946–58) than Italy over the same period, and, let me remind you, it collapsed. What kind of impact or consequences on the functioning of the Italian political system and on the quality of its democracy has governmental instability had in the past and throughout its history? Which solutions, if any, have been suggested, formulated, attempted or enacted? Before I tackle those three major and complex questions, let me start with a general remark that aims to provide a snapshot of the entire history of governments in the first long phase of the Italian Republic. It is a snapshot that, to a large extent, has retained its validity, with various ups and downs, for most of the period covered by the second phase of the Republic, from 1992 up to now.

Not unlike all the other European parliamentary democracies, from the very beginning Italy acquired all the necessary elements and features of what is called *party government*. As defined by Katz, the main features of party government are:

> Firstly, all major governmental decisions must be taken by
> people chosen in elections conducted along party lines, or by

individuals appointed by and responsible to such people. Secondly, policy must be decided within the governing party, when there is a "monocolour" government, or by negotiations among parties when there is a coalition ... Thirdly, the highest officials (e.g. cabinet ministers and especially the prime minister) must be selected within their parties and be responsible to the people through their parties. Positions in government must flow from support within the party rather than party positions flowing from electoral success.

(Katz 1986: 43)

All these features fit neatly, regularly and consistently, with only a very few exceptions, into the life and works of all Italian governments from 1946 until 1992 (Pasquino 1987). Slowly, but inexorably, over time Italian party government degenerated into *partitocrazia* (partyocracy), which I would define as a situation in which Italian parties have extended their power to control the economic sphere and social and cultural organizations, have colluded in sharing available state resources ("spoils") and have appropriated them for the almost exclusive benefit of their organizations, their supporters and their leaders. Even after the collapse of the party system in the period between 1992 and 1994, what remained of the Italian parties succeeded in keeping alive a miniaturized version of partyocracy, which, of course, contributed to the resentment and the irritation of quite a number of voters, later largely channelled into and by the Five Star Movement.

Table 5.1 illustrates several significant elements concerning the composition of governments with reference to ministers and volatility with reference to parties. Following a long period of stability and continuity of both elements, the turmoil started in 1992, opening the path to a wide variety of situations and outcomes. In a way, they are all a tribute to the institutional imagination of Italian political and party leaders attempting to dominate the parliamentary fragmentation emerging from civil society and to give civil society representation and governability.

Box 5.1 The formation of the government

Article 92: The President of the Republic appoints the President of the Council of Ministers and, on his/her proposal, the ministers.
Article 94: The Government must have the confidence of both Houses.

Table 5.1 Governmental composition and volatility, 1953–2018

Year	Legislature	Government	Party of Prime Minister	Cabinet size	Technocratic and independent ministers	Ministers from new parties	Ministers from existing parties	Governmental volatility
1953	II	Pella	DC	19	0.00%	0.00%	100.00%	0.00%
1954	II	Fanfani I	DC	19	0.00%	0.00%	100.00%	0.00%
1954	II	Scelba	DC	21	0.00%	0.00%	100.00%	28.57%
1955	II	Segni I	DC	21	0,00%	0.00%	100.00%	0.00%
1957	II	Zoli	DC	21	0.00%	0.00%	100.00%	28.57%
1958	III	Fanfani II	DC	22	0.00%	0.00%	100.00%	18.18%
1959	III	Segni II	DC	24	0.00%	0.00%	100.00%	18.18%
1960	III	Tambroni	DC	23	0.00%	0.00%	100.00%	0.00%
1960	III	Fanfani III	DC	23	0.00%	0.00%	100.00%	0.00%
1962	III	Fanfani IV	DC	24	0.00%	0.00%	100.00%	12.50%
1963	IV	Leone I	DC	20	0.00%	0.00%	100.00%	12.50%
1963	IV	Moro I	DC	24	0.00%	16.67%	83.33%	37.50%
1964	IV	Moro II	DC	24	0.00%	0.00%	100.00%	4.17%
1966	IV	Moro III	DC	23	0.00%	0.00%	100.00%	7.97%
1968	V	Leone II	DC	22	0.00%	0.00%	100.00%	34.78%
1968	V	Rumor I	DC	25	0.00%	0.00%	100.00%	16.00%
1969	V	Rumor II	DC	23	0.00%	0.00%	100.00%	16.00%
1970	V	Rumor III	DC	26	0.00%	0.00%	100.00%	34.62%
1970	V	Colombo	DC	26	0.00%	0.00%	100.00%	3.85%
1972	V	Andreotti I	DC	25	0.00%	0.00%	100.00%	38.46%

Year	Leg.	Government	Party	N	%	%	%	%
1972	VI	Andreotti II	DC	27	0.00%	0.00%	100.00%	29.63%
1973	VI	Rumor IV	DC	29	0.00%	0.00%	100.00%	27.59%
1974	VI	Rumor V	DC	26	0.00%	0.00%	100.00%	6.90%
1974	VI	Moro IV	DC	25	0.00%	0.00%	100.00%	38.46%
1976	VI	Moro V	DC	22	0.00%	0.00%	100.00%	20.00%
1976	VII	Andreotti III	DC	21	4.76%	0.00%	95.24%	4.76%
1978	VII	Andreotti IV	DC	22	4.55%	0.00%	95.45%	0.22%
1979	VII	Andreotti V	DC	22	0.00%	0.00%	100.00%	22.73%
1979	VIII	Cossiga I	DC	25	0.00%	0.00%	100.00%	16.00%
1980	VIII	Cossiga II	DC	27	0.00%	0.00%	100.00%	44.44%
1980	VIII	Forlani	DC	27	0.00%	0.00%	100.00%	11.11%
1981	VIII	Spadolini I	PRI	28	0.00%	0.00%	100.00%	5.29%
1982	VIII	Spadolini II	PRI	28	0.00%	0.00%	100.00%	0.00%
1982	VIII	Fanfani V	DC	28	0.00%	0.00%	100.00%	10.71%
1983	IX9	Craxi I	PSI	29	0.00%	0.00%	100.00%	12.07%
1986	IX	Craxi II	PSI	29	0.00%	0.00%	100.00%	0.00%
1987	IX	Fanfani VI	DC	26	23.08%	0.00%	76.92%	48.28%
1987	X	Goria	DC	30	3.33%	0.00%	96.67%	46.67%
1988	X	De Mita	DC	31	0.00%	0.00%	100.00%	3.98%
1989	X	Andreotti VI	DC	31	0.00%	0.00%	100.00%	3.23%
1991	X	Andreotti VII	DC	32	0.00%	0.00%	100.00%	10.08%
1992	XI	Amato I	PSI	26	7.69%	0.00%	92.67%	10.58%
1993	XI	Ciampi	Technocratic	28	32.14%	14.29%	53.57%	38.74%

(Continued)

Table 5.1 (Cont.)

Year	Legislature	Government	Party of Prime Minister	Cabinet size	Technocratic and independent ministers	Ministers from new parties	Ministers from existing parties	Governmental volatility
1994	XII	Berlusconi I	FI	26	7.69%	76.92%	15.38%	76.92%
1995	XII	Dini	Technocratic	25	100.00%	0.00%	0.00%	92.31%
1996	XIII	Prodi I	Ulivo / Indep.	24	20.83%	12.50%	66.67%	79.17%
1998	XIII	D'Alema I	DS	26	11.54%	7.69%	80.77%	33.33%
1999	XIII	D'Alema II	DS	27	7.41%	7.41%	85.19%	16.24%
2000	XIII	Amato II	Technocratic	25	12.00%	0.00%	88.00%	13.78%
2001	XIV	Berlusconi II	FI	24	12.50%	0.00%	87.50%	79.67%
2005	XIV	Berlusconi III	FI	25	4.00%	0.00%	96.00%	19.00%
2006	XV	Prodi II	Ulivo / Indep.	27	14.81%	11.11%	74.07%	82.15%
2008	XVI	Berlusconi IV	PDL	25	4.00%	0.00%	96.00%	94.15%
2011	XVI	Monti	Technocratic	20	100.00%	0.00%	0.00%	96.00%
2013	XVII	Letta	PD	22	13.64%	4.55%	81.82%	86.36%
2014	XVII	Renzi	PD	17	11.76%	0.00%	88.24%	19.25%
2016	XVII	Gentiloni	PD	19	0.00%	0.00%	100.00%	19.50%
2018	XVIII	Conte	Independent	19	31.58%	42.11%	26.32%	100.00%
2019	XVIII	Conte	Independent	21	14.33%	42.50%	57.50%	50.00%

Source: Adapted from Calossi and Cicchi (2018).

Why has Italy had so many governments?

From 1946 to the time of writing, June 2018, Italy has had sixty-five governments. However, there have been only twenty-nine Prime Ministers.[2] This means that several Prime Ministers have led more than one government: Christian Democrat Alcide De Gasperi was Prime Minister eight times between December 1945 and March 1954; at different points in time, from February 1972 to June 1992, Giulio Andreotti was Prime Minister seven times; again, in different periods between July 1958 and July 1987, Amintore Fanfani was Prime Minister six times. Other notable cases are: five governments led by Aldo Moro between December 1963 and July 1976; and more recently four governments led by Silvio Berlusconi between May 1994 and December 2011. A preliminary comparative remark is useful. The long tenure of Alcide De Gasperi was an incommensurable blessing for the new Italian Republic. Similar to the even longer tenure (1949–63) of the German Christian Democrat Chancellor Konrad Adenauer, the uninterrupted period of De Gasperi's premiership contributed in a highly significant way to the consolidation of the newly born Italian parliamentary democracy. There are good reasons to believe that too many and too frequent changes of Prime Minister in neighbouring France (between 1946 and 1958 there were more governments in France than in Italy) significantly weakened the Fourth Republic. It may also be of some interest to underline that De Gasperi, Andreotti, Fanfani and Moro, all Christian Democrats, led governments supported by different parliamentary coalitions (see Table 5.2). Looking at those coalitions, one finds a very intriguing Italian paradox: changing Italian government coalitions have been, at the same time, part of the problem – that is, the instability of governments – and part of the solution: that is, the (relative) stability of many Prime Ministers and several ministers. In any case, all of them were capable of keeping together the various coalition partners and of implementing a variety of important public policies.

Also to be taken into account are two phenomena that have received somewhat inadequate attention. First, all Italian governmental coalitions characterized different, but relatively long, periods of time, easily accommodating the game of musical chairs played by some Prime Ministers and several ministers. Second, the return to government of Christian Democratic Prime Ministers and ministers who retained political power within their parties also meant continuity and avoided a leap into the dark. Berlusconi's and Prodi's comebacks must be analysed differently. For the former, it was

Table 5.2 Phases of coalition government in the Italian Republic, 1945–2018

Government formula	Years	Parties involved	Number of cabinets	Sub-phases and Prime Ministers	Major policy issues
Democratic instauration	1945–47	DC, PCI, PSI, PLI, PRI	4	Parri 1945 De Gasperi 1946	Constitutional setting
First party system Centrism	1947–60	DC, PLI, PSDI, PRI	13	Preparation: De Gasperi 1947 Central period: De Gasperi 1948–53 Crisis: De Gasperi 1953; Pella 1953; Fanfani 1954 New stabilization: Scelba 1954; Segni 1955 Final crisis: Zoli 1957; Fanfani 1958; Segni 1959; Tambroni 1960	International alliances, economic reforms
Centre-left	1960–75	DC, PSI, PSDI, PRI	17	Preparation: Fanfani 1960–62; Leone 1963 Central period: Moro 1964–68 Crisis: Leone 1968; Rumor 1968–70 New stabilization: Colombo 1970	Nationalizations, enlargement of the public sector, social reforms

National solidarity	1976–79	DC, PCI, PSI, PSDI, PRI, PLI	3	Attempts to change the coalition: Andreotti 1972–73 Decline and final crisis: Rumor 1973; Moro 1974–76 Preparation and central period: Andreotti 1976–78 Crisis: Andreotti 1979 New stabilization: Scelba 1954; Segni 1955 Final crisis: Zoli 1957; Fanfani 1958; Segni 1959; Tambroni 1960	Economic crisis, terrorist emergency
Five-party	1980–92	DC, PSI, PSDI, PRI, PLI	14	Preparation: Cossiga 1979–80; Forlani 1980 Central period: Spadolini 1981–82; Fanfani 1982; Craxi 1983–86 Crisis and renegotiation: Craxi 1986; Fanfani 1987; Goria 1987; De Mita 1988 New stabilization: Andreotti 1989–91 Final crisis: Amato 1992	Correction of state intervention, public debts, inflation

(Continued)

Table 5.2 (Cont.)

Government formula	Years	Parties involved	Number of cabinets	Sub-phases and Prime Ministers	Major policy issues
I Transition					
Transitional cabinet	1993–94	DC, PSI, PSDI, PLI (PDS, Greens, PRI, LN)	1	Ciampi 1993	Economic crisis, institutional reforms
Second party system					
Centre-right attempt	1994–95	FI, AN, LN, CCD	1	Berlusconi 1994	Institutional reforms, federalism, privatizations
Technocratic cabinet	1995–96	PDS, PPI, LN (FI, CCD, AN)	1	Dini 1995	Institutional reforms
Olive Tree coalition	1996–2001	PDS, PPI, Greens, RIN	4	Prodi 1996–98; D'Alema 1998–99; Amato 2000	European policies, reform of the welfare state, institutional reforms
Berlusconism I	2001–06	FI, AN, LN, UDC	2	Berlusconi 2001	Federalism, immigration, institutional and electoral reforms
Centre-left interruption	2006–08	DS, Margherita, IdV, RC, Greens, Partito Radicale, UDEUR	1	Prodi 2006	Economic reforms, liberalization, institutional and electoral reforms
Berlusconism II	2008–11	PDL, LN, MPA	1	Berlusconi 2008	Federalism, educational reform, institutional reforms

II Transition					
Transitional technocratic cabinet	2011–13	PDL, PD, UDC	1	Monti 2011	Economic crisis, austerity measures, electoral reform
Third party system					
Centrist-mainstream coalition	2013–15	PD, PDL/NCD, UDC, SC	2	Letta 2013–14; Renzi 2014–15	Economic crisis, institutional and electoral reforms
Populist coalition	2018–19	M5S, League	1	Conte 2018–19	Reform of the welfare state, immigration, law and order
New centre-left	2019–	M5S, PD	1	Conte 2019–	Europe, immigration, employment

Source: Adapted from Cotta and Verzichelli (2010) and Valbruzzi (2013) and updated.

a sign of his personal strength and resilience; for the latter, it was a sign of weakness of the centre-left galaxy, which was unable to find a viable alternative leadership between 1998 and 2006. Sharply different results followed. The extremely abundant high-quality literature on coalition governments (Laver 1996; Müller and Strøm 2000; Mershon 2002) confirms that such governments are inherently less stable and less durable than one-party governments. In coalition governments, all the parties (in some instances, Italy being one, party factions have to be taken into account as well) continue jockeying for visibility, in order to get better offices, to advance their policies and to demonstrate publicly how influential and indispensable they are. More precisely, the minor coalition partners in particular have to rock the boat in order to make it clear and visible to their voters, to the media and to public opinion more widely that they are important players and could do more and better were they to acquire greater political and institutional power.

There was also something specific, though not unique, to Italian parties that affected the stability of Italian governments. Beginning with the Christian Democrats, all Italian parties were internally divided, accommodating several, more or less organized, factions (Sartori 1973). Of course, the Communists prohibited factions, but internal semi-organized groups always existed. The very formation of a coalition government implied several stages of negotiation: first, among the factions within each party, then among the secretaries of the parties that had reached a preliminary agreement to instigate the government. The balance of power within each party and within each faction – especially, of course, within the more complex Christian Democratic Party – was bound to change frequently with reference to two variables: the outcome of party conventions and the overall dynamic of the governments: that is, their capabilities, their achievements and their liabilities. When some factions in a party became ascendant, they would immediately attempt to translate their newly acquired power within the party into government offices. Which, of course, often meant a more complicated redistribution of offices and spoils among the various parties and a change in the Prime Minister and the reshuffling of some of the ministers and the undersecretaries. Essentially, it was a not particularly painful process of readjustment to which Italian public opinion was largely acquiescent, even though it was often denounced by the mass media. It was the task of the Communist opposition to criticize severely governmental crises motivated solely by parties' and factions' greed at the expense of the general interests of the country. To no avail.

Since changes in the distribution of power within the (four or five) governing parties and their factions occurred frequently, governmental crises followed just as frequently. However, almost all those crises had quasi-predetermined outcomes: the same coalition, often with the same Prime Minister as well and most ministers staying in office, often the very same office. Indeed, in key offices such as Foreign Affairs, Defence and Home Affairs, Italian ministers could often boast a longer tenure than British ministers.[3] Table 5.3 ranks the seven Italian Prime Ministers who have enjoyed the longest uninterrupted tenures.[4]

A few selected comments may be enough to illuminate some of the most important features of Italian governmental instability (see Table 5.4). Four out of the six longest-lasting Italian governments have appeared in the second post-1992 phase of the Italian Republic. The two longest governments of all have been led by Berlusconi, whose Forza Italia party was a stabilizer par excellence, being firmly under his control. Also, the other major coalition partners – National Alliance and the Northern League – each had one undisputed leader. For several reasons, not only political,[5] Berlusconi has repeatedly proved to be an excellent coalition-maker. He was also in full control of his party, in which, of course, no faction ever appeared. The second government he led could have achieved the record of being the only one ever to last for the entire parliamentary term. Its crisis came as the consequence of the restlessness of some former Christian Democrats in the Union of the Democratic Centre. The man who guided the rebellion, Marco Follini, has been out of politics since then. The fourth government led by Berlusconi was weakened by a haemorrhaging of parliamentarians who abandoned his coalition partly because they

Table 5.3   Tenures of the longest-lasting governments

Government	Period	No. of days	Effective no. of days*
Berlusconi II	11/6/2001–23/4/2005	1,412	1,409
Berlusconi IV	8/5/2008–16/11/2011	1,287	1,283
Craxi I	4/8/1983–1/8/1986	1,093	1,058
Renzi	22/2/2014–12/12/2016	1,024	1,019
Prodi I	18/5/1996–21/10/1998	886	874
Moro III	24/2/1966–25/6/1968	851	831
Prodi II	17/5/2006–8/5/2008	722	617

Note: * The number of days between the government taking office and its resignation, the revocation of confidence or the death of the President of the Council.

Table 5.4 Tenure of the Presidents of the Council of Ministers in Italy, 1945–2017

President of the Council	No. of cabinets	Days in office	Average days in office per cabinet
Giuliano Amato	2	699	350
Giulio Andreotti	6	2,206	368
Silvio Berlusconi	4	3,312	828
Carlo Azeglio Ciampi	1	259	259
Emilio Colombo	1	527	527
Giuseppe Conte	1	455	455
Francesco Cossiga	2	405	203
Bettino Craxi	2	1,275	638
Massimo D'Alema	2	546	273
Alcide De Gasperi	8	2,651	331
Ciriaco De Mita	1	401	401
Lamberto Dini	1	355	355
Amintore Fanfani	6	1,371	229
Arnaldo Forlani	1	220	220
Paolo Gentiloni	1	467	467
Giovanni Goria	1	227	227
Giovanni Leone	2	285	143
Enrico Letta	1	300	300
Mario Monti	1	500	500
Aldo Moro	3	2,216	739
Giuseppe Pella	1	151	151
Romano Prodi	2	1,593	797
Matteo Renzi	1	1,019	1,019
Mariano Rumor	5	963	193
Mario Scelba	1	527	527
Giovanni Spadolini	2	440	220
Fernando Tambroni	1	116	116
Adone Zoli	1	371	371
Average	2.2	852	400

were disturbed by his less than admirable personal life and partly because they were preoccupied by the bleak prospect of the interruption of their parliamentary careers.

Socialist secretary Bettino Craxi's long tenure was the product of both the severe electoral defeat suffered by the Christian Democrats in June 1983, and also – and more significantly – of his leadership style and his ruthless ability to oblige his party to remain united in what was promising to be a turning point in the history of the PSI and its revitalization (it was not to be, but it did reach a turning point later for other reasons). In spite of the many tensions and conflicts with his party's internal minorities, which he regularly manhandled and mistreated, Renzi's government might have lasted until the end of the parliamentary term, something that no other leader of the Democratic Party had ever achieved, had he not gambled with the referendum on constitutional reform. Nevertheless, as we saw at the beginning of this chapter, Renzi's resignation was followed by the swift formation of an almost carbon-copy cabinet. The first government led by Romano Prodi in 1996 remains the only Italian government ever to fall because it was defeated in a confidence vote the Prime Minister himself had called, unnecessarily. Finally, deep in the history of the first phase of the Italian Republic, one finds a government led by Aldo Moro, one of the most respected Christian Democratic politicians, whose termination coincided with the end of the parliamentary term (February 1966–June 1968).

Types of governing coalition

The several cases of long-lasting Italian governments that have nothing to envy most governments of the other European parliamentary democracies for (for comparative evidence, see Magone 2015) suggest that it is necessary to look at the type of coalition in which they were embedded. The existing literature has identified three types of governing coalition: minority, minimum winning and oversize. Between 1946 and 1994, the Italian Republic witnessed the appearance and formation of all three types (see Table 5.5). The ranking both in number of days and

Table 5.5   Duration of Italian governments by cabinet type

Cabinet type	No. of cabinets	Duration in office (average no. of days)
Minimum-winning coalition	10	680
Non-partisan cabinet	2	432
Oversize coalition	26	413
Single-party minority	6	406
Coalition minority	7	369
Total/average	51	459

Note: The figures exclude caretaker or "interim" governments.

in percentage of cabinets is oversize, minimum winning, minority. Since definitions are important, let me state at the outset that oversize coalitions are those coalitions that include a party that is not numerically necessary to attain an absolute majority in Parliament. Minimum-winning coalitions are those coalitions in which all the parties are needed to attain a majority; if one party abandons the coalition, the government loses its parliamentary majority and is obliged to resign. Finally, minority governments are simply those governments that do not have an absolute majority of seats in Parliament. Although, of course, there is a difference between a single-party minority government and minority governments made up of more than one party, the former being potentially more cohesive and more stable, the Italian situation has offered exclusively instances of single-party minority governments made up of and supported by parliamentarians who all belong to the Christian Democratic party. The most notable of these minority governments were those led by Andreotti between August 1976 and March 1979 in the period called National Solidarity.[6]

Minority governments have been rather frequent both in Sweden and in Norway, because there is no constitutional need for an explicit vote of confidence.[7] Both the Labour Party in Norway and the Social Democratic Party in Sweden have long been the largest parties in their political systems, never extremist in their policies, and reliable because their previous governmental experiences have not exceeded acceptable though not well-defined limits. Moreover, if they "misbehaved", they could have been brought down at any moment by the combined vote of the Communists and the bourgeois parties. However, the opposition parties could not work together and give rise to an alternative government and both considered a Labour–Social Democratic government the lesser evil in the circumstances. A similar reasoning held sway in the Italian case. The Christian Democrats were as large a party as the two Scandinavian left-wing parties. They were experienced, moderate and reliable. Their minority government(s) could be brought down at any point in time, but any alternative coalition government would have been possible only under the exacting conditions of parties including the Communists. The only obstacle to the inauguration of a minority DC government was the constitutional requirement that it had to win a vote of confidence in both Houses. This meant that, in the Chamber of Deputies, a large number of parliamentarians had to abstain in order to allow a minority government to come into existence. As Andreotti memorably remarked, his first minority government, which lasted from August 1976 to March 1978, was "floating on a sea of abstentions".

The Senate rule that abstentions count as negative votes meant that a number of Senators simply had to leave the floor in order not to be counted among those, usually the Neo-Fascist extreme right, who opposed the government.

In addition to the two minority governments of the phase called "National Solidarity" (July 1976–March 1978; March 1978–March 1979), a few other Christian Democratic minority governments were created either just before the general elections or immediately after them. Here, one finds the most compelling political motivations. Often minority governments were created some months before the forthcoming general election because DC's allies wanted to distance themselves from the Christian Democrats in order to campaign with their hands free and to be able, more or less credibly, to eschew any responsibility for much of what had been done by the government of which they had been part. Minority governments were also created (or prolonged) after general elections so that some decompression time could be allowed in order to heal the wounds of bitter electoral campaigns and so that negotiations could start without any pressure to reach an early conclusion.[8]

When aiming to form a governmental coalition, the priority of the Christian Democrats was never just to attain a minimum-winning outcome. Although, of course, spoils mattered for all Christian Democratic factions, the party as a whole and its leaders at different points in time were more interested in having partners sincerely willing to collaborate and to support a cabinet led by a Christian Democrat. If one measures, as I have suggested, the "size" of the coalition with reference to the number of parties (and not of seats) necessary to reach a parliamentary majority, there were many possible minimum-winning coalitions. But – and this is the point I want to stress – the DC decision to form a coalition started from the identification of preferred partners. Though important, parliamentary numbers were always a secondary consideration. Minimum-winning coalitions were neither less stable nor less productive than oversize coalitions. They were subject to the same challenges and problems as all Italian coalitions. The jockeying for more and better offices conducted by Christian Democrat factions and their partners went on as usual in the knowledge that "objective" conditions – that is, the lack of true alternatives – would make it necessary to build yet another, similar coalition if there were to be a governmental crisis. One additional element acted in favour of the reproduction of a similar coalition: the knowledge that all the partners were necessary, in one way or another, and none could therefore be easily dislodged.

In Italy, oversize coalitions have been slightly more frequent than minority and minimum-winning coalitions. The story began in earnest when, in spite of the biggest electoral victory ever of the Christian Democrats in 1948, De Gasperi decided not to create a government composed of DC ministers only (which, in any case, would have encountered problems in the Senate),[9] but deliberately chose to call upon the minor centrist parties. It was a wise decision and took into account two political considerations. First, the DC alone could not represent significant parts of Italian society and ran the risk of a perilous confessional drift and, equally importantly, of being intensely pressured by the Vatican. Second, minor parties had something to contribute to the coalition not only in terms of socio-political representativeness, but also of ideas and personalities. There probably was one additional preoccupation. De Gasperi was aware that Christian Democratic parliamentarians were not going to be assiduously present nor highly disciplined. Hence, an oversize coalition could work as an insurance policy for the government. Oversize coalitions contained a hidden safety valve. Some parliamentarians can express their dissent by being absent or even voting against the government (thus pleasing some interest groups or some organized voters and retaining their useful support) without automatically causing the fall of the government.

The most important of Italian oversize coalitions was the one that comprised five parties (*pentapartito*): from right to left, the Liberals, Christian Democrats, Republicans, Social Democrats and Socialists. This was in office from 1980 to 1992 and saw a succession of governments. At the very beginning, for the first time in the history of postwar Italy, a non-Christian Democrat, Giovanni Spadolini, the secretary of the small Republican Party, became Prime Minister (1980–82).[10] Then, the time came for Bettino Craxi, the secretary of the Socialist Party, who was Prime Minister in what became the longest-lasting government (1983–86) in the first phase of the Italian Republic. The *pentapartito* period also witnessed the longest interval between the fall of a government – the one led by Ciriaco De Mita, the secretary of the Christian Democrats – and the formation of its successor, led by Giulio Andreotti. The crisis lasted an unprecedented sixty-five days. The negotiations between Craxi and Andreotti were protracted because they also entailed the allocation of important offices at the local level.

No matter which coalition was in government, there always existed a tense political discussion concerning the boundaries of the governing majority. The Christian Democrats always wanted to make it clear to the public that their coalition governments were self-sufficient, that there was no need for any outside support, and especially not from the Neo-Fascists, who were always excluded because they were not part of the "constitutional arc" (which encompassed only those who had participated in the drafting and approval of the Constitution), or from the Communists, because they were subservient to a foreign power. The Christian Democrats and the Socialists always claimed that the various government coalitions could function and produce significant reforms autonomously, without taking into account what the Communists were proposing. The Socialist stance had some, perhaps inevitable, elements of ambiguity. On the one hand, they were largely opposed to the recognition of any positive role by the Communist Party and its parliamentarians – and even more opposed to them playing an indispensable role – because the Socialists themselves claimed not only that they could represent the Communist, working-class electorate to some extent, but also that they could effectively translate those requests into public policies. On the other hand, the Socialists constantly entertained the hope that Communist voters would shift their support to the Socialist Party, a consequence that was somewhat feared by the Christian Democrats, who preferred not to deal with a stronger Socialist Party. Their hopes did not materialize and no positive electoral consequences ever followed for the Socialists. Under Craxi, the Socialists totally reversed their strategy. In order to show that the Communists were irrelevant to the functioning and the policies of the coalition, the five-party government became for all intents and purposes a locked-down, armoured parliamentary majority.

So far, I have claimed that Italian governments on the whole were much less unstable than many have thought and have written, and that there were several good reasons for changes within and from the various types of cabinet: minority, minimum winning, oversize. Those types of cabinets also made their appearance through the different coalition phases. Starting from 1948 and ending in 1992, there have been four coalition phases: centrism (PLI, DC, PRI, PSDI) from 1948 to 1960; centre-left (DC, PRI, PSDI, PSI) from 1962 to 1976; National Solidarity (two monocolour DC governments) from 1976 to 1979; and *pentapartito* (PLI, DC, PRI, PSDI, PSI) from 1980 to 1992 (for a good in-depth analysis, see Verzichelli and Cotta 2000). With the exception of the National Solidarity governments, which were meant to be an emergency solution to the challenges of left- and right-wing terrorism and high inflation/high unemployment, the various coalitions have been characterized by a remarkable stability in their respective time in office. Minor changes in the protagonists, party leaders and governmental office holders have never produced a situation of serious political anxiety concerning the very survival of Italian democracy. Unstable cabinets were often replaced by stable ones in an overall framework of limited and restrained change. During a forty-four-year trajectory, only five parties held governing positions while several political and institutional personalities replaced each other, mainly because of generational turnovers: in the 1987–92 Parliament there were many, still quite powerful, parliamentarians who had been elected for the first time in 1946, 1948 and 1953. Once more, "political instability" is most certainly not the best phrase to describe the Italian 1946–92 trajectory, and even "governmental instability" should be used with caution.

Together with people and coalitions, there is a third element to be taken into consideration when focusing on stability/instability: public policies. Unstable cabinets do not have the opportunity or the power to enact and implement public policies nor to evaluate their performance and, when necessary, to revise them. A frequent turnover of cabinets and ministers may lead to the overturning of major policies and/or to "stop and go" policies (an experience no British audience needs to be reminded of). In Italy, not only were there few significant changes in policies, mainly during the only truly reformist wave launched by the centre-left (1962–64), but most of the most important public policies were initiated by centrist governments and were sustained and implemented by all subsequent governments.[11] Here, I will emphasize only that this was very true for Italian foreign policy and economic policy, while the welfare state was shaped through many uncoordinated interventions (a modality still at work). To become a member of NATO and to be among the six states that gave birth to the European political unification process were the two major goals pursued and successfully achieved by De Gasperi's cabinets in the late 1940s and early 1950s. With the passing of time, full acceptance of NATO and loyal participation in the activities of European institutions were the two indispensable tickets for admission to the governmental area, first for the Socialists and then for the Communists. This process of acceptance seems at work for the Five Star Movement as well.

As for the economy, the Christian Democrats quickly accepted some Keynesian ideas, thanks to some of their professors of economics (although one should not forget that the principles of a mixed economy and the role of the state are written into the Constitution), and they proceeded to launch several public programmes to substitute for what private entrepreneurs were not doing and, with full autonomy, to pursue the goal of developing the South of Italy. They went so far as to create a special Ministry for State Participation, which, of course, also enjoyed the approval and the support of the left. The story to be told is not that this ministry was (rightly) abolished by a referendum in 1993, because it had also been used to channel funds to the governing parties, but that it worked unchallenged from 1956 to the early 1990s. In the light of government instability, the continuity of Italian public policies is more than remarkable. It contributes powerfully to challenge the view of a political system torn apart by conflicts, plagued by governmental crises, and prey to politicians who have no time to look forward or plan their activities. It explains why, by 1990, Italy had become one of the five most industrialized countries in the world (even today, 2019, Italy still belongs to the G8).

The impossibility of governmental alternation, the long tenure of ministers (and party leaders) and the lack of innovation in public policies all contributed to what amounted almost to political stagnation, especially in the 1980s. A tremendously important exogenous event, the fall of the Berlin Wall and of Communism, led to the collapse of the parties and the party system as well as of the Italian model of government in 1992–94.[12] Highly significant political changes have taken place in the 1994–2018 period, but an overall appraisal indicates that, from the point of view of governmental stability, change has not necessarily meant improvement. In a twenty-year period, in which six national elections have been held, there have been thirteen governments, but also four of the five longest-lasting cabinets. Above all, governmental alternation made its first appearance and was practised in three of the six elections. The political imperatives to build pre-electoral coalitions that had to be as encompassing as possible – and therefore too often, and inevitably, quite heterogeneous – meant that government coalitions were very vulnerable to intra-coalition dissent. In fact, most governmental crises were the product of this kind of dissent. Less significant were intra-party conflicts and dissenting views, because all the electoral laws had given party leaders the power to designate parliamentarians (and also to re-select them or not), therefore favouring the formation of disciplined parliamentary groups. This kind of expedient and compulsory discipline was bound to diminish when new elections were in sight because, then, many parliamentarians began repositioning themselves. The reasons to be dissatisfied with the stability of governments and their performance were somewhat different from those of the 1946–92 period, but they still led to yet another round of attempts to change the Constitution.

The post-1994 period: instability and alternation

How much has changed in the process of government formation and termination, in the kind of coalitions winning elections, in the nature and overall working of Italian governments after 1994? The most important change that took place after 1994 was the appearance of *alternation*, of rotation in government among different parties and party coalitions, something that had eluded the Italian political system during the entire first phase of the Italian Republic (Pritoni 2011; see also Table 5.6). The premise is that, by 1994, neither the PCI, which had transformed itself into the Democratic Party of the Left, nor the MSI, which became the basis of National Alliance, could be excluded from participation in government. No Italian party had to be considered truly "anti-system" any more. All Italian parties became available for the formation of government coalitions: that is, they were, as the Germans and Austrians put it, *Koalitionsfähig*.

Starting with the critical elections of 1994, because of the electoral system, governing coalitions had to be formed not in Parliament after the vote, but in public before the vote, so to speak, and they could be positively or negatively "sanctioned" by the voters themselves. It was also taken for granted that the leader of the winning coalition(s) would become Prime Minister, but no change was made to the Constitution or to the formal power of the President of the Republic to appoint the Prime Minister (and, according to Article 92, "on his proposal", the ministers). Understandably, what was needed was a short period of experimentation, of trial and error – and the newcomer to politics, Berlusconi, certainly tried and made quite a number of errors, but so too did the old leftists. In this period, Italy had a government composed entirely of non-parliamentarians, a fully non-party government led by Lamberto Dini, whose only practical political experience had been seven months in office, from May to December 1994, as Berlusconi's Minister of the Treasury.

The four national elections of 1996, 2001, 2006 and 2008 have been characterized by the bipolar competition pitting the centre-left

Table 5.6 Type of government replacement in Italy, 1946–2018

	No.	Percentage
No change	13	26.6
Micro-substitution	27	55.1
Semi-rotation	3	6.1
Alternation	6	12.2
Total	49	*100.0*

Note: For the definition of the type of cabinet replacement, see Valbruzzi (2011).

against the centre-right and by the occurrence of alternation. The 2013 election was an unexpected harbinger of the 2018 elections, characterized by a bitter tripolar competition. The centre-left gained a sizable majority in 1996, but it suffered a serious defeat in 2001. The centre-left barely won in 2006 and was resoundingly defeated in 2008 by Berlusconi's centre-right coalition, which obtained the largest parliamentary majority in the history of the Republic. That majority was eroded by Berlusconi's governmental inadequacy (already in April 2001, just before the national elections, *The Economist* had declared Berlusconi "unfit to lead Italy") and his less than dignified personal behaviour. Suddenly appointed Senator for life, Mario Monti, Professor of Economics and former EU Commissioner, was appointed in November 2011 by President of the Republic Giorgio Napolitano to lead a non-partisan government quite similar in its composition to the one formed by Dini in 1995: that is, none of the ministers were members of Parliament. Following the general elections of 2013, the Democratic Party could count on a large parliamentary majority in the Chamber of Deputies, although this was only thanks to the majority bonus contained in the electoral law, but it did not have even a working majority in the Senate. President Napolitano masterminded the formation of a government of the "grand coalition" type: that is, including both the Democratic Party and its traditional, quite weakened, opponent, Forza Italia (see Box 5.2).

It is impossible to detect a pattern behind the processes of government formation and termination that occurred between May 1994 and March 2018. Leaders, parties, coalitions and governments changed so frequently that only two words can meaningfully capture the sequence

Box 5.2 Mario Monti

Professor of Economics at the Bocconi University of Milan, Mario Monti (born 1943) was a European Commissioner from 1995 to 2004. He was appointed Senator for life on 16 November 2011 by the President of the Republic, Giorgio Napolitano, who, a few days later nominated him to be President of the Council of Ministers. Monti remained in office from 16 November 2011 to 28 April 2013, leading a non-partisan cabinet. In December 2013 he constructed an electoral vehicle called Civic Choice that obtained slightly more than 8 per cent of the votes in the 2013 general elections. It no longer exists.

of events: improvisation and, borrowing a leaf from the books of the late Polish sociologist Zygmunt Bauman, "liquidity". The only element of continuity was Berlusconi's constant presence on the political scene, despite suffering ups and downs in terms of political power, who still produced a confrontation between his supporters and those who were definitely anti-Berlusconi. As I have already noted, at the other end of the continuum, all the problematic occurrences were the consequences and products of a party system in disarray.

Uncharted waters

The 2013–18 Parliament has seen three governments all revolving around the Democratic Party. All have been of the same type – minimum-winning coalitions[13] – and all composed largely of the same ministers. Once more, as I argued at the start of this chapter, the formal instability of the three 2013–18 governments has been more than counterbalanced by the prolonged tenure of the same ministers and by the fundamental continuity of public policies. However, the entrance of the Five Star Movement in full sail into Parliament, making it more difficult to create a minimum-winning coalition, combined with internal tensions and mistakes made by the leadership of the Democratic Party motivated the reluctantly re-elected President of the Republic, Giorgio Napolitano, to prod Parliament to search for and enact significant constitutional and electoral reforms.

Somewhat surprisingly, the constitutional reforms, initially shared by Matteo Renzi, then the secretary of the Democratic Party, and Silvio Berlusconi, were fundamentally focused on the streamlining of the legislative process, a reduction in the number of parliamentarians ("cutting the armchairs") and the lowering of the costs of politics. The writing of a new electoral law was also part of the package. Nothing was explicitly oriented towards making Italian governments more stable, not to mention creating the conditions for policy innovations. The strengthening of the government had to be the consequence of the so-called governability bonus contained in the electoral law called Italicum (several of whose features were later declared unconstitutional by the Constitutional Court), the trimming of the power of Parliament, especially of the opposition, to monitor the behaviour of the government, and the concentration of legislative powers in the Chamber of Deputies (firmly in the hands of a cabinet endowed with a large majority). In this way, the allegedly longed-for governability would finally come to the Italian political system! Of course, with some sorrow, the "reformers" confessed

that a "trade-off" between representation and governability had to occur
to the expense of representation, but, according to them, this is what globalization imposes on all political systems, especially those shaped in the
immediate post-World War Two period and influenced by the left, or the
Communists. Those who have read the report to the Trilateral Commission (Crozier, Huntington and Watanuki 1975), written more than forty
years ago, may remember that the roots of the crisis of governability
were found in the dynamic relationships between existing political institutions and a highly mobilized, effervescent society. It was said that
demand overloads could not be accommodated by the existing institutions. Generally speaking, the answer was not looked for principally in
strengthening the government,[14] but in reaching a better equilibrium
between society's demands and institutional decision-making capabilities.
In fact, one cannot find a theoretical background to the proposal that, in
order to obtain governability, it is absolutely necessary to reduce representation. On the contrary, it is more than reasonable to hypothesize that
citizens who feel that they are adequately represented will be more
inclined to support the activities of their government(s). To its own detri-
ment, Renzi's majority in the Democratic Party took the opposite view.

Improving Italian governments

The fact that all parliamentary governments might encounter some
problems[15] concerning their formation, functioning and duration is not
a recent discovery. On 4 September 1946, in the Italian Constituent
Assembly, the decision to reject both the presidential government and the
directorial government and to adopt a parliamentary model was accompanied by a unanimous recommendation, known as *ordine del giorno*
Perassi, stating the need to find "constitutional measures appropriate to
protect the requirements of stability for the action of the government and
to avoid the degeneration of parliamentarism".[16] The member of the
Republican Party, Tomaso Perassi, Professor of International Law at the
University of Rome, together with the other distinguished members of
the Constituent Assembly, had in mind the experience of pre-Fascist Italian governments, but, above all, the tragic trajectory of the Weimar
Republic (1919–33). What was not found in the Italian Constituent
Assembly, and was not even looked for in the many subsequent decades
of unstable governments in a framework of stable coalitions and
the continuity of policies, has since become one of the most
important institutional innovations. This innovation was devised
less than a year later, in 1949, by the Germans when writing their

Grundgesetz: the *constructive vote of no confidence*. Having been voted into office by the absolute majority of the members of the Bundestag, no German Chancellor can be ousted unless, first, he or she has been rejected by an absolute majority and, second, he or she is replaced within forty-eight hours by another Chancellor voted in by the absolute majority of the Bundestag.

No *crisis in the dark* is possible or likely in the German parliamentary democracy. Indeed, none has ever taken place, and, together with post-1977 Spain, which adopted the constructive vote of confidence from the outset, Germany is the political system that has had the lowest number of heads of government in the 1949–2019 period: just eight. In both cases, the stability of the head of government and his or her cabinet has clearly demonstrated itself to be a very important precondition for decision-making efficacy (which is, of course, greatly dependent on personal qualities as well) and "governability".

Even though Renzi had sharply criticized governmental instability and lack of governability, somewhat surprisingly in the constitutional reforms formulated by his government there was no provision for the constructive vote of no confidence. The illusion that a parliamentary majority inflated by the bonus of seats provided by the electoral law is preferable to a clearly defined and successfully tested constitutional mechanism has not disappeared from the Italian public debate. In the meantime, Italian governments are bound to remain relatively unstable, most Italian ministers, junior ministers and undersecretaries will continue to retain their offices, public policies will be affected only in a limited way, and the system will cope by exhibiting a fair amount of the political and institutional flexibility that is the hallmark of parliamentary democracies. Indeed, Italian governmental crises will serve two essential purposes. On the one hand, they may break stagnation and immobilism – exactly the charge Renzi wrongly levelled against his predecessor Enrico Letta when replacing him at the end of February 2014. On the other, governmental crises, especially when they take place in situations in which everybody knows that the next government will be formed more or less by the same protagonists, represent opportunities for change, reshuffles and revitalization. Some – a few – ministers will depart. Some – a few – new ministers will arrive. Some old ministers will be repositioned, at least once. The new government may even enjoy a honeymoon period with its parliamentary majority, the mass media and public opinion. In sum, "more of the same" is the normal conclusion of a governmental crisis.

Turning point or interlude?

Following the stunning results of the 4 March 2018 general elections, numerically four government coalitions were possible.

I rank the possible coalitions in Table 5.7 with reference to the number of seats they would have: centre-right plus Five Star Movement; centre-right plus PD; Five Star plus League; Five Star plus PD. Politically, two of these coalitions were immediately ruled out. The Five Star Movement was adamantly opposed to any coalition including Berlusconi because of, among other reasons, his permanent conflict of interests. The Democrats were unwilling to join a coalition with the centre-right, and, to a lesser extent, the opposite also applied: the League was opposed to any government in which the PD were to be present. Once – in fact, almost immediately – the declaration by the outgoing PD secretary Matteo Renzi that his party had been forced into opposition by the voters was understood as his unwillingness even to start a process of bargaining with the Five Star Movement, the only remaining alternative was a Five Star–League government. Both relying on the fact that they had gained a significant number of votes and both sharing, though with different emphases, an anti-system sentiment, the Five Star Movement and the League succeeded in finding common ground. Inevitably, it took some time for them to give birth to what Five Star's "political head" Luigi Di Maio called a "government of change". On 1 June, the government led by neophyte Professor of Civil Law Giuseppe Conte saw the light. Not a member of Parliament, Conte was chosen by the Five Star Movement once it became clear that the President of the Republic was opposed to appointing either leader of the two coalition partners. What also counted was that neither of them was willing to yield the office to his competitor/partner. Di Maio and

Table 5.7   Numerically possible government coalitions after the 2018 elections

	House (absolute majority 316)	Senate (absolute majority 158)
Centre-right plus Five Star Movement	488	248
Centre-right plus Democratic Party	397	189
Five Star Movement plus League	352	169
Five Star Movement plus Democratic Party	339	163

Salvini chose to become Deputy Prime Ministers and, at the same time, ministers of, respectively, Labour and Economic Development and the Interior.

Technically, Conte's government was a minimum winning coalition, made up of 18 ministers, 13 men and 5 women. 8 belonged to the Five Stars, 5 to the League, 5 had no party affiliation. Contrary to what the PD stated, it was not the 'most right-wing government' in the post-war Italian political history[17]. For a while, Di Maio and Salvini succeeded in pursuing their quite different political and economic perspectives. Buoyed by his highly positive results in the European elections, Salvini broke the coalition August 8, 2019, hoping to obtain snap elections. Not so: the Five Stars and the PD were quick in reaching an agreement that led to the formation of the Conte 2 government, yet another minimum winning coalition, made of 21 ministers, 14 men and 7 women. Ten belonging to the Five Stars; 9 to the PD, 1 to Liberi e Uguali, 1 independent. For now, Salvini has been put out in the cold.

To conclude, it may be interesting to remark that, so far, there has unfortunately been no attempt to evaluate or rank in a scholarly way all the Italian governments with reference to their performance. Nor has there been an attempt to evaluate the costs of governmental crises: that is, of the interruptions to the functioning of governmental activities. Although I would reject the often repeated statement that Italy fares better when there is no government, I would be equally critical of those who believe that the Italian problem has been and still is that of governmental instability. On the contrary, most of the time, changes in the composition of Italian governments and even governmental crises have been the oil that has kept the political system running, transforming itself, adapting to challenges.

This chapter has explained why Italy has had so many government since 1946. It has found good reasons for governmental instability and has argued that, instead of being a significant problem for the political system, instability (plus ministerial reshuffles) has served as a surrogate for alternation and, more recently, as a way of periodically (re)synchronizing politics with society. Usually in the hands of party leaders, the processes of government formation and termination have recently seen the incisive and even decisive participation of another institution, in a largely unpredictable manner, in cooperation with Parliament and the government(s): that is, the Presidency of the Republic. The following chapter is devoted to the Presidents, the interpretation they have given to their task, and the way in which they have fulfilled their constitutional (and political) role.

Notes

1 A different counting method is possible if the old government is not considered out at the time of its resignation, but when the new government is formed. According to this method, Gentiloni's government was in office from 12 December 2016 to 1 June 2018, hence 536 days (one year, five months and twenty days), and not very short-lived.

2 The official title of the head of the Italian government is President of the Council of Ministers: that is, he is just a *primus inter pares*. Leaving aside the really un-byzantine discussion concerning the more limited amount of power that a *primus inter pares* has vis-à-vis, for instance, a *primus supra pares*, throughout I will use the term Prime Minister for reasons of brevity. I dare not engage in a comparison that calls into question the difference between Cabinet government and Prime Ministerial government. However, I must remark that the shorter tenure of British ministers has essentially been and remains a by-product of a two-party competition in which the formation of a single-party government implies the replacement of all previous ministers, most of them never to return, and opens the way to new ministers, many of them first-time office holders. On the contrary, for a pool of Italian politicians who have reached the heights of political power, only the passing of time has put an end to their ministerial careers.

3 Neither Christian Democrat Alcide De Gasperi, who was Prime Minister eight times from December 1945 to August 1953, nor Christian Democrat Giulio Andreotti, Prime Minister seven times between February 1972 (the shortest Italian government, at seventeen days) to June 1992, appear in the table because the duration of each of their cabinets was inferior to those ranked here.

4 An affable man surrounded by an aura of personal charisma, a shrewd TV communicator, quite generous with his friends and collaborators, Berlusconi could be very convincing in all negotiations. Although it did not enjoy much editorial success, the book by Fiori (1995) is by far the best, coldly critical analysis of how Berlusconi became so powerful. Why and how he remained powerful for almost twenty years require a specific explanation that must start with the paucity and inadequacy of the political leaders of the centre-left.

5 All the ministers were Christian Democrats or "close" to the DC. Given important offices in Parliament – that is, chairs of parliamentary committees and the speakership of the House of Deputies (Pietro Ingrao, 1976–79, and Nilde Iotti, 1979–92, proved to be admirably fair and capable) – the Communists were more than instrumental; they were decisive in allowing the formation and functioning of Andreotti's governments.

6 See the pathbreaking comparative analysis by Strøm (1990).

7 In some cases, the pre-electoral minority government just prolonged its existence for another three or four months.

8 The 1948–53 Senate was packed with parliamentarians appointed for having been discriminated against, oppressed and repressed by Fascism.

9 This was in the wake of the discovery of a conspiracy by the Masonic lodge P2 (Propaganda 2) involving many politicians, military men, top bureaucrats, journalists and entrepreneurs. Berlusconi, too, had been admitted to the P2.

10 The positive and negative faces of policy continuity find a convincing explanation in the analytical framework put forward by Mancur Olson (1982).

11 The reasons why the collapse of Communist regimes had such an impact on Italian parties and the party system are analysed in Chapter 4.

12 Technically, even the so-called "grand coalition" government led by PD Enrico Letta (28 April 2013–22 February 2014) was a minimum-winning coalition since the withdrawal of any single party would have plunged the government below the absolute majority of seats in both Houses. Indeed, when Berlusconi abandoned the coalition it took a split of his party to keep the government alive.

13 It may be of some interest to recall that in the 1983–85 Committee for Institutional Reforms there was widespread agreement that the problem was, indeed, the crisis of representation. Only the Socialists, whose leader, Bettino Craxi, was at the time Prime Minister, suggested that governability could be obtained almost exclusively by giving more power(s) to the head of government (Pasquino 1985).

14 Should I have put a question mark after the heading? Anyway, what is improving? Does it refer to the stability of the government or to its performance? These are not trivial distinctions, since Renzi's reformers and collaborators, as well as too many journalists and commentators, thought that any improvement had to start by providing, no matter how, an ample parliamentary majority to the preferably single-party government. The question of performance was practically never part of the discussion.

15 In the past twenty years, however, Juan Linz (1994) has decisively addressed serious criticisms of Presidential Republics because of their institutional rigidity. Once an incompetent and dangerous crook is elected President, there is no way to get rid of him until the end of his term. Only the Latin American solution exists: a military coup. Linz praised parliamentary democracies precisely because they are flexible and are capable of peacefully replacing their heads of government and their cabinets according to rules and procedures, and of performing according to the preferences of voters.

16 The degeneration of parliamentarians was imputed not so much to *trasformismo* but to frequent changes in the composition of governments, to their short durations and to the opening up of what Italians have defined a "crisis in the dark", meaning the ousting of a government without a quick, ready-made alternative solution.

17 The first government led by Andreotti in 1972 and the two governments led by Berlusconi in the 2001–06 period qualify as being the most right-wing. In any case, in terms of understanding, explaining and predicting what the Di Maio–Salvini government is and will do, there is not much to be gained by applying the "most right wing" label. For an excellent, balanced assessment, see Valbruzzi (2018).

References

Calossi, E. and Cicchi, L. (2018). The Italian Party System's Three Functional Arenas after the 2018 Election: The Tsunami after the Earthquake. In *Journal of Modern Italian Studies* 23 (4), pp. 437–459.

Cotta, M. and Verzichelli, L. (2000) *Political Institutions in Italy*. Oxford: Oxford University Press.

Crozier, M., Huntington, S. P. and Watanuki, J. (1975). *The Crisis of Democracy: Report on the Governability of Democracies to the Trilateral Commission*. New York: New York University Press.

Fiori, G. (1995). *Il venditore: storia di Silvio Berlusconi e della Fininvest*. Milan: Garzanti.

Katz, R. S. (1986). Party Government a Rationalistic Conception. In F. G. Castles and R. Wildenmann (eds) *Visions and Realities of Party Government* (pp. 31–71). Berlin and New York: Walter de Gruyter.

Laver, M. (1996). *Making and Breaking Governments: Cabinets and Legislatures in Parliamentary Democracies*. Cambridge: Cambridge University Press.

Linz, J. J. (1994). Presidential or Parliamentary Democracy: Does It Make a Difference? In J. J. Linz and A. Valenzuela (eds) *The Failure of Presidential Democracy* (pp. 3–87). Baltimore and London: Johns Hopkins University Press.

Magone, J. M. (ed.) (2015). *Routledge Handbook of European Politics*. London: Routledge.

Mershon, C. (2002). *The Costs of Coalition*. Stanford: Stanford University Press.

Müller, W. C. and Strøm, K. (eds) (2000). *Coalition Governments in Western Europe*. Oxford: Oxford University Press.

Olson, M. (1982). *The Rise and Decline of Nations: Economic Growth, Stagflation, and Social Rigidities*. New Haven and London: Yale University Press.

Pasquino, G. (1985). Teoria e prassi dell'ingovernabilità nella Commissione per le Riforme Istituzionali. In *Stato e Mercato* 15 (3), pp. 365–96.

Pasquino, G. (1987). Party Government in Italy: Achievements and Prospects. In R. S. Katz (ed.) *Party Governments: European and American Experiences* (pp. 202–42). Berlin and New York: Walter de Gruyter.

Pritoni, A. (2011). Italia: dal pluralismo polarizzato all'alternanza "esagerata". In G. Pasquino and M. Valbruzzi (eds) *Il potere dell'alternanza: Teorie e ricerche sui cambi di governo* (pp. 91–120). Bologna: Bononia University Press.

Sartori, G. (ed.) (1973). *Correnti, frazioni e fazioni nei partiti politici italiani*. Bologna: Il Mulino.

Strøm, K. (1990). *Minority Government and Majority Rule*. Cambridge: Cambridge University Press.

Valbruzzi, M. (2011). Misurare l'alternanza, la sua pratica e la sua mancanza. In G. Pasquino and M. Valbruzzi (eds) *Il potere dell'alternanza: Teorie e ricerche sui cambi di governo* (pp. 303–34). Bologna: Bononia University Press.

Valbruzzi, M. (2013). Not a Normal Country: Italy and its Party Systems. In *Studia Politica: Romanian Political Science Review* 13 (4), pp. 617–40.

Valbruzzi, M. (2018). When Populists Meet Technocrats: The Italian Innovation in Government Formation. In *Journal of Modern Italian Studies* 23 (4), pp. 460–80.

Verzichelli, L. and Cotta, M. (2000). Italy: From "Constrained" Coalitions to Alternating Governments. In W. C. Müller and K. Strøm (eds) *Coalition Governments in Western Europe* (pp. 433–97). Oxford: Oxford University Press.

The accordion of the Presidents **6**

For too long, the powers of the Italian President have been underestimated. His role was supposed to be that of a ceremonial figure. When Italian parties started their irresistible decline, it became clear that the constitutional figure envisioned by the drafters of the Constitution could successfully perform a variety of important tasks. This chapter will explore when, why and how these tasks have in fact been fulfilled and will assess the overall political and institutional performance of the Italian Presidents.

The Presidency of the Republic is the highest institutional office in Italy. It has always been coveted by most Italian politicians, possibly with two exceptions, Luigi Einaudi and Carlo Azeglio Ciampi,[1] as the culmination of a protracted and successful political career. For a long time, most of the scholars and commentators thought that the President of the Italian Republic had fundamentally to be a ceremonial figure, enjoying little or no political or institutional power. In fact, the members of the Constituent Assembly had converged only in rejecting the proposal by Piero Calamandrei of a Presidential Republic in which the power(s) of the President would have been counterbalanced by strong local governments. They were very suspicious of a powerful figure, but, at the same time, they felt that the Presidency had to be a substantial role, because, after all, he had to replace the monarchy (ousted by the 2 June 1946 referendum), and he would be entrusted with significant institutional powers. In the end, those powers are many, but their significance and impact change according to variables that are not all in the hands of the President himself.[2]

The elections

The President, who must be at least fifty years of age, is elected by an assembly of Deputies, Senators and representatives of the Regional Councils (1,011 people) for a seven-year term. He can be re-elected, but, as we will see, although some of the incumbents aspired to remain at the Quirinale, even though they could not say so overtly, only Giorgio Napolitano in 2013 accepted a request to serve for an additional short period. A two-thirds majority is needed in the first three ballots; then, an absolute majority is required. No presidential election has ever been easy. Only two Presidents have been elected on the first ballot, following a complex round of negotiations among the major parties: the Christian Democrat Francesco Cossiga (1985–92) and the unaffiliated Carlo Azeglio Ciampi (1999–2016). In most instances, quite a number of ballots have been necessary. Only in one case did the governmental majority succeed in translating into a presidential majority – in the 1971 election of Giovanni Leone – but even in that case the votes of the Neo-Fascist party proved to be decisive. Table 6.1 provides the pure statistical information, but often presidential elections have amounted to a political drama (Pasquino 2015); for a major overview, see Cassese, Galasso and Melloni (2018).

The political class never formulated precise criteria to be applied to the presidential elections. Once more, it was the wisdom of the Christian Democratic leader Alcide De Gasperi that created a precedent. Although in 1948 the DC was by far the largest party, coming quite close to the absolute majority needed to elect the President, De Gasperi succeeded in convincing his parliamentarians that the first President of the Republic had to be a non-Christian Democrat (although, paradoxically, in the end it was not his preferred candidate who won). He wanted to send an important message to the DC's governmental allies and to Italian public opinion: the DC did not want to obtain or maintain a monopoly on political and institutional power. From this followed the first, unwritten and never formalized criterion: alternation. A non-Christian Democrat President had to be followed by a Christian Democrat, and so on. Of course, both the Neo-Fascists and the Communists were in principle excluded: the former because, in addition to the fact that they represented a past that should not be revived, they had opposed the Constitution and remained critical of it; the latter for international reasons – that is, their continuous, unshakable support for Soviet foreign policy. The second subordinate and informal criterion was that the candidate to the Presidency, although

Table 6.1 Presidents of the Italian Republic, 1948–2018

Year	No. of ballots	President elected	Age	Votes	Electoral college	Percentage of votes	Party of the President
1948	4	Einaudi	74	518	900	57.6	Liberal Party
1955	4	Gronchi	68	658	843	78.1	Christian Democracy
1962	9	Segni	71	443	855	51.8	Christian Democracy
1964	21	Saragat	66	646	963	67.1	Social Democratic Party
1971	23	Leone	63	518	1,008	51.4	Christian Democracy
1978	16	Pertini	82	832	1,011	82.3	Italian Socialist Party
1985	1	Cossiga	57	752	1,011	74.4	Christian Democracy
1992	16	Scalfaro	74	672	1,015	66.2	Christian Democracy
1999	1	Ciampi	79	707	1,010	70.0	Independent
2006	4	Napolitano I	81	543	1,009	53.8	Former PCI/Olive Tree
2013	6	Napolitano II	88	738	1,007	73.3	No party affiliation
2015	4	Mattarella	74	665	1,010	65.9	Former Democratic Party

Source: Author's calculation based on the information available at www.quirinale.it.

he might have had a distinguished political career, should not still be significantly active in day-to-day politics at the time of his candidacy.[3]

In order to get the full picture of presidential elections, the two informal criteria should be combined with two important "regularities": that is, two types of expected behaviour. The first concerned the constant attempts by the Communists and the Neo-Fascists to prove that their votes could be decisive and make a difference. While the Communists cannot claim to have been decisive in the election of any President (with the exception, perhaps, of Cossiga), in one case, the very difficult and controversial election of Giovanni Leone (in 1971) on the twenty-third ballot, the Neo-Fascists did indeed cast the decisive votes.[4] The second "regularity" refers to the very difficult fate of all the "official" candidates chosen by the Christian Democrats (or their secretary), who were always expected to win the ballot. In 1962, Antonio Segni won, but only because of a couple of favourable circumstances, one being that the DC did not recognize his predecessor, Giovanni Gronchi, as being chosen by them. In 1971, Giovanni Leone became President, but the majority that elected him was not the one envisaged by the Christian Democrats (several of whom would have preferred Aldo Moro). Finally, in 1985, Francesco Cossiga's election was wisely pre-negotiated by DC secretary Ciriaco De Mita with the secretaries of several parties, including the PCI.

Duties and powers

Once at the top of the political system, nurturing no further political ambitions, the President has, according to Article 87 of the Constitution, the duty "to represent the national unity" – nothing less and nothing more. The task of representing the "national unity" is both extremely demanding and difficult to define. Certainly, this difficulty is one of the reasons why the adjectives "enigmatic and elusive" were used by Livio Paladin (1986), one of the outstanding Italian post-war constitutional lawyers and at one point Chief Justice, to capture the essence of the Italian President. The paradox is that, when they came to define the powers to be entrusted to the President of the Republic, the same members of the Italian Constituent Assembly who did not want a strong President were quite generous, to say the least. Probably at the back of their minds, some of them held the conviction that the President would be obliged to deal with political parties in his exercise of any and all of those powers. Therefore, he had to be adequately equipped. Article 87 also clearly spells out the many institutional and political powers the President enjoys. Much to the surprise of Italian politicians, commentators and scholars, those powers became very visible and their impact quite momentous when, for a variety of reasons from the 1990s onwards, some Presidents felt it their duty to activate and to exercise them in many areas.

In fact, the Italian President of the Republic already has significant powers when it comes to legislation. He authorizes the presentation to Parliament of all bills coming from the government and, at the end of the legislative process, he has the power to sign bills into law – or not. However, he may also send bills back to Parliament accompanied by a message containing his reservations and criticisms. Both powers are rarely used in an explicit and visible manner, but there is a scholarly consensus that in several instances the governments concerned have undertaken previous consultations with him and that quite often the President has given his advice in an informal, but no less incisive, manner. The sore point in the relationship between the President and the government relates to decrees. Too often, practically all governments have resorted to legislating by decree because of delays and mistakes of their own making. Too often, the President has felt compelled to ratify what the government has done in order to avoid worse consequences, especially further delays, stalemates and conflicts. Not even the repeated invitations and statements by the Constitutional Court to strictly abide by Article 77 (which states that decrees have to deal exclusively with homogeneous matters in cases of absolute necessity and urgency) have led to significant improvements. The point is that, whenever the President would like to, he can block decrees. Hence, his predictable behaviour automatically works as a brake on the government, the head of government and ministers whenever they decide to engage in hasty and erratic legislative gestures.

Finally, the President of the Republic enjoys the full discretionary right and power to appoint some life Senators and five constitutional judges. However, it has become more and more difficult to justify this in the eyes of the public, and such appointments tend to be based on some shared criteria: for instance, especially for judges, personal and professional qualifications and the appointee's capability to represent not just different schools and disciplines in a period when even juridical knowledge is fragmenting, but different evanescent political cultures (Liberal, Democratic Catholic, Socialist, Federalist and so on). In the light of the growing "political" importance of the Constitutional Court, Italian Presidents have been invested with high expectations and carry delicate responsibilities when selecting and appointing the five judges. To be sure, so far, no presidential appointment has been made in questionable or partisan manner; professional credentials and style have been the foremost criteria utilized by Presidents.

Here I offer my quasi-theoretical interpretation of the ups and downs of presidential activism and its impact based on the analytical framework that I call "the accordion".[5] The accordion must be understood as an elastic container of a panoply of powers. It is meant to indicate that any and all Italian Presidents are, in principle, in a position to "play" their institutional and political powers from zero to the maximum depending essentially on the strength of the parties, their leaders and the coalition governments they have formed. If and when the parties are strong and cohesive, the President may not even attempt to exercise his own powers. Whenever the parties are divided and weak, all Presidents enjoy the opportunity of playing the accordion of their powers as much as the circumstances require and their own personality allows them to. Of course, when the incumbent President decides to activate his powers – that is, to play the accordion, following to my metaphor – then attention has to shift to the reactions of the parties and their leaders, which may pave the way for a constitutional tug of war (see Box 6.1).[6]

For the entire period I have described as a partyocracy (1948–92), Italian political parties were strong and cohesive enough and capable of steering the course of the government and of dissuading the President from any attempt to influence politics, coalitions or policies. This situation is best reflected in the title of a book published at the end of his term by the first Italian President, Luigi Einaudi (1948–55): *Prediche inutili* (*Wasted sermons*). Highly respected, following a long and successful professional (Professor of Economics, editorial writer for, at the time, the most important Italian daily, the *Corriere della Sera*, and Governor of the Bank of Italy) and political career (he was one of the

---

Box 6.1 The accordion of the Presidents

In this metaphor, the "accordion" can be considered a precious tool containing all the many significant powers granted by the Constitution to the Presidency. However, when the parties and their leaders are cohesive, know what they want and act in unison, following the Constitution, the President must abide by their desires and their decisions. Weakened parties and litigious leaders open up a significant space for Presidents to use all their constitutional and political powers to the full: that is, to play their accordion as much and as well as they can.

leaders of the small Italian Liberal Party, deputy Prime Minister and Minister of Finance), Einaudi is unanimously considered the least "interventionist" of all Italian Presidents. His book reveals that he did, indeed, keep a low profile, but also that he did not refrain from making his opinions known to the political and institutional protagonists by resorting to a practice that Italian scholars have decided to call "moral suasion". Although Einaudi's own evaluation of his impact on political events is rather minimal, it is impossible to know whether his moral suasion worked, for instance in terms of anticipated reactions: that is, politicians and governmental power holders refraining from objectionable behaviour for fear of President Einaudi's critical scathing "sermons" and reprimands.

To make a long story short (for more details, see Pasquino 2015), however, there have been many episodes of Presidents trying to influence the course of political events in a variety of ways. Some of them derived their political power from the support of a political party or of informal networks of politicians. None of them acquired enough power to pursue their goals against the wishes of the parties. One President, Giovanni Leone, was obliged to resign in 1978 because he was allegedly involved in a corruption scandal.[7] On the whole, until 1991, no President, not even the flamboyant and maverick Socialist Sandro Pertini (1978–85), who interpreted his role as "President of the people" (criticizing and counterbalancing the government) and frequently went further than his powers allowed, clashed fully with party politics. Nevertheless, Pertini was responsible for breaking the Christian Democratic monopoly on the office of Prime Minister. In 1980, he appointed the first non-Christian Democrat Prime Minister, Senator Giovanni Spadolini, secretary of the Republican Party, and, in 1983, after a serious electoral defeat of the Christian Democrats, Pertini appointed the Socialist secretary, Bettino Craxi. That is, Pertini fully exercised his constitutional power to appoint the Prime Minister (Article 92), when the Christian Democrats, despite remaining the majority party, started undergoing an electoral and political decline. No doubt President Pertini played his accordion to the full, with much gusto.

A significant clash between the President and the parties came at the end of Cossiga's term (1985–92). A seasoned politician (several times a minister, once Prime Minister, and at the time of his election Speaker of the Senate), President Cossiga sensed that the parties were trying to get rid of him: they were going to "ask" him to step down before the end of his term in order to rearrange the allocation of the most important institutional offices. But, more than anybody else, he also thought that, in the wake of the fall of the Berlin Wall, Italian politics needed to transform itself profoundly. The end of the Cold War was bringing to completion the first phase of the Italian Republic, characterized by the confrontation between the DC and PCI and by the impossibility of governmental alternation because the PCI was technically and politically an anti-system party. Making explicit reference to Article 87 of the Constitution, which states that the President "may send messages to the Houses",[8] Cossiga took advantage of this constitutional opportunity. The message he sent on 26 June 1991 focused on institutional reforms, an issue that had become very important since the end of the 1970s and extremely divisive, and one on which all political parties, with the exception of some second-rank politicians, were taking a conservative position and an overly cautious and defensive attitude. Not Cossiga – which provided one more reason for the parties to try to oust him. Interestingly, Cossiga continued to play what remained of his accordion, chastising all the party leaders for their inadequacy and inability to foresee the future.

All Presidents of the Italian Republic are expected to abide by the Constitution and to facilitate its implementation as it is, but not to suggest reforms or propose solutions. The main purposes of presidential messages are fundamentally to highlight an issue that is considered of major importance, to encourage Parliament to deal with it, to explain why some aspects of a law or of a decree are objectionable and have to be rewritten, and possibly to communicate with the public (one should never forget that the President represents the "national unity") in order to inform people impartially. Cossiga aimed to accomplish all of these purposes, but he exposed himself to abundant criticisms and was accused of interfering in the political debate. In the meantime, he had not spared many political figures in his sarcastic and scathing (often well-taken) criticisms. The newly born Democratic Party of the Left started the procedure necessary to proceed to the impeachment of the President of the Republic, accusing him of subverting the Constitution because he had indicated the need to modify some major features of the Italian parliamentary democracy. Cossiga was partially vindicated when the newly elected Parliament in 1992 simply dropped the impeachment request and immediately appointed a special bicameral commission to deal with the burning issue of institutional reforms.

The second instance of an important and timely presidential message to Parliament occurred on 23 July 2002 in the midst of a persistent and bitter confrontation on the issue of the "conflict of interests" affecting Prime Minister Silvio Berlusconi, a conflict that was especially applicable to his ownership of half the Italian telecommunications system. On 15 December 2003, President Carlo Azeglio Ciampi (1999–2006) sent a message on "Pluralism and Impartiality of Information" to Parliament, indicating the paramount need for the bill on information under discussion to be inspired precisely by those two criteria: pluralism and impartiality. The message, balanced and delicately argued, was immediately followed by an uproar on the part of Berlusconi's supporters and his government, whose sizable parliamentary majority went on to approve a law that essentially allowed the Prime Minister's conflict of interests to continue unabated and unregulated. No subsequent law has been approved so far. The point I am making is that, through his messages to Parliament, the President performs a sort of pedagogical function, but he wields little or no political power if Parliament and the government decide to ignore his messages. Reiteration may be an option, but this may lead to a perilous inter-institutional confrontation to be adjudicated by the Constitutional Court. So far, however, no President has pushed his disagreements with Parliament and the government to an outright, open clash. However, it must be stressed that Ciampi had no party of his own, that Berlusconi's coalition relied on a large parliamentary majority and that, generally speaking, Italian public opinion is not particularly sensitive to the existence of "conflicts of interest".

1992: a pivotal election

In between Cossiga's 1991 and Ciampi's 2003 messages, the Italian political system had gone through major events. No new Republic (that is, no Second Republic) was born, but a wave of popular referendums, the judicial investigation called Clean Hands (*Mani Pulite*) and a new electoral law had all dramatically affected Italian parties and the party system, producing their sudden collapse. Even the election of the successor President to Cossiga had been significantly influenced by a traumatic external factor. In 1992, there were three candidates for the Presidency of the Republic: the secretary of the Christian Democrats, Arnaldo Forlani; the incumbent long-term Prime Minister, Giulio Andreotti; and the secretary of the Socialist Party, Bettino Craxi. The old criterion that a non-Christian Democrat should follow a Christian Democrat (Cossiga) had been somewhat erased by the results of the 1992 parliamentary elections, in which all the traditional parties performed very poorly. The situation was made even more unmanageable, on the one hand, by Craxi's strong desire to be reappointed Prime Minister and his distrust of Andreotti (whom he had labelled an old, and treacherous, fox) and, on the other hand, by the fact that Andreotti, well aware that the 1992 presidential election was going to be his last chance, for reasons of age (he was already seventy-three) and because of the decline of the Christian Democrats, was thoroughly mobilizing his many supporters in all parties, including within the ranks of the former Communists – no minor feat. Because of the bitter conflict between Craxi and the former Communists, the latter were against Craxi's election to the Presidency, but they were also against Forlani, who might have appointed Craxi to the office of Prime Minister. Therefore, the 1992 presidential election became an unprecedented power game concerning not just the careers of three important politicians, but the future of the Italian political system.[9]

After fifteen acrimonious ballots, it became clear that Parliament was frozen in a duel between the reluctant Forlani and the manoeuvring Andreotti. Only an unpredictable outside event could decide the presidential election. The stalemate was broken by the assassination of Judge Giovanni Falcone, an icon of the anti-Mafia battle, his wife and their bodyguards, masterminded and carried out by the Sicilian Mafia on 23 May 1992.[10] Reacquiring some of their lost dignity, parliamentarians quickly reacted, electing Christian Democrat Oscar Luigi Scalfaro, who had had a long political and ministerial career. A few years before he had served as Minister of Internal Affairs, and a few days before his election to the Presidency he had become Speaker of the House of Deputies. Immediately, President Scalfaro made use of his institutional powers, choosing the Prime Minister from a roster of three candidates that, at his explicit request, had been submitted to him by the Socialist secretary Craxi. Thus, Giuliano Amato, former Minister of the Treasury and deputy secretary of the Socialist Party, became the last Prime Minister of the first phase of the Italian Republic, only to resign one year later in the wake of several referendums because he had expressed his strong and explicit disapproval of the referendums on the electoral law, declaring them to be, in his opinion, "very unconstitutional". Hence, President Scalfaro appointed the Governor of the Bank of Italy, Carlo Azeglio Ciampi (in office April 1993–March 1994) as the first non-partisan Italian Prime Minister ever. Ciampi's cabinet was made up of party and non-party members. Scalfaro was also largely responsible for deciding the early dissolution of a Parliament that had lasted just two years (1992–94), following approval of the electoral law at the referendum, and the budget law.

By then, it had become clear that no Italian party was any longer in a position to prevent the President from playing to the full the accordion of his constitutional powers. The parties' weaknesses allowed, encouraged and even made it necessary for the President of the Republic to take the two most important "institutional" decisions: appointing the Prime Minister and dissolving Parliament (or not). It is a paradox that the new "presidential" phase was inaugurated by an old Christian Democratic conservative politician known for defending Parliament and for extolling its fundamental role. Scalfaro's presidential powers were decisively tested again when Berlusconi's first government (May 1994–December 1994) lost its parliamentary majority because it was "betrayed" – that is, abandoned – by the parliamentarians of the Northern League, most of them elected in single-member districts thanks to the votes for the coalition masterminded by Berlusconi himself.

Wrongly[11] claiming that he had been elected by the people (an immodest dose of populism was always present in Berlusconi's public declarations) – that is, by voters – and that therefore it was up to the voters to pass judgement on the betrayal by some of his governmental allies, Berlusconi asked President Scalfaro to dissolve Parliament immediately and to return power to the voters. Scalfaro rejected this request, stating that as long as Parliament was capable of producing a government and supporting its activity, no dissolution was constitutionally acceptable, permitted or necessary. However, Scalfaro recognized the right and privilege of Berlusconi as leader of the party that had won the 1994 elections (Forza Italia) to suggest the name of the Prime Minister. Lamberto Dini, who was not a member of Parliament but was a former Minister of the Treasury in Berlusconi's government, became the second non-partisan Italian Prime Minister. Moreover, Scalfaro requested that none of his ministers be a parliamentarian so that Dini's government could not be criticized as having totally subverted the outcome of the 1994 elections. Indeed, in Parliament, the government received the votes of both Berlusconi's centre-right coalition and the centre-left. In February 1996, President Scalfaro was once more obliged to dissolve Parliament early when it became clear that the parties and parliamentarians were unable to formulate or approve institutional reforms.

Scalfaro's interpretation of the Constitution, his institutional powers and even his own consistency were once more put to the test by the unpredictable vagaries of Italian politics. In October 1998, the Prime Minister of the Olive Tree governing coalition, Romano Prodi, lost a vote of confidence. Claiming in a manner that was very similar to what Silvio Berlusconi had argued four years earlier – that is, that he had received a popular mandate and that his parliamentary majority had been betrayed by a coalition partner, hence making a return to the polls almost mandatory – Prodi asked Scalfaro for an early dissolution of Parliament. Scalfaro's answer was fully consistent with his previous behaviour: no dissolution would follow if Parliament proved capable of voting its confidence in a new government and supporting its activities. Consequently, Scalfaro appointed to the office of Prime Minister Massimo D'Alema, secretary of the Leftist Democrats, the largest party of the Olive Tree coalition, on whose candidacy an absolute majority of parliamentarians had indicated their willingness to agree. There is no doubt that all of Scalfaro's decisions were enabled by the weakness of the parties. Both Berlusconi's and Prodi's coalitions were anything but cohesive. D'Alema's government was made possible by the decision of approximately eighty Deputies and Senators to leave the centre-right parties in whose ranks they had been elected and join the centre-left, something that would have been unthinkable before 1989.

Scalfaro's unobjectionable constitutional behaviour illustrates a glaring paradox. A top political personality, who all his life had been an admirer of "absolute" parliamentarism[12] in which the President of the Republic has a limited role, he was obliged by political events to transform into a "presidentialist", or, looking at the case of the Fifth French Republic, into a "semi-presidentialist" President, who was required to play a very active role and who willingly obliged. Working for the health of the political system required him to decide whether or not to dissolve Parliament and which personality to appoint to the office of Prime Minister, almost disregarding the preferences of the different parties. There is no doubt that Scalfaro provides an excellent test of the accordion theory of presidential powers. Changed times required the President fully to exercise his institutional powers and he could respond and perform within the Constitution; this shows that, when the parties are weak, divided and unable to coalesce, as a consequence the President becomes very strong and finds himself in a position to fill their political space, working according to the rules.

In a way, Scalfaro's election had been a break from the pattern that up to then had been informally applied to the election of the Presidents of the Italian Republic: a (conservative) Christian Democrat succeeding another (though progressive) Christian Democrat, Francesco Cossiga.[13] Next, it might have been the turn of someone coming from the Communist Party, which had just changed its name, possibly a woman. Nilde Iotti had been a widely respected Speaker in the House of Deputies for an unprecedented length of time, from 1979 to 1992, but three factors militated against her election. First, at the time, the *pentapartito* was not inclined to recognize the former Communists as influential actors; second, Iotti's party had become very weak; and, third, the power struggle within the DC and between the DC and the PSI prevented any outcome that rewarded someone not coming from their ranks. In any case, Scalfaro's election was not accompanied by the identification or stipulation of new criteria in a phase that looked transitory and out of control. Seven years later, the lack of agreed criteria was even more glaring.

In 1999, for the first time, even an extra-parliamentary candidacy made an appearance: Emma Bonino, one of the leaders of the small Radical Party, former European Commissioner, passionate promoter of human rights, highly esteemed personality and, last but not least, a woman. Largely in order to prevent a parliamentary stalemate that might have opened a wide space for Bonino's candidacy, Walter Veltroni, then secretary of the Party of the Democratic Left, attempted to build significant parliamentary support for someone not coming from the ranks of professional politicians: Carlo Azeglio Ciampi, at the time no longer a minister. Having reached an agreement with Berlusconi (who had no candidate of his own), Veltroni secured Ciampi's election on the first ballot. As already remarked, this was an extraordinary achievement.

Much less experienced than Scalfaro, the new President was blessed with a period of relative political and institutional tranquillity. Ciampi's Presidency had to deal first with two minor government reshuffles within the centre-left, but these involved no conflict. Then, unparadoxically, his life was made easy by the electoral victory of a large centre-right parliamentary majority led by Prime Minister Berlusconi, a majority that lasted for the entire parliamentary term (2001–06), although it went through another minor governmental reshuffle that did not require any action by the President because it was quickly solved by the parties in the governing coalition. If anything, this event provided decisive evidence that when the parties are "strong" and cohesive, willing and able to coordinate their behaviour, there is little room and no need for an autonomous initiative by the President of the Republic. There is neither the necessity nor the possibility of him playing his accordion. Even though he was courted to accept an unprecedented re-election, very wisely Ciampi declared that he was not available. Hence, in the absence of any criterion, with the impossibility of relying on past occurrences, in a situation in which no candidate could openly campaign for fear of sabotaging his (or her) chances, and where no one was powerful or credible enough to seek a solid inter-party agreement, the 2006 presidential election was thrown wide open.

Much to the surprise of the candidate himself, the long story of the exclusion of the Communists from the top institutional office of the Republic[14] came to a sudden end. On 10 May 2006, the former leader of the Communist reformist wing Giorgio Napolitano, aged almost eighty-one, was elected the eleventh President of the Italian Republic on the fourth ballot, receiving 543 votes (53.8 per cent). The incoming centre-left coalition, which had just – barely – won the April 2006 parliamentary elections, had indeed searched for a convergence with the centre-right. In the end, however, Berlusconi decided to deny his votes to Napolitano.[15] Life Senator at the time of his election, Napolitano had had a long and very successful political career. Elected by the PCI to the House of Deputies for the first time in 1953, he had been continuously re-elected until 1994. Speaker of the House of Deputies from 1992 to 1994, he served as Minister of Internal Affairs in the Ulivo government from 1996 to 1998. In 1999 he was elected to the European Parliament and served as chair of the Committee on Constitutional Affairs until 2004. Also thanks to his parliamentary career, which included being head of the Communist Deputies, Napolitano had a profound knowledge of the formal and informal rules guiding the activities (and the idiosyncrasies) of parliamentarians and their party leaders. Hence, he was eminently suited for a very demanding job, especially in a situation of head-on confrontation between the centre-left composite coalition called Union led by Romano Prodi and the centre-right coalition called Freedom's People (Popolo della Libertà) led by Berlusconi. The combination of Napolitano's political and constitutional knowledge with the most difficult circumstances of Italian politics goes a long way to explaining why he felt obliged to play a highly interventionist role in an extremely turbulent period – something that the President repeatedly did with a fair amount of political, institutional and even personal pleasure.

Napolitano's Presidency

From the very beginning of his Presidency, Napolitano (see Box 6.2) was required to make important decisions. First, in mid-February 2007, he helped Prime Minister Prodi reacquire control over his razor-thin parliamentary majority, but at the end of January 2008 Napolitano was

Box 6.2 Giorgio Napolitano

Napolitano (born in 1925), one of the most important leaders of the reformist wing of the Italian Communist Party, was elected to the House of Deputies uninterruptedly from 1953 to 1994. For several years head of the House parliamentary group of the PCI, he served as Speaker of the House of Deputies from 1992 to 1994 and as Minister of Home Affairs from 1996 to 1998. Elected to the European Parliament in 1999, he became chair of the Committee of Constitutional Affairs. In May 2006, he was elected the eleventh President of the Italian Republic. The only President ever to have been re-elected (in April 2013), he resigned in January 2015.

obliged to accept the termination of Prodi's second governmental term, one that had been marked and marred by constant clashes within the centre-left's extremely diversified and disjointed parliamentary coalition. The early dissolution of Parliament in 2008 opened the way to Berlusconi's return in style to Palazzo Chigi, the headquarters and residence of the Prime Minister. When, for several political and non-political reasons, Berlusconi proved unable to keep his coalition united and to govern in a satisfactory way,[16] and when the haemorrhaging of his Freedom's People parliamentarians was on the verge of depriving his government of its absolute majority in the House of Deputies, President Napolitano proceeded to construct the preliminary conditions for a new government. First, he nominated life Senator Mario Monti, Professor of Economics at Bocconi University and, most importantly, former European Commissioner (appointed at the time by Berlusconi). Then, he invited Berlusconi to resign in order to avoid losing a vote of no confidence that might have had to be followed by an inevitable, constitutionally grounded request of the centre-left for yet another early dissolution of Parliament. Finally, he appointed Monti Prime Minister of a non-partisan government supported mostly by parliamentarians belonging to the centre-left as well as many coming from the centre-right. Napolitano's main, but undeclared, motivation was twofold. On the one hand, he wanted to avoid general elections that might have further destabilized the Italian political system, and, on the other, he wanted to empower a government capable of making a number of unpopular reforms in the full knowledge that a non-partisan government could achieve a lot, partly because it did not have to be exposed to the risks of electoral accountability. The facilitating conditions were that, first, Berlusconi's Freedom's People was in a state of disarray and that, second, the various political actors of the centre-left were just muddling through.

In more than one way, President Napolitano threw his political prestige and weight behind Monti's governmental action, only to be bitterly disappointed by the Prime Minister's unexpected decision in December 2012 to launch his own political vehicle (called Scelta Civica or Civic Choice) in order to take part in the February 2013 elections. Subsequently, Monti's rather poor electoral results were not Napolitano's most important post-election preoccupations. In fact, the distribution of parliamentary seats made the formation of a new government anything but easy. Once more it became crystal-clear that when the parties are weak, the President of the Republic acquires and enjoys enough constitutional power to make up for them. In this particular instance, although Pier Luigi Bersani, the secretary of the Partito Democratico, could rely on a sizable majority in the House of Deputies, but only because of the majority bonus, Napolitano denied him the opportunity of creating a government because it was less than certain that he could obtain the indispensable support of an absolute majority in the Senate as well. This was a momentous decision. Napolitano wanted to avoid a situation in which the government would be permanently exposed to floating majorities in the Senate, and where the PD and its official allies could not count on a majority. Bersani's potential government would therefore constantly remain vulnerable to the threats and blackmails of the Five Star Movement. When it became clear that Bersani could not confirm the existence of a reliable centre-left majority in the Senate, another unprecedented event took place that laid bare the weakness of Italian political parties and opened up a large window of opportunity for the President to exploit.

Both for personal (old age) and institutional reasons – that is, not to create the precedent of a re-election – Napolitano had repeatedly declared that he was not seeking a second term and was not willing to accept one. Following the election of the new Parliament in February 2013 and a few weeks before the end of his term, Napolitano resigned in order to open the way for the election of a new President of the Republic, whose first paramount task had to be the appointment of the Prime Minister. It was up to the secretary of the largest parliamentary party, Bersani, to start the process, and, following some consultations with other party leaders, to designate a candidate to the Presidency. The situation was made more complicated than in the past, not so much because no acceptable criteria existed any longer to choose the President from many possible candidates, none of them outstanding or untainted, but because the new entrants to the Italian Parliament – that is, the Five Star Movement – loudly claimed that they should have a say in the process. To no avail. A couple of quite clumsy attempts by the centre-left followed. First, the candidacy of the former Speaker of the Senate, Franco Marini, who belonged to the Christian Democratic tradition, was put forward. But Marini's actual votes were significantly below the number of all those who were expected to support him and his candidacy was immediately dropped. Then, it was up to the former centre-left Prime Minister Romano Prodi, who, understandably, was not acceptable to Berlusconi; he was defeated by the divisions within the centre-left itself, or, more precisely, within the Democratic Party.

On the verge of political desperation and a systemic crisis, practically all the party leaders, with the exception of the Five Star Movement's,[17] appealed to Napolitano to accept re-election. On the sixth ballot, on 20 April 2013, Napolitano received 738 votes coming from many parliamentary sectors, but not from the Five Star Movement (whose votes were among the 217 that went to the leftist professor of law Stefano Rodotà), the Northern League or the right. Once re-elected, President Napolitano masterminded the formation of a new government; this was led by Enrico Letta, deputy secretary of the Partito Democratico, and, more importantly, enjoyed the initial support of Berlusconi's Forza Italia. In a way, then, Letta's government was simultaneously a grand coalition Italian-style and a "government of the President": that is, it relied on Napolitano's open support. In exchange for his personal "sacrifice", Napolitano requested that party leaders and parliamentarians devote themselves to institutional reforms and to redrafting the electoral law, which was deemed largely responsible for the fact that in the House of Deputies there was a clear majority, while in the Senate no viable majority existed (see Chapter 2). What had been considered inappropriate twenty years before for Cossiga – that is, to suggest in a formal message to Parliament the institutional reforms to be made – had now become a privilege for President Napolitano to enjoy. Institutional and constitutional reforms were put among the priorities in the new government's agenda.

The next phase was characterized by Berlusconi being ousted from the Senate because he had been convicted of financial fraud. There followed a split of Forza Italia, one wing remaining in the government, and the seemingly irresistible ascent of Matteo Renzi. The young Florentine politician, first, following Bersani's resignation, was elected secretary of the Democratic Party; next, he undermined Letta and replaced him at the helm of the government on 22 February 2014. When the Democratic Party, the strongest and, at the time, still the most cohesive party in Parliament, decided to inform the President of the Republic that only a different government would have a chance of surviving and working (thriving would be too optimistic), the President felt obliged to abide by those wishes and indications. This is not to say that no other options were possible. For instance, Napolitano might have sent Prime Minister Letta to Parliament in order to check whether he still enjoyed the confidence of a majority. If not, he could have opened the way to a formal governmental crisis. In the knowledge that the keys to the inauguration as well as the solution of the crisis were in the hands of the secretary of the Partito Democratico, President Napolitano accepted Letta's resignation and Renzi's immediate ascent to the office of Prime Minister, probably in the hope that the process of institutional reform would start right away in a more favourable environment.

In more than one way, from the very beginning, in interviews, in frequent declarations and in official statements, Napolitano behaved not as an impartial referee. He was an active participant, supporting all the institutional (and electoral) reforms drafted by the Partito Democratico, his secretary and his government. When all those reforms appeared to be well under way, their first parliamentary reading having been completed, Napolitano kept his word and resigned on 14 January 2015. The only President ever to be re-elected, he had served for almost nine dense, turbulent years in which five governments had been made and unmade (overall evaluations of Napolitano's presidential performance are offered by *Paradoxa* (2015) and Lippolis and Salerno (2016)). In his public life, he continued giving a full and unreserved positive evaluation of the institutional reforms formulated by Renzi's government and approved by Parliament, always stressing the importance of the constitutional referendum through which Italian voters were asked to ratify or reject them. Following a defeat in the constitutional referendum, he felt that the voters' clear rejection of the reforms was also a blow to his intense, prolonged commitment.

Folding the presidential accordion

The election of a new President was relatively easy – or at least easier than expected. It is likely that, again unusually, Napolitano himself had prepared the ground for a smooth succession. Perhaps many parliamentarians had learned the lesson of 2013 and decided to avoid additional blame and discredit. Though not necessarily pursuing a full-blown attempt to reach an agreement with Berlusconi, the Partito Democratico put forward the name of Sergio Mattarella. A constitutional judge at the time and a former left-wing Christian Democrat, Mattarella had served in several important ministerial positions. He was also well known for having been the rapporteur of the electoral law that carried his name. In spite of the fact that Berlusconi, who had indicated his preference for Giuliano Amato, decided not to support his candidacy, Mattarella was elected on 31 January, at the fourth ballot, by a larger than expected number of votes – 665 (65.9 per cent). It is too early to judge soft-spoken Mattarella's performance (Figure 6.1 gives a preliminary assessment of the Italians' trust in him and in his predecessors), but his inclination to refrain from visible political interventions and actions has already been put to exacting tests. He immediately made known his unwillingness to dissolve Parliament in the wake of the constitutional referendum. He has offered his encouragement to the drafting of a new electoral law with homogeneous features for the House and the Senate. He has recognized the right of the largest party – at the time, the Democratic Party – to steer the actions of the government. He has made clear attempts to keep a balance between the political preferences of the governmental majority and the national interests, which, in his view, include Italy's implementation of EU rules and obligations.

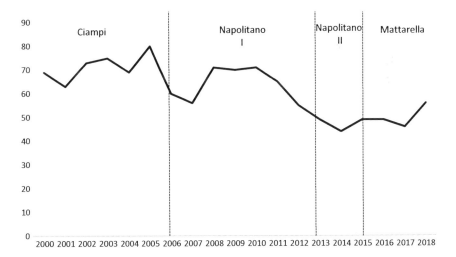

Figure 6.1   Trust in the President of the Republic (percentage)

Note: The percentages are of respondents who declare that they have "much" or "very much" trust in the President of the Republic.

Source: Author's own elaboration based on data provided by Demos (www.demos.it).

The results of the 2018 elections have inevitably posed a significant challenge to Mattarella's accordion: that is, to his possibility of fully utilizing his constitutional powers in the formation of an unusual government. During the formation of the yellow–green government, President Mattarella has protected and exercised his constitutional prerogatives vis-à-vis both the Five Star Movement and the League. Among other less well-known gestures, he has suggested the names of some ministers and has successfully vetoed one of them for his anti-EU statements. The two coalition partners seem to be less than inclined to allow the President to play his accordion, but in the first period of their government, they have been obliged to listen and to abide by the constitutional music that President Mattarella has played so far. Chances are that he will continue to play for the rest of his term until January 2022.

Ranking the Presidents

Italian scholars, historians and political scientists have not (yet) compiled an overall comparative evaluation of the performance of the eleven Presidents of the Republic. It is true that, until recently, Italian Presidents were not considered particularly interesting. Though not necessarily just grey figures, their exercise of political and institutional powers appeared somewhat limited, checked by the parties; they seemed to be largely uninfluential, and their impact on the course of Italian politics appeared occasional and minor, not affecting the politics of the parties. However, since President Scalfaro (1992–99), and especially with President Napolitano, one may confidently state that the actions of the Presidents have very significantly affected and changed the course of Italian politics. It may be a good idea to ask whether, had Scalfaro and Napolitano yielded to the requests of, respectively, Berlusconi in 1994, Prodi in 1998, the centre-left in 2011 and Bersani in 2013, the Italian political system would find itself in a better or worse shape. Well-argued and persuasive answers to these legitimate questions are not easy to reach, but they would definitely be illuminating. However, the main point I have made throughout this chapter is that it is high time to recognize that the Presidents of the Italian Republic are endowed by the Constitution with considerable political and institutional powers, and that, because of the decline of the power of Italian political parties, a lot of space has become available to them to intervene actively in Italian politics. When necessary, they have made good use of that space.

Analyses of Italian politics that do not take into account those powers and the conditions in which they can and have been exercised are doomed to fail in fully appreciating the evolution and transformation of Italian politics. Observing the apparently confused dynamics of Italian politics at the beginning of the 1960s, General de Gaulle, who had just inaugurated "his" Fifth French Republic, was quoted as saying "L'Italie en est à la Cinquième" (Italy is on the verge of the Fifth Republic), meaning that, in his opinion, Italy was in need of a shift from a weak parliamentary democracy to a "strong" semi-presidential regime. Maybe not, but if Italian parties do not reconstruct themselves and do not create a decent party system, Italian Presidents will increasingly need to resort to the autonomous wielding of their most important institutional powers, beginning with the appointment of the Prime Minister and the dissolution of Parliament – the two defining powers of the Presidents of the Fifth French Republic – and to influence the drafting and even the approval and enactment of the most important pieces of legislation. Those who do not accept the improvised jargon of the journalists who have been speaking for almost twenty years of a Second Republic that never was may well remember that semi-presidentialism French-style was seriously considered by the Bicameral Commission on Institutional Reforms chaired by D'Alema in 1996–98. It remains an option in the best-informed discussions on what to do in order to improve the functioning of the Italian political system. Renzi's reforms took a different path, and failed. Perhaps, a more incisive and more convincing process of constitutional reforms could be launched once a full understanding of the powers of the Italian Presidency and their systemic consequences is reached.

This chapter has focused on the constitutional and political powers of the Presidents of the Italian Republic. It has shown that, more than any other President of a contemporary parliamentary democracy, the Italian President can play a significant political role. Indeed, some of them have felt obliged to do so for the well-being of the political system. Especially since the collapse of the Italian party system in 1994, Italian Presidents have actively intervened in a significant and positive way to safeguard the Constitution and to improve the working of the Italian political system.

Notes

1 In fact, Einaudi also had a political "biography", as a prominent leader of the Italian Liberal Party, Governor of the Bank of Italy (1945–48) and Minister of Finance (1947–48). Ciampi, although Prime Minister (1993–94), Minister of

the Treasury (1996–98) former Governor of the Bank of Italy (1979–93), had neither any previous political experience nor a political "basis" (see Pasquino 1999; Giannini 2006).

2 No single adjective can convey the complexity of the role Italian Presidents are in a position to play. "Ambiguous" has a negative connotation that most certainly does not reflect what the members of the Constituent Assembly wanted to achieve. Flexible, adaptable and elastic are closer to the institutional reality, but quite vague. So is adjustable. In this chapter I will analyse the presidential powers, making reference to an accordion. Here, let me state with some emphasis that the Italian President has been shown to be the most powerful of the Presidents in all parliamentary democracies (Grimaldi 2012).

3 In 1971 this criterion played against the very powerful Christian Democratic leader Aldo Moro. In addition, he was accused, wrongly, to be working in order to create the political basis for an opening to the PCI, which was, indeed, ready to vote for him. In the light of subsequent events, Moro's non-election was a turning point in the history of Italy.

4 Leone received 518 votes out of 1,008. Hence, his election was due to the thirty-five Neo-Fascist votes because otherwise he would not have passed the required absolute majority of 505 votes. The Neo-Fascists immediately received their longed-for reward: the first early dissolution of the Italian Parliament, which allowed them to cash in the electoral benefits of their "law and order" campaign against mounting Italian terrorism, which, paradoxically, also involved right-wing groups bordering with the party.

5 The idea that "the set of institutional powers available to the President of the Republic are similar to an accordion" (Pasquino 2012: 847) was imaginatively put forward by Giuliano Amato, Professor of Constitutional Law, a minister several times and twice Prime Minister, now a constitutional justice, in a public conference whose location and date neither of us remembers. With Amato's consent and approval, I have elaborated on the idea that, with the passing of time, has become commonplace. Many scholars have freely made use of it without appropriately quoting the sources (several instances can be found in Cassese, Galasso and Melloni (2018)). Authorized by Amato, I am happy to claim full responsibility for its formulation, adaptation and implementation.

6 It is a war of many battles, never decisive, that suggest that the politico-constitutional system of the (Italian) parliamentary democracy contains several important elements of flexibility. It is exactly this kind of flexibility that goes a long way to explaining the functioning and the persistence of the Italian political system as we know it and Italy's democracy.

7 In addition to the discovery that the Lockheed company had given money to Leone's trusted lawyers and associates, a variety of factors made it impossible for him to remain at the Quirinale, among them the revulsion

felt by several sectors of the public against the authorities for having been unable (if not unwilling) to rescue Aldo Moro from the Red Brigades' homicidal hands.

8 By that time, the preconditions for a new political "game" had come into existence. The PCI had already changed its name and was no longer sub-servient to the foreign policy imperatives of the Soviet Union, which had collapsed. The new party, PDS (Democratic Party of the Left), had also been seriously weakened by a split.

9 A more detailed analysis can be found in Pasquino (1993).

10 Many rumours regarding personal as well as indirect ties between him and the Sicilian Mafia immediately swept away any remaining chance for Andreotti.

11 The only constitutional condition for the formation and existence of a government in Italy is that it must have and retain the confidence of a parliamentary majority in both Houses.

12 In fact, Scalfaro was voted into the presidential office largely because he seemed to be in a position to revitalize the Italian Parliament: that is, to restore a working relationship between Parliament and the government(s). He did just that.

13 Remember that the old parties, the old political class and the old political habits were approaching their Armageddon.

14 The very Republic they had contributed to establishing, as the Commun-ists never ceased reminding all party leaders and the Italian public.

15 Berlusconi's candidate at this time, and, as would become known later, in the 2015 election as well, was Giuliano Amato, who proved to be unacceptable both then and later to most parliamentarians of the PDS and the PD because of his Socialist past and the prominent and crucial role he played in Craxi's party and government.

16 The most significant indicator of the declining confidence in Berlusconi's government by the banks, rating agencies and economic operators was the growing spread between Italian and German state bonds, which had gone above quota 600.

17 The Five Star parliamentarians stuck to their decision to the end. Even in the last ballot they supported the left-wing Professor of Law Stefano Rodotà, member of the House of Deputies from 1979 to 1994 and former chair of the Italian Data Protection Authority, who consistently received more than 200 votes. It is a legitimate question to ask whether a different outcome might have followed had the Five Star Movement been willing to search for allies.

References

Cassese, S., Galasso, G. and Melloni, A. (eds) (2018). *I Presidenti della Repubblica: Il Capo dello Stato e il Quirinale nella storia della democrazia italiana*. Bologna: Il Mulino. 2 vols.

Giannini, M. (2006). *Ciampi: Sette anni di un tecnico al Quirinale*. Turin: Einaudi.

Grimaldi, S. (2012). *I Presidenti nelle forme di governo: Tra Costituzione, partiti e carisma*. Rome: Carocci.

Lippolis, V. and Salerno, G. M. (2016). *La presidenza più lunga: I poteri del capo dello Stato e la Costituzione*. Bologna: Il Mulino.

Paladin, L. (1986). Presidente della Repubblica. In *Enciclopedia del Diritto* (Vol. 35, pp. 185–242). Milan: Giuffré.

Una storia presidenziale (2006–2015). (2015). *Paradoxa* IX (1), January/March.

Pasquino, G. (1993). Electing the President of the Republic. In G. Pasquino and P. McCarthy (eds) *The End of Post-war Politics in Italy: The Landmark 1992 Elections* (pp. 121–140). Boulder: Westview Press.

Pasquino, G. (1999). The Election of the Tenth President of the Italian Republic. In *Journal of Modern Italian Studies* 4 (3), pp. 405–415.

Pasquino, G. (2012). Italian Presidents and their Accordion: Pre-1992 and Post-1994. In *Parliamentary Affairs* 65 (4), pp. 845–860.

Pasquino, G. (2015). The Presidents of the Republic. In E. Jones and G. Pasquino (eds) *The Oxford Handbook of Italian Politics* (pp. 82–94). Oxford: Oxford University Press.

Civil society   7

Citizens deserve the government they get. This famous sentence can be interpreted in many ways. While most Italians have always thought that they deserve a better government, there are good reasons to believe that Italian governments are, and have always been, not only the genuine product of a society that has many drawbacks, but also effectively representative of their citizens' preferences and feelings. In this chapter, I explore and assess those drawbacks, their continued existence, their impact on politics and their consequences.

Associational propensities and capabilities

The politics of all political systems is always, more or less decisively, influenced – if not considerably shaped – by civil society. Of course, not all citizens deserve the governments they get, but, especially in a democracy, most of them are responsible in several ways for the ascent to office of the various government coalitions, the quality of their performance and the overall conditions of the political system. Leaving aside the precise quantity and quality of associations present in Italy, there is no doubt that there exists a significant amount of pluralism. Groups are born; groups compete, win and lose; groups merge, with total freedom to do so; groups disappear; new groups surface. Generally speaking, there is also a fair amount of competition among the many groups, although, in Italy, one might have reservations concerning competition in the field of mass media and concerning the procedures of state financing of cultural associations and non-governmental organizations. Also, as Table 7.1 shows, Italians do engage in a fair number of social activities. However,

Table 7.1 Frequency of social activities in Italy, 2001–16 (percentage)

Year	Meetings in associations: ecological, civil rights, peace	Meeting in associations: cultural, recreational, other	Free activities in voluntary associations	Free activities in non-voluntary associations	Free activities for a union	Donate money to an association
2001	1.8	8.4	8.4	3.2	1.5	17.3
2002	1.7	7.6	8.0	2.9	1.4	15.2
2003	2.3	8.9	8.5	3.3	1.3	16.5
2005	2.0	8.8	8.9	3.4	1.3	18.1
2006	2.0	9.0	8.8	3.2	1.4	17.1
2007	1.9	9.1	9.2	3.4	1.3	16.7
2008	1.6	8.8	9.0	3.3	1.4	15.8
2009	1.8	9.3	9.2	3.1	1.2	16.7
2010	1.8	9.6	10.0	3.4	1.3	17.6
2011	1.9	9.7	10.0	3.7	1.2	16.8
2012	1.6	9.0	9.7	3.5	1.2	14.8
2013	1.5	8.2	9.5	3.0	1.1	12.9
2014	1.6	8.8	10.1	3.6	1.1	14.5
2015	1.8	9.4	10.6	3.5	1.2	14.9
2016	1.7	8.9	10.7	3.5	1.1	14.8

Source: Author's own compilation based on data provided by Istat (www.istat.it).
Note: Percentages are of people aged fourteen and over who performed at least one of the above activities in the last twelve months.

it is unclear how much all this affects, in a more or less substantial way, Italian politics. Moreover, the table does not contain data on the existence or activities of social movements (for a good introduction to this topic, see della Porta 2015). As expressions of discontent and channels of activism, though not without their mistakes and inadequacies, social movements have played a role in mobilizing various sectors of Italian society, especially the young and industrial workers, but, more recently, also the bourgeoisie, or the so-called reflexive middle classes.

It remains to be seen how the presence and activities of many associations and the reflexive middle classes actually translate into the formation of a civil society that is "robust and vibrant", to use two adjectives often used in the past to refer to a US society. In fact, there are several reservations concerning the type of society that exists in Italy. At this point in time, I can say that what is clear is that in Italy the relationships between civil society and the political sphere are undergoing some significant transformations, also due to the role played by social networks. All this makes it very difficult to understand and analyse the processes behind the formation of Italian public opinion, how much they depend on social networks and how much they are exposed to manipulation and the circulation of fake news. Given this, it is undeniable that all explorations and analyses of civil societies are rather complicated exercises, but they are indispensable in order to understand politics. The Italian case is not necessarily more difficult to explain than other cases, but it has several peculiarities worth being noted, measured and evaluated for their consequences.

For a full understanding of the type of civil society that exists in contemporary Italy, one must start from two preliminary considerations. The first is the impact of Fascism – its rule and its consequences. The second is a highly controversial, though very powerful and influential, interpretation: that of "amoral familism", which was put forward two political generations ago (Banfield 1958) but which needs to be critically assessed and constantly reassessed.[1]

From Fascism to amoral familism

In its totalitarian drive, which remained unachieved,[2] Fascism (1922–43) deliberately tried to destroy all existing associations. On the whole, it was largely successful, but it encountered an insurmountable obstacle in the Catholic Church. The Fascist regime was obliged to come to a compromise through which Catholic associations covering many areas were allowed to survive as long as they did not openly engage in political activities. Taking advantage of the suppression of all their competitors, Catholic associations continued unchallenged in their work in the social, educational, economic and cultural fields. The consequences for post-war Italian politics were highly significant. From the very beginning, the wide network of Catholic associations could and did provide a national hinterland in which the Christian Democratic Party was born, promoted, nourished and sustained. It received abundant "ideological" support and all kinds of resources, including the possibility of recruiting a large number of capable, well-trained and ambitious personalities from a variety of associations, and it thrived. In contrast, when Fascism was finally ousted in 1943, the left had to work very hard, though not entirely from scratch, to rebuild its pre-Fascist associational networks. The unions made their immediate return, but they quickly split along partisan lines. The two left-wing parties, the Socialists and the Communists, cooperated in establishing and staffing several types of association with an emphasis on mutual help and cultural and recreational activities and on pursuing a strategy of hegemony: that is, acquiring consensus in society as the foundation for winning political power. This strategy was designed by Antonio Gramsci (1891–1937), the most original Communist theoretician.

In the Cold War period, to be able to rely on flanking associations was an absolute political necessity for both the Christian Democrats and the Communists. Of course, the Christian Democrats always enjoyed the advantage of informal, but easy, access to private and public money, which was more than useful – it was necessary in order to finance their flanking associations, to keep their support and to obtain their votes. Although they could rely on some sources available through local governments, especially in the Red Belt (the five regions long governed by the left) and, to a minor extent, in northern industrial areas, the fundamental resource the PCI could mobilize was the devotion and generous efforts of party members motivated by the Communist ideology, which was revised again in the light of Antonio Gramsci's thinking, and by the promise and expectation of major social, political and economic international transformations.[3]

With the passing of time and the appearance of the post-war generation, two phenomena surfaced in the late 1960s. On the one hand, secularization, and on the other, the decline of ideology not only gradually weakened the ties between many associations and the two major parties, but were also responsible for the shrinking of the number of members in those associations and for the spread of social fragmentation. The final blow came with the disappearance at the beginning of the 1990s of both the DC and the PCI. In a way, this signalled the "liberation" of Italian associations of all types from the need to have a partisan representative, but this freedom has also brought several problems, paramount among them what I call a "selfish turnaround". Most of the "liberated" associations do not pursue goals of national interest, such as improvements in the functioning of the political system, social justice, cultural advancement or equality of opportunities. They have come to seek almost exclusively the immediate fulfilment of the demands of their members (privileges, rejection of state interference, preservation of the status quo, and so on – as discussed later in the chapter), often at the expense of competing associations. What is at work here is often a zero-sum game in which what one association gains[4] is considered lost by other associations. In any case, the frequency with which Italians engage in social activities, though not to be underestimated, appears to be somewhat limited (see Table 7.1).

The second preliminary consideration for the study of Italian civil society concerns the impact and importance of a specific trait attributed to Italian political culture:[5] *amoral familism*. When conducting research in the small, rather isolated, quite poor town Edward Banfield called Montegrano in the southern Italian region of Basilicata in 1955–56, one could not expect to find a hustling, bustling society. Social relations were determined by traditions and by hierarchical structures and had probably been reinforced by Fascism, especially in terms of personal distrust. The inhabitants of Montegrano had learned that positive change was slow, difficult to achieve and had a high price. The authorities and their fellow citizens could not be trusted. Moreover, their personal experience led them to believe that most of the time any type of change was a zero-sum gain: what a family gained was lost by another family. No surprise then that the Montegranesi's rule of conduct was very simple, elementary: "maximize the material, short-run advantage of the nuclear family; assume that all the others will do likewise" (Banfield 1958: 83).

From certain points of view, in their given conditions, the behaviour of the inhabitants of Montegrano was quite rational. Outside observers, coming from very different situations, such as the American political scientist Edward Banfield,[6] may have been at least partially justified in considering that the specific type of amoral familism which was the overarching principle of individual behaviour contained several elements that would produce negative consequences for the community: no crosscutting association was created; no public goals were pursued; there was no check on the behaviour of public officials. Above all, "in a society of amoral familists it will be assumed that whatever group is in power is self-serving and corrupt" (Banfield 1958: 99). There is no reason to doubt that life in Montegrano was as described by Banfield and that the label "amoral familism" was quite appropriate to describe the reactions of the Montegranesi to the context of a stagnant society in which the lack of interpersonal and interfamily trust prevented any possibility of cooperation. When it came to politics, each of the various families proved more than willing to exchange their votes for resources that were promised and later possibly provided by candidates and office holders. Competitive clientelism has characterized public life in a very large number of Italian towns, by no means not only those located in the South, which have generally been marked by socio-economic and behavioural features similar to Montegrano's. Interestingly, many of the same features have been found, analysed and criticized by one of the most innovative Italian cultural anthropologists: Tullio-Altan (1986, 1997).

Leaving aside the criticisms of some Italian sociologists – for instance Alessandro Pizzorno came close to praising the inhabitants of Montegrano for acting rationally in following the principles of amoral familism, arguing that nothing else was possible or advisable but the protection and the promotion of the interests of their respective families – two questions can still be asked legitimately. First, was amoral familism a feature peculiar to southern Italian culture and, therefore, not present in most non-southern communities? Second, has amoral familism been overcome and abandoned with the passing of time and replaced by something resembling civic culture? Unfortunately, Banfield's study was not replicated in any other local Italian community, either by American or by Italian sociologists, anthropologists or political scientists.[7] However, the conviction that, indeed, the culture of many southern areas was imbued and characterized above all by amoral familism has probably not yet died. Indeed, from time to time in a variety of contexts, the family remains the unit of behaviour and the point of reference for many activities. From time to time, especially in some criminal activities, the family is, so to speak, the most valuable hub.

In a way, families are the nucleus of organized crime, of the Sicilian Mafia, of the Neapolitan Camorra, of what remains of the Sacra Corona Unita in Apulia, and, perhaps even more so, of Calabria's 'Ndrangheta (for an excellent synthetic view, see Paoli 2015; for data concerning their entrenchment region by region see Figure 7.3). In any case, a very large number of southern voters either enter into patron–client relationships and rely on favours received from office holders or riot and protest against the authorities. With few exceptions, they do not follow in the least what Tocqueville discovered, much to his bewilderment, in the US: "when there is a problem Americans get organized" (de Tocqueville 2000). Amoral familism has proved quite unlikely to transform itself and to become a solid ground on which to build a decent, strong society capable of pursuing its own goals without relying on political favours, even less so in those situations when serious socio-economic difficulties make their appearance (Catanzaro 2018). Figure 7.1 provides comparative data regarding the relationship between politics and society, indicating how much the political sphere relies on patronage ties. In a way, one can read in the data not only the subservience of society, but also the power of the parties.

Paradoxically, largely going against the ascertained truth that Italians have a low propensity to join associations, organized crime reveals that, under some conditions, Italians trust each other and are capable of creating powerful and lasting organizations. I do not want to put too much cynical emphasis on this phenomenon, but until recently criminal organizations, especially the Mafia, appeared to be not only entrenched but cohesive and almost impenetrable. Table 7.2 indicates the presence of the different organizations in the Italian regions. The Sacra Corona Unita monopolized criminal activities in Apulia; Calabria is the home turf of 'Ndrangheta, which has also proved capable of penetrating Valle d'Aosta, Piedmont, Liguria and Emilia Romagna. The Camorra has its home in Campania but has

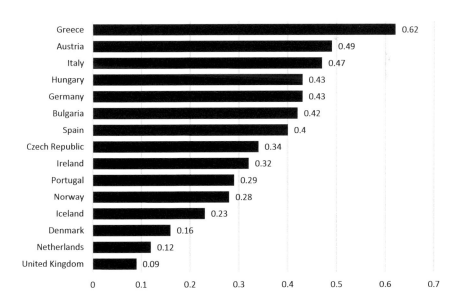

Figure 7.1 Index of patronage in fifteen European democracies

Note: The expert survey was conducted in 2008–09.

Source: Adapted from Di Mascio (2014: 9).

Table 7.2 Organized crime presence in Italy by type and region (percentage)

Region	Cosa Nostra	Camorra	'Ndrangheta	Apulian organized crime	Other organized crime	Total
Abruzzo	8.9	80.6	6.0	4.5	0.0	100
Basilicata	0.0	0.0	0.6	0.0	99.4	100
Calabria	0.0	0.1	99.9	0.0	0.0	100
Campania	0.0	99.8	0.2	0.0	0.0	100
Emilia-Romagna	8.8	24.4	66.8	0.0	0.0	100
Friuli-Venezia Giulia	73.9	24.3	1.8	0.0	0.0	100
Lazio	31.0	35.6	30.4	0.8	2.2	100
Liguria	22.7	7.0	70.3	0.0	0.0	100
Lombardy	11.6	29.2	53.1	5.0	1.1	100
Marche	7.0	21.5	54.8	16.7	0.0	100
Molise	0.2	93.4	2.7	3.7	0.0	100
Piedmont	2.9	1.1	95.2	0.0	0.8	100
Apulia	0.0	0.0	0.0	100.0	0.0	100
Sardinia	0.0	71.0	27.7	0.0	1.3	100
Sicily	91.1	0.0	0.5	0.0	8.4	100
Tuscany	5.9	57.7	34.9	1.5	0.0	100
Trentino-Alto Adige	0.0	0.0	100.0	0.0	0.0	100
Umbria	5.6	59.0	35.4	0.0	0.0	100
Valle d'Aosta	0.0	0.0	100.0	0.0	0.0	100
Veneto	5.4	12.5	37.3	0.9	43.9	100

Source: Adapted from Calderoni (2014).

expanded its activities in several other regions, namely tiny Molise but also Tuscany and Umbria. Finally, Cosa Nostra (the Mafia), the epitome of organized crime in Italy, is, of course, almost a monopoly in Sicily but has also acquired a presence in several northern regions. To somewhat soften this very bleak picture, it is fair to say that some welcome counter-mobilization of civil society against organized crime, especially against the Mafia, is taking place. Its effectiveness remains to be assessed.

1968: its impact, its aftermath

Largely encapsulated by or embedded in the two major parties, Italian civil society was shocked by the 1968 student and workers' movements (Tarrow 1989). In Italy, the long-lived Sessantotto was substantially a generational revolt, against political, social and cultural hierarchies and, later, against patriarchy as well, but the events and their participants also brought to light the fact that significant social and cultural changes were being made, changes that Italian parties had either underestimated or, more likely, not understood at all. Indeed, it was the Christian Democrat Aldo Moro who realized and proclaimed that "the future is no longer in our [perhaps not only the DC's] hands". As for the Communists, it took almost a decade for their secretary, Enrico Berlinguer, to come to a less hostile view of these movements, and especially of the feminist movement.[8] It is impossible to review all the positive and negative interpretations of the 1968 movement in Italy, when a new generation of students and workers, and later of women, launched their protest against partyocracy and a paternalistic society. The "Movement" lasted for more than a decade, rejecting any attempt at institutionalization: for instance, a role in the governance of universities. When it entered into its inevitable decline, some of its more militant components chose the path of "armed struggle", which also lasted almost a decade (see Figure 7.2), and some offshoots lingered right up to recent times. Left-wing terrorism is obviously not an instance of "associability".[9] Still, some, not unimportant, family and peer facilitators have made their appearance in these movements and their significance should not be underestimated.

   In all likelihood, the best interpretive key to the 1968 movements can be found even in the Italian context in the slow and gradual emergence of post-materialist values within the post-war generations.[10] Of course, the student movement had plenty of post-materialists in its ranks, while the workers' movement comprised a large number of

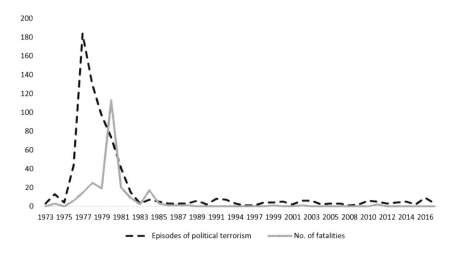

Figure 7.2 Political terrorism in Italy, 1973–2016

Source: Author's own compilation based on data provided by the Global Terrorism Database (www.start.umd.edu/gtd).

young workers with high expectations concerning their life chances, which led them to challenge the unions' frozen organizational hierarchy. Admittedly, neither movement was "Tocquevillian". The students never gave their protests or activities the goal of producing an association, while the young workers introduced conflicts and tensions within existing associations. Both were cases of collective action addressed against the authorities: university authorities and employers (and, frequently, union bureaucracies too). In the background, and not particularly hidden, it was clear that two important sectors of society were indirectly challenging the way in which the Italian state had structured itself and, caught off guard, that state proved unable to offer satisfactory responses. If there ever was a lethal challenge to Italian democracy, it came both from left-wing terrorism and its supporters in certain petty bourgeois and "intellectual" sectors of society and from right-wing Neo-Fascist terrorism, which enjoyed support and connivance from within the public apparatus. It is almost impossible to say whether and how the fifteen-year-long trajectory of the Red (left-wing) and Black (right-wing) terrorists and the response of the state had an impact on Italian civic and political culture.[11] The always present, large grey zone may have absorbed and swallowed a phenomenon that in fact affected the evolution of Italian politics in an extremely significant way,[12] and, precisely for this reason, the phenomenon cannot be either understood or explained. It must first be fully located within the political history of Italy, its unsolved problems and its contradictions. On the one hand, one must focus on the failure or the unwillingness to purge from the top positions in the bureaucracy and the judiciary all those who had supported and collaborated with Fascism. On the other hand, one must point to the inability or unwillingness of the left to get rid of the false conception of the Resistance as an unfinished revolution to be completed through a "romantic", Leninist or Tupamaros-style armed struggle.

It is the contention of this chapter that Italian civil society has shaped itself in a relationship both with state institutions and with political parties. Hence, amoral familism, as "discovered" and labelled by Banfield, appeared in a context in which public institutions were fundamentally inoperative and political parties fundamentally absent. The family was simultaneously the only association that, on the one hand, could provide protection and goods and, on the other, could be a place where relational ties could be created, maintained and put to work, and the only organizational form capable of producing good consequences or preventing negative outcomes. From this perspective, amoral familism was, indeed, a rational reaction in the specific environment of Montegrano (and in many other Italian municipal communities sharing similar characteristics) to the lack of opportunities and the absence of associational experiences. Much of this remains very true and hinders the appearance of idealized civil society, pitting citizens who have created overlapping and cross-cutting associations against the state and its bureaucrats and political party authorities – "those who do not care about what we need", the classic response of alienated citizens in all public opinion surveys, and just one step away from a syndrome conducive to populism. Let us see whether and why differences have manifested themselves and how distrust has been limited and with what consequences.

Here, I suggest that there exists a measure both of the lack of trust of the Italians towards each other and the state and of their amoral behaviour: tax evasion. The much revered statement by the American patriots in their revolt against Great Britain ("No taxation without representation") has no meaning in Italy or for many Italians. Through free and fair parliamentary elections, all Italians enjoy political representation and, thanks to their Deputies and Senators, they can exercise some influence on the processes and modes of taxation. They also enjoy a generous welfare state of good quality, even comparatively. Still, the percentage of Italians who do not pay their due and who, one way or another, succeed in cheating on their income and defrauding the state is scandalously high. Unofficial data have been suggesting that between one-quarter and one-fifth of Italians do not file a tax return containing correct data on their earnings. Figure 7.3 shows that, among the member states of the EU, Italy is the country whose citizens have the highest level of tax evasion. The comparison is merciless with regard to what is, I believe, probably the worst Italian vice, and one that has tremendous consequences.

To better understand the phenomenon, two points must be stressed. First, one can find Prime Minister Silvio Berlusconi publicly declaring in 1994 that the level of taxation in Italy made him "morally author-ized to evade [taxes]". Second, there is the declaration of impotence on the part of Italian state and governmental authorities signalled by the number of tax amnesties of all kinds in the past forty years: there have been at least twelve. To give a few recent examples: the volun-tary disclosure of capital illegally held abroad in 2014; tax amnesties in 2016, 2017 and 2019; and the so-called graveyard amnesty in 2018. Needless to say, all these tax amnesties have been sending a clear message to would-be taxpayers: "Never mind, continue evad-ing and sooner or later you will be 'pardoned'." The inefficiency of the state plus privileges for some categories of people in the form of loopholes and deductions, plus a fair amount of corruption in finan-cial transactions and in a variety of tax assessments, end up with state authorities accepting defeat. In the meantime, the Italian public debt has not stopped growing; it is well above 132 per cent of the gross public income. There is a lot to be worried about, but a reassuring message comes from the data regarding the wealth of Italian families (Figure 7.4). One is tempted to say that Italy is perhaps the best

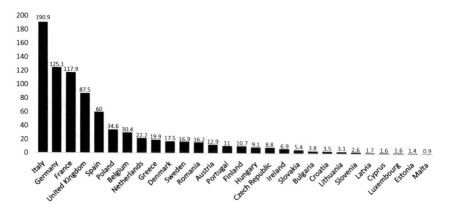

Figure 7.3 Estimated level of evaded taxes in EU countries (billion euros)

Source: University of London for Socialists and Democrats Group in the European Parliament.

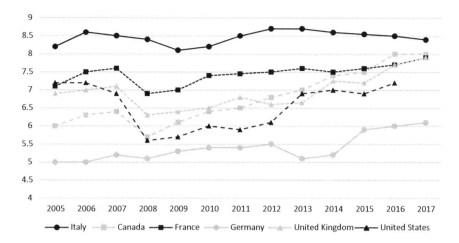

Figure 7.4 Wealth of families as a percentage of gross national product

Source: Istat and Bank of Italy for Italy; OECD (Organisation for Economic Co-operation and Development) for other countries.

contemporary example of a country in which public misery is accompanied by private wealth, much to the satisfaction of Bernard Mandeville and his eighteenth-century satire *The Fable of the Bees: Or, Private Vices, Publick Benefits*.

Summing up, I would say that, looking at these data and their evolution through time, one appears justified in saying that Italian civil society carries its own responsibility for the state of the economy as well as for the political system. Perhaps, I could add first that it is wrong to contrast a supposedly healthy Italian society with a degraded politics. They go together and no improvement will follow unless and until a joint effort is undertaken.

Institution building and social capital

A Machiavellian combination of *luck* (that is, the possibility and capability of taking advantage of the existing conditions) and *virtue* (a specific knowledge of Italy and mastery of research techniques) led Robert Putnam, Raffaella Nanetti and Robert Leonardi to study the long-awaited establishment[13] of Italian regional governments in 1970. The three scholars were not interested in regional institutions per se, but in analysing the performance of their governments. Putnam discovered that, after several years of existence, regional governments in the Centre and the North of Italy had clearly outperformed regional governments in the South. This result could not be attributed to the institutions themselves, because their design and their powers were more or less the same throughout the entire country. Therefore, he hypothesized that the differences might depend on the type and quality of civic and political culture prevalent in the various regions.

Hence, Putnam decided to look into the political history of several selected regions to provide a convincing explanation. Since the eleventh century, the Normans had imposed their top-down rule on some southern Italian regions, especially Sicily, Puglia and Calabria, never allowing space for autonomous initiatives or activities by their subjects. More or less in the same period, most communes in the Centre and North of Italy were enjoying autonomy and self-government and could shape their own future and life, allowing citizens to participate and to influence any decisions to be taken. According to Putnam, both traditions continued well into the 1970s (see Figure 7.5). Their unabated existence goes a long way to explaining both the persisting difference between the South and the Centre/North of Italy and the gap in the performance of regional institutions. Individuals accustomed to wait for top-down decisions and orders are far less capable of making institutions work satisfactorily than individuals accustomed to participating and to translating their preferences into practical activities.

In a way, Putnam innovatively redefined amoral familism by characterizing the relationships between citizens in the Centre and North as creating and reproducing social capital while those in the South are negatively affected by a lack of trust that prevents joint action and cooperation and, at the same time, cannot be conducive to supporting the activities of the authorities. The gap between North and South makes an appearance in the most likely and unlikely places. Recently, though somewhat unaware of all the implications, one of the two most important Italian dailies, *Corriere della Sera*, ran two pages on earthquakes and reconstruction in the last seventy years (24 August 2017, pp. 2–3). The subtitle was "Spese lievitate, infiltrazioni criminali" (Soaring costs, criminal infiltrations). The contrast in terms of the speed of the response and reconstruction in northern areas with the slowness in southern areas could not be starker. The explanation is largely to be found in the active, often autonomous and voluntary participation by northerners in reconstruction in their territory while southerners expect all solutions to come from the state and public authorities.

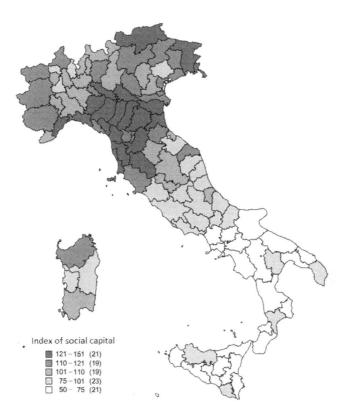

Figure 7.5 Distribution of social capital in the Italian provinces
Source: Adapted from Cartocci (2012).

Many historians have objected that Putnam's *longue durée* is really exaggeratedly long, and does not allow for the appearance of intervening variables such as the role played by the Kingdom of the Two Sicilies in the South and of Catholic Church rule. Some political scientists have drawn attention to the independent role played by organized, largely left-wing, party organizations, for instance in changing the political culture of Emilia-Romagna, which was ruled by the Pope for about four centuries, and making it highly civic and progressive. Be that as it may, Putnam formulated an important explanation for both the North–South divide and the impact of civil society culture on the functioning of institutions. Of course, there is also a dark side to Putnam's assessment. When and how will southern Italian culture change, shaped and reinforced as it is by events over almost a millennium? Also, in the light of massive waves of migration from the South to the North, and even abroad, probably depriving the South of its most dynamic, ambitious and forward-looking daughters and sons, where will the stimulus come from to shape a different, participatory, more modern political culture? Putnam's answer is that the key is "building social capital" (1993: 185). Twenty-five years have elapsed since the publication of his seminal book and not even the most benevolent observers would say that enough social capital has been built in most of southern Italy.

A different answer was possible. It had already been formulated more than a decade before the publication of Putnam's book by Ronald Inglehart (1977). Largely the product of generational changes, profound and essentially irreversible transformations in the political culture of Western nations have made their appearance. The values held by new, post-1945 age cohorts were quite different from those of their fathers and mothers. A silent revolution (the title of his book) was under way, characterized by a major shift from materialist to post-materialist values.[14] This shift, tied as it was to increasing levels of education and growing prosperity, was more apparent in northern areas. Therefore, in a way, it exacerbated the distance in terms of cultural (and political) attitudes between the North and the South, the latter continuing to lag behind. The growing number of post-materialist citizens also produced important consequences for their social and political behaviour. Many of the post-materialists did not translate their resources into associational activities. This was due neither to a lack of interpersonal trust, as in the "traditional" South, nor to a lack of opportunities. On the contrary, it derived from a surplus of confidence among the post-materialists in their own personal capabilities. They had come to believe that they did not need associations to protect or promote their interests. They had already acquired positions and qualities from which they could easily access the resources necessary and useful for their personal goals.

If it is appropriate to interpret the 1968 movements as also a generational revolt or rebellion against the authorities, institutions, parties and unions, there is no doubt that the Italian example contained and exhibited all these elements. The rebellion took place mainly outside and against Italian political parties, especially left-wing parties, and soon found support among younger industrial workers. Although there were some southern urban areas in which "rebellious" activities took place, the 1968 movement was mainly located in the North (and in the capital city, Rome). Of course, insofar as the transition from materialist to post-materialist values was at work in Italy (see Figure 7.6), it could have started only in the northern areas, where the wind of socio-economic development had been blowing

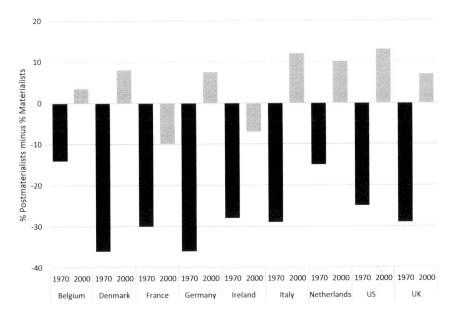

Figure 7.6 Shift towards post-materialist values among the publics of nine Western societies, 1970 and 2000 (percentage points)

Source: Adapted from Inglehart and Welzel (2005).

hard for some time. Having said this, what is important for our discussion is that once more the North–South divide manifested itself in full view.

The students' movement and the workers' movement were followed by the feminist movement. All three, but especially the first two, shared an aggressive anti-institutional drive, although the feminists had no visible counterpart but the elusive, though no less pervasive, patriarchal society. The students went through successive, but not successful, phases, while the workers, thanks to the unions, which were strengthened by their protest, obtained lasting institutional gains embedded in the Charter of Workers' Rights (1970), especially concerning job security and automatic wage indexing (both subsequently eroded). By the end of the 1970s, a decade also marked by domestic terrorist activities of the left and right wing, a sea change had taken place. Italian parties had largely lost their quasi-monopoly on the representation of interests. Most associations had taken into their own hands the task of bargaining with the state, with national governments and with Parliament. Socio-economic modernization had been accompanied by the proliferation of professional associations that were almost exclusively interested in protecting the status and promoting the preferences of their membership. Increasingly unable to aggregate a plurality of interests, Italian parties had become self-referential and self-centred. At the same time, a process of fragmentation was at work in Italian society. This was especially true for the middle strata (Bagnasco 2016) and for the unions (Regalia and Regini 2018). Several repeated attempts to build a single unified national union of workers had failed, but in the meantime small, aggressive groups had made their appearance, representing specific sectors of private and public employees. These groups were often strategically located, and their activities unscrupulously exploited their blackmailing power in some areas: for instance, transportation (buses, underground, taxis, railways, planes), where their strikes could be very costly not only for the employers but for the population at large and for the political system.

All this had an impact on the relationship with politics. Generally, civil society constitutes both an interlocutor of the state and a check on the behaviour of the government. Its associations often perform both roles. Although the trade unions and, perhaps to a lesser extent, Confindustria and the Confederazione Nazionale dell'Artigianato (CNA) would probably object to being lumped together with interest and pressure groups, there is no doubt that they all want to be recognized as legitimate interlocutors of the government in all issues concerning employment, economic policies and the welfare state. For a long time, both Confindustria and the trade unions acted through political parties, Confindustria being at an advantage because it had powerful advocates for its interests within the Liberal Party as well as within the Christian Democratic Party. While CISL also had easy access to the Christian Democrats and UIL to the Social Democrats and the Socialists, CGIL had to work mostly through the Communists in opposition. Incidentally, on most issues concerning labour, contrary to widespread opinion, the so-called transmission belt went from CGIL leaders to the Communist Party, which, most of the time, accepted *in toto* what the union leaders told them to do. Until 1968, top union leaders were often elected to Parliament, where they could make their voices heard. Informal negotiations between the unions, the government and Confindustria, often joined by the moderately progressive CAN, took place in the offices of ministers, on a one-to-one basis, and, of course, were rarely made public. Otherwise, it was up to parliamentary committees to provide a forum for discussion and compromise, for the reconciliation of interests.

Attempts to reach tripartite agreements began only in the mid-1970s, under duress, because of the appearance of high rates of inflation and high levels of unemployment, the combination of which was appropriately called the "misery index" by the economist Arthur Okun. It was only in January 1983 that the government, the unions and Confindustria jointly signed a commitment on income policy. This was not what goes under the name of neo-corporatism in some Scandinavian countries – a not insignificant difference in Italy was that the major left-wing party was never part of the government – but it represented a remarkable step forward in terms of tasks to be performed by the three signatories and of the predictability of socio-economic policies. Although what was then called *concertazione* (prolonged negotiations in order to reach shared decisions) had its ups and downs and went no further, the practice of (perhaps too) prolonged government consultations with the unions, Confindustria, CNA and a variety of associations has since characterized the Italian process of policy-making, especially in the economic and welfare fields.

It was only in 2015 that, due to his personal exasperation with what he considered exaggeratedly exacting and inconclusive negotiations, Prime Minister Matteo Renzi decided to discontinue these meetings. The time had come, he said, for "disintermediation". The government would acquire on its own the information it needed, then it would evaluate it and proceed to make decisions. It is difficult to say how much disintermediation has followed in practice, partly because Renzi had to resign about a year later. But the relationships between the government and all the associations representing civil society remain a controversial issue – it could hardly be otherwise. Moreover, probably more than in other democratic countries, protest movements have made their appearance, challenging government policies. I mention only one of them here – one that has lasted a very long time and is continuing its activities.

Starting in 1995, a group of activists in Val di Susa, Piedmont, launched a protest against the building of the infrastructure for a high-speed train going to France. Their collective name is NO TAV (No treno ad alta velocità – No high-speed train). They have resorted to road blocks, sabotage, intimidation and clashes with the police. In many ways, this is one of the most revealing instances of the "not in my backyard" (nimby) syndrome. Interestingly, a counter-mobilization has recently followed organized by six middle-class, middle-aged women living in Turin, the capital city of the Piemonte region, where the high-speed train will run. Derisively, they have been called *madamine* by their opponents. *Madamine*, a word of French origin used in the dialect spoken in Piedmont, contains a more or less explicit reference to women of little importance, unmarried (though not necessarily spinsters), performing not very demanding jobs. The ladies involved accepted the challenge and decided proudly to refer to themselves as *madamine*.

All Berlusconi's governments were the target of actions and mobilizations by the diffused left. In 2002 in Milan, utilizing the internet for the first time, upper-middle-class women (and men) organized a protest against Berlusconi and his attempt to subdue the judges by surrounding the Tribunal with a ring-a-ring o' roses the Tribunal. Quickly imitated in other Italian cities, they were labelled *girotondini*. This was a short-lived phenomenon designed to awaken the left rather than to challenge Berlusconi's government, which was supported by a sizable parliamentary majority. A different form of protest, and much more imposing, was the union demonstration led by the Secretary General of CGIL, Sergio Cofferati, in March 2002 against the repeal or rewriting of Article 18 of the Workers' Charter (Statuto dei Lavoratori) that requires the existence of a "just cause" to sack a worker. The government abandoned its intention, but it was not weakened by the union's show of strength. The real winner was Sergio Cofferati, who was appointed leader of the broad social left-wing opposition that challenged the weak and meek official opposition in Parliament; two years later, he was elected mayor of Bologna, at the time the quintessentially "red" city. Interestingly, Article 18 was subsequently rewritten by Renzi's government (in 2015), drastically reducing protection for workers. Ironically, a centre-left government passed a reform quite close to what Berlusconi's centre-right coalition had not been able to accomplish.

In a way, of course, the unions are part of civil society and ought to be taken into consideration when discussing the associational propensity and willingness of the Italians. Moreover, the unions' activities reveal something important concerning the relationships between civil society in the guise of organized labour and the state (the government). But, due to the configuration of Italian politics and the party system, in the past Italian unions formed too close a relationship with the major Italian parties, as did the "Christian Democrat" union CISL with the DC-led government (on this relationship, and much more, LaPalombara (1964) provides an excellent analysis). The numbers of union members are often contested, rarely up to date, and have been in decline following the post-2008 economic crisis. CGIL claims to have about 5,700,000 members, slightly less than half of them retired workers. CISL has approximately 4,500,000 members and UIL 2,200,000. Finally, UGL claims 2,300,000 members (see Box 7.1). Although it must be noted that these numbers are not reliable, on the

Box 7.1 Italian trade unions, 2014

CGIL: Confederazione Generale Italiana del Lavoro – left – 5,748,269 members
CISL: Confederazione Italiana Sindacati del Lavoro – centre, moderately progressive – 4,542,354 members
UGL: Unione Generale del Lavoro – right – 2,377,529 members
UIL: Unione Italiana del Lavoro – centre, moderate – 2,184,911 members
CONFSAL: Confederazione Sindacati Autonomi Lavoratori – conservative – 1,818,245 members
COBAS: Sindacati Unitari di Base – mostly left – membership unknown
Total known union membership: 16,671,308
Percentage employed: 33.8%
Percentage retired: Between 40% and 50% (the Sindacato Pensionati Italiani (Italian Pensioner Trade Union, part of CGIL) has approximately 2,500,000 members)

whole, somewhat surprisingly, more than a third of Italian workers appear to be unionized. While, of course, there is strength in numbers, Italian unions cannot be considered very powerful, partly because they are divided and often play the game of overbidding (or underbidding). In very many instances, they have negative power, blocking or more frequently postponing some unpleasant decision. Rarely do they succeed in getting the policies they want. Italian unions have been on the defensive whenever changes are proposed by the government on welfare measures, especially those concerning retirement benefits and the regulation of the labour market. As I hinted earlier, the unsolved issue remains how to establish new rules for negotiations between the unions and the governments (on all this, see Regalia and Regini 2018).

To some extent, Italian unions have always been channels for political participation and several union leaders have also played significant political roles, becoming parliamentarians and party leaders. In a period of party decline, the unions have retained a relatively high number of members (as shown in Figure 7.7). In a way, they fill a socio-political void and, without exaggerating their impact, they still contribute to the political information and the political socialization of millions of Italian workers. An important, recent example is offered by the electoral campaign for the 4 December 2016 constitutional referendum. Together with several sectors of Italian civil society, foremost among them the National Association of Italian Partisans

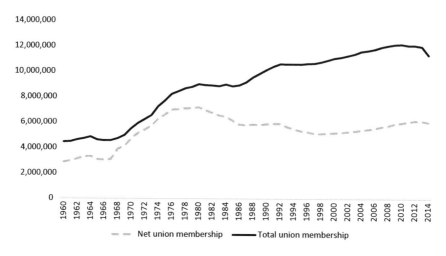

Figure 7.7 Total and net union membership in Italy, 1960–2014

Note: Net union membership is measured as the total union membership minus union members outside the active, dependent and employed labour force.

Source: Author's own compilation based on data provided by ICTWSS database (http://uva-aias.net/nl/ictwss).

(ANPI), CGIL launched a major and, in the end, successful mobilization against the government's constitutional reforms. On the whole, the electoral campaign was a period of exceptional effervescence, but the "Committees for No" have not succeeded in transforming themselves into associations devoted to tasks other than the defence of the Italian Constitution. Nevertheless, those committees deserve to be singled out as an example of the vitality of Italian civil society that should not be underestimated (Pritoni, Valbruzzi and Vignati 2017).

This leads our attention to an emerging problem suggested, albeit from a different perspective, by Olson (1982). The appearance, existence and competition of several associations – that is, pluralism – are decisive components of a thriving democratic life. Perhaps more attention should be focused on the internal life of these associations. Internal democracy is a request to be made of all organizations in the public sphere, especially those engaged in the highly significant tasks of articulating and aggregating interests. There is a lot to be said and much to be learned in analysing the activities of interest groups and lobbies: what they represent and how, and even their "legitimacy" (on this and much more, see the collection of articles in Valbruzzi (2016), especially the introduction by the editor). Lobbying agencies tell those interested in politics much about the structure of a political system, its functioning, the distribution of political power, the processes of decision making and, indeed, the robustness and vibrancy of civil society.

While admitting that there is such a thing as the "general or common interest", not as a static target but as a goal to be pursued, this is never just the sum of special interests. The situation in the USA may not represent Italy's future, but the power of special groups and their lobbying capabilities teach scholars and citizens something very important (Lehman Schlozman, Verba and Brady 2012): that, often, these associations are responsible for unfair imbalances, undue advantages, and skewed distribution of political, social and economic power. This may not be a recent phenomenon, but it is now completely clear that in Italy some associations have acquired an amount of political and social power sufficient to prevent or block any type of change. The contemporary terminology would identify them as *veto players*. In the Italian case, there is one additional element to be taken into consideration: the way in which some existing associations protect their privileges and promote their interests no matter what.

Some time ago, a not very lively debate appeared regarding the "social responsibility of entrepreneurs". What is lacking is a similar debate concerning the behaviour of some associations whose activities affect all citizens (my attempt can be found in Pasquino 2017): those who are employed in the world of mass media, those who administer the law, those in the field of education from elementary schools to universities, state and local government bureaucrats, and associations of judges.[15] Increasingly, in the void left by the decline in the capability of political parties to perform the role of aggregating interests, these associations have drifted into pursuing almost exclusively their special interests, a shift that has often been identified with the non-interference by the law in their internal activities or in what their members do. It is an unfolding story whose episodes are easily found in daily reports. I believe I am justified in summarizing the tendency at work in Italy as a transition from amoral familism to amoral corporatism. Powerful associations that never think in terms of the more general interest but defend their members no matter what cannot contribute to the shaping of a democratic civil society. Worse, their behaviour indicates that cohesive associations sharing one well-defined goal are capable of offering a successful resistance against any state attempt to regulate their activities. The continuing tensions in the world of communication, the poor and ineffective reforms of the educational system and the total failure of the proposals to improve the functioning of the judiciary stand as a monument to the strength of Italian amoral corporatism.

Conclusion

Good-quality democracies rely on a robust and vibrant society. In this chapter, I have fundamentally argued and documented that in Italy there are quite a number of associations of all types. However, on the one hand, many Italians still act first and foremost to advance the interests of their families (amoral familism); on the other, several existing associations behave following what I have called the principle of amoral corporatism – that is, putting their own interests above everything else. In addition, there is also a high degree of political corruption, plus the presence of organized crime in many parts of Italy. All this means that there is a lot to do to renew Italian politics.

Notes

1 The 1961 translation, edited at the time by a young, promising, now well-established, sociologist, Domenico De Masi, contains several review articles by Italian and non-Italian scholars – F. Cancian, G. A. Marselli, A. J. Wichers, A. Pizzorno, S. F. Silverman, N. S. Peabody, J. Davis, J. Galtung and A. Colombis – providing a thorough evaluation of Banfield's thesis.

2 Juan Linz (1964) provided a path-breaking definition and analysis of authoritarian regimes with reference to the case of Spain. Their most important components – limited, not responsible, not competitive pluralism – apply perfectly to the case of Italian Fascism as well. Mussolini's attempt to "fascistize" the bureaucracy and the armed forces and to subjugate the monarchy and the church failed. The regime had to abandon its totalitarian goal.

3 The critics would immediately add "and Soviet money", which is, of course, true, but it was counterbalanced by US dollars channelled to the DC (and some centrists parties) and its union, CISL.

4 The competition among the various associations rarely entails the recruitment of more members. It is marked by the ability to get access to parliamentary and governmental authorities and the bureaucrats who are in charge of implementing decisions and translating them into public policies.

5 Although I am not able to pursue the subject here, there are many scholars, historians and literary critics who believe that both the historian Francesco Guicciardini (1483–1540) and, even more so, the poet Giacomo

Leopardi (1798–1837) have captured important Italian psychological and behavioural features. The first positively emphasized the Italian's search for the *particulare* (personal advantages), while Leopardi's *Discorso sopra lo stato presente dei costumi degli Italiani* (1824) critically highlighted some permanent and pernicious traits of the Italian national character.

6 Banfield was accompanied by his wife Laura. She was of Italian descent and played an important role not only in translating documents and speeches, but probably also in providing the necessary interpretation of certain feelings and behaviours expressed in body language.

7 This lack of replication of a truly important research project with all its insights as well as its weaknesses is an interesting feature of the sociology of knowledge in Italy.

8 The PCI had always recruited women into its ranks, but true political power remained firmly in the hands of male politicians up to the dissolution of the party.

9 Right-wing, Neo-Fascist terrorism had a different origin in the past, among the "nostalgics", and found support in some sectors of the state: the bureaucracy, the secret services and the judiciary.

10 To his enduring merit, it was Ronald P. Inglehart (1977) who first discovered the phenomenon and who intelligently provided a comparative explanation.

11 The analysis of Red and Black terrorist movements is usually quite limited in books devoted to the post-1945 history of Italy; they are often relegated to few pages as a sort of extraneous phenomenon. To be fair, there are several good books on both types of terrorism, but none that can be considered a landmark study. For comprehensive views, see Galli (2014) and Cento Bull (2015).

12 Aldo Moro's murder by the Red Brigades on 9 May 1978 deprived Italian politics of an outstanding protagonist. Certainly, what was committed by the Red Brigades changed the course of the gradual evolution of the Communist Party and of the relationships between the Christian Democrats and the PCI. In a way, it also disrupted the political system. It is true that the Red Brigades were defeated but it is wrong to say that their bloody actions were inconsequential. On the contrary, they succeeded in preventing any agreement between the DC and the PCI and opened up the path to a five-party coalition (1980–92) that decisively sidelined the Italian Communist Party.

13 Foreseen in the 1948 Constitution, regional councils were elected only in 1970 and no rearrangement of the state bureaucracy followed. After fifty years, the overall evaluation of their performance remains less than positive.

14 Materialist values are maintaining order in the nation and fighting rising prices. Post-materialist values are giving people more say in important political decisions and protecting freedom of speech. Their changing combinations have affected different generations of voters and their party preferences.

15 The most recent case (on 30 May 2019) of what is more than just an instance of "amoral corporatism" regards the indictment of Luca Palamara, no less than the former president of the National Association of Magistrates, who was accused of having received money and gifts in order to interfere in the process of appointing and promoting several judges, together with a couple of powerful politicians.

References

Bagnasco, A. (2016). *La questione del ceto medio: Un racconto del cambiamento sociale*. Bologna: Il Mulino.

Banfield, E. C. (1958). *The Moral Basis of a Backward Society*. New York and London: The Free Press.

Calderoni, F. (2014). Mythical Numbers and the Proceeds of Organised Crime: Estimating Mafia Proceeds in Italy. In *Global Crime* 15 (1–2), pp. 138–163.

Cartocci, R. (2012). Il capitale sociale. In M. Almagistic D. Piana (eds) *Le parole chiave della politica italiana* (pp. 267–282). Rome: Carocci.

Catanzaro, R. (2018). After and Beyond Amoral Familism: The Impact of the Economic Crisis on Social Capital Italian-Style. In *South European Society and Politics* 23 (1), pp. 47–62.

Cento Bull, A.. (2015). Terrorist Movements. In E. Jones and G. Pasquino (eds) *Oxford Handbook of Italian Politics* (pp. 658–667). Oxford: Oxford University Press.

della Porta, D. (2015). Social Movements. In E. Jones and G. Pasquino (eds) *Oxford Handbook of Italian Politics* (pp. 644–655). Oxford: Oxford University Press.

Di Mascio, F. (2014) Exploring the Link Between Patronage and Party Institutionalization. An Historical and Institutional Analysis of the Italian Transition. *Democratization* 21 (4), pp. 678–698.

Galli, G. (2014). *Piombo rosso: La storia completa della lotta armata in Italia dal 1979 ad oggi*. Milan: Baldini & Castoldi.

Inglehart, R. (1977). *The Silent Revolution: Changing Values and Political Styles among Western Publics*. Princeton: Princeton University Press.

Inglehart, R. and Welzel, C. (2005). *Modernization, Cultural Change, and Democracy: The Human Development Sequence*. Cambridge: Cambridge University Press.

LaPalombara, J. (1964). *Interest Groups in Italian Politics*. Princeton: Princeton University Press.

LaPalombara, J. (1965). Italy: Fragmentation, Isolation, and Alienation. In L. W. Pye and S. Verba (eds) *Political Culture and Political Development* (pp. 282–329). Princeton: Princeton University Press.

Lehman Schlozman, K., Verba, S. and Brady H. H. (2012). *The Unheavenly Chorus: Unequal Political Voice and the Broken Promise of American Democracy*. Princeton and Oxford: Princeton University Press.

Linz, J. (1964). An Authoritarian Regime: The Case of Spain. In E. Allardt and Y. Littunen (eds) *Cleavages, Ideologies, and Party Systems* (pp. 291–341). Helsinki: The Westermarck Society.

Olson, M. (1982). *The Rise and Decline of Nations: Economic Growth, Stagflation, and Social Rigidities*. New Haven and London: Yale University Press.

Paoli, L. (2015). Mafia, Camorra, and 'Ndrangheta. In E. Jones and G. Pasquino (eds) *Oxford Handbook of Italian Politics* (pp. 668–681). Oxford: Oxford University Press.

Pasquino, G. (ed.) (2017). Le società (in)civili. *Paradoxa* XI (2), April/June.

Pritoni, A., Valbruzzi, M. and Vignati, R. (2017). *La prova del NO: Il sistema politico italiano dopo il referendum costituzionale*. Soveria Mannelli: Rubbettino.

Putnam, R. D. (1993). *Making Democracy Work: Civic Traditions in Modern Italy*. Princeton: Princeton University Press.

Regalia, I. and Regini, M. (2018). Trade Unions and Employment Relations in Italy during the Economic Crisis. In *South European Society and Politics* 23 (1), pp. 63–79.

Tarrow, S. (1989). *Democracy and Disorder: Protest and Politics in Italy, 1965–1975*. Oxford and New York: Oxford University Press.

de Tocqueville, A. (2000) Democracy in America. Translated by H. Mansfield and D. Winthrop. Chicago: University of Chicago Press.

Tullio-Altan, C. (1986). *La nostra Italia: Clientelismo, trasformismo e ribellismo dall'Unità d'Italia a oggi*. Milan: Feltrinelli.

Tullio-Altan, C. (1997). *La coscienza civile degli italiani: Valori e disvalori*. Udine: Gaspari.

Valbruzzi, M. (ed.) (2016). Maledetto lobbying! La società aperta e le sue lobby. *Paradoxa* X (4), October/December.

Italy and the European Union   **8**

Where would the Italian political system be if Italy had not joined at their inception the most important European institutions? This is the preliminary question to ask in order to understand the trajectory of the complex relationships between Italy and the subsequent incarnations of those institutions. The second question concerns what Italian policymakers have been willing and able to do in the international organizations of which Italy has been part for many decades. Finally, one has to look at what Italian citizens see and would like to see, at what they believe Italian governments should contribute and what they would like to obtain in exchange from Italian membership, specifically of the EU. This chapter will also deal with some of the changes produced by the appearance in the Italian political system of a quasi-majority of sovereignists, its meaning and its consequences.

A defeated country, humbled and in shambles, Italy reacquired some dignity thanks to two important decisions made by the Christian Democratic Prime Minister De Gasperi (December 1945–August 1953) and his ruling centrist coalition: to join NATO at its foundation in 1949 and to be part of the six countries (Belgium, France, the Federal Republic of Germany, Italy, Luxembourg and the Netherlands) that in 1951 launched the first European institution, the European Coal and Steel Community, the predecessor of all subsequent European institutions. Since then, Italy has never wavered in its overall support for both – yet another striking indication that the instability of governments has not affected the continuity of major policies. Together, NATO and the European unification project have constituted the cornerstones of Italian "foreign" policy. Their full acceptance was also considered the litmus test for participation in the Italian government.

From the beginning, and for a long period of time, the PCI voiced its opposition to both. In the early 1970s it came gradually to accept Italian membership in the EU and NATO as inevitable, even beneficial, because of the persistence of the Warsaw Pact. In a famous interview in 1976, Enrico Berlinguer, the secretary of the Communist Party, declared that he felt safer on "this" side of the iron curtain. In the mid-1970s, also because of the vigorous and unrelenting battle fought by Altiero Spinelli,[1] the PCI changed its attitude towards the process of European unification. Since then, former Communists (outstanding among them Giorgio Napolitano) have always expressed themselves in favour of the process of European political unification and have behaved accordingly. Napolitano himself was elected to the European Parliament in 1999 and, in recognition of his European "stature", was chosen as chair of the Committee on Institutional Affairs.

Once the two watershed decisions had been made, Italian authorities never questioned them, but most of the time they have distinguished themselves only by playing the passive, though loyal, role of "followers": no additional initiatives, no vigorous dissent, no dynamic leadership, no proposals for improvement, no opposition (in Moravcsik's (1998) excellent, though controversial, analysis, Italy almost does not appear). Still, some individual Italian personalities were more than merely reliable: for instance, Ambassador Manlio Brosio, who, chosen as General Secretary of NATO, served from 1 August 1964 to 1 October 1971. More or less in the same time frame, in July 1970 Franco Maria Malfatti was appointed President of the European Commission, only to resign in March 1972 without completing his term in order to run for the Italian Parliament, a decision deplored by the heads of government of the other member states. Fortunately, there have also been two other important events that saw Italy playing the role of protagonist. First, Italy organized the Conference of Rome on 25 March 1957, during which a major treaty was signed that must be considered the true breakthrough in the process of European political unification. Second, Italy sponsored the meeting of the European Council in Milan in June 1985 that led to the adoption, on 1 January 1987, of the Single European Act, which contained important modifications to the Treaty of Rome and several measures necessary to complete the single market by 1992, plus the criteria for a common foreign policy. In all other instances, the merits of subsequent Italian governments have fundamentally consisted in not opposing or delaying agreed changes and in following and supporting initiatives taken by other European authorities. For instance, Italy was quick – twenty-five years after the fact there are many who would say "too quick" – to underwrite the Maastricht Treaty in 1992.

In his desire not to be left behind, Prime Minister Romano Prodi joined the euro at its inauguration in 1998, accepting what some Italian economists still consider a rather unfavourable exchange rate with the Italian lira, the price to be paid to those in Europe who considered Italy not fully reliable. Overall, Italian behaviour remained consistent with the founding principles of its foreign policy: to join, to be present, to become and remain part of supranational organizations, not to be left behind and never to rock the boat. As for taking (an active) part in the evolution and transformation of those organizations, the record of Italian governments is not particularly flattering or exciting. However, the Europeans have been more than willing to recognize the importance of Italy and to appoint several Italians to prominent roles in the EU (in recent times, Prodi, Mogherini, Draghi, Tajani and Sassoli).

The story of Italy's involvement in European affairs is marked by significant accomplishments, but also by serious shortcomings as well as by potential changes. Throughout the long period leading to Maastricht, Italian public opinion was largely supportive of all efforts made by subsequent Italian governments, so Italy was rightly considered as one of the most pro-European countries. Probably, the highest point and the best measure of the amount of support "for Europe" was offered by the results of a popular referendum. The Italian Parliament promoted a consultative referendum in which Italian voters were asked whether they were in favour, first, of transforming the European Communities into an effective Union, endowed with a government responsible to the European Parliament, and, second, of giving the European Parliament a mandate to draft the project of a European Constitution, to be then submitted to the ratification of the member states. Held on 18 June 1989, the same day as elections to the European Parliament, the Italian referendum was a resounding success. Turnout was quite high at 80.68 per cent. Those in favour were 29,158,656 (88.03 per cent); those against 3,964,086 (11.97 per cent). It was not a surprising outcome because, at the time, there existed widespread public support for the European institutions, and, in practice, there was no organized opposition. I subscribe to the hypothesis that Italians were taking for granted that the functioning of their political system would continue to be not very satisfactory and that the only possible improvements would have to come from the rules and regulations formulated at the European level and "imposed" on Italian politicians' behaviour, what came to be known as *il vincolo europeo* (the European constraint). My suggestion is that the Italian consensus for strengthening the European institutions should be interpreted as the product of a combination of, on the one hand, a (healthy) scepticism towards Italian political authorities and their ability to perform, and, on the other, an, admittedly somewhat exaggerated and idealized, confidence in the strength, capabilities and effectiveness of European authorities and institutions.

The foundations for Italian participation in the European institutions (and in NATO) had been clearly and farsightedly stated in Article 11 of the Constitution, according to which Italian national sovereignty could be curtailed in favour of international organizations pursuing "peace and justice among the Nations". It is wrong to say, as some commentators do, that Italy has lost her sovereignty, supposedly "stolen" by European institutions. In practice, all transfers of sovereignty from Italy to international and supranational organizations must be and have been approved by large majorities in the Italian Parliament. Nevertheless, the current Italian debate on "losing" (or being expropriated of) versus "transferring" sovereignty is indicative of profound changes within the political elites and in Italian public opinion as well. These changes have often been fuelled by the criticisms coming from many Italian politicians, in the government and in the opposition, addressed towards the EU as such. The decline of public support, down to slightly more than 50 per cent, may also suggest a great deal of dissatisfaction with the overall behaviour exhibited by Italian policymakers and representatives within the European institutions. This is a topic of some interest because it significantly affects the overall credibility of Italy at the European level. I will have to be rather selective in choosing examples and explaining their relevance. One finds some Italians who have held important positions within the European institutions (see Box 8.1), but, at the same time, there have been many Prime Ministers and ministers who routinely took part in the activities of the Council, Ecofin (Economic and Financial Affairs Council) and other Councils of Ministers but were ill-prepared and lacking proposals, only to find themselves on the losing side.

Box 8.1 Italians in top European offices

Romano Prodi, President of the European Commission: 1999–2004
Mario Draghi, President of the European Central Bank: 2011–19
Federica Mogherini, EU Vice President and High Representative for Foreign Affairs and Security Policy: 2014–19
Antonio Tajani, Speaker of the European Parliament: 2017–19
David Sassoli, Speaker of the European Parliament: 2019–

Over time, some Italian Commissioners, a couple of exceptions aside, have played a significantly positive role, recognized by all their colleagues. Two Commissioners stand out, Emma Bonino (1994–99) and Mario Monti (1994–2004), for their achievements, respectively, in the areas of civil and social rights and of economic competition and anti-trust activities.[2] Without doubt, by far the most influential Italian in a formal role within the European institutions has been Mario Draghi, named President of the European Central Bank in 2011. Reappointed in 2015, he remained in office until the end of October 2019. Obviously, it is too early to provide a substantial evaluation of what Draghi has done for the euro[3] and for the EU in difficult times, but there is no doubt that he has steered the course of the European economic recovery in an independent, persuasive and successful manner without any specific concession to Italian policymakers.

Following the election of the European Parliament in May 2014 (see Viola 2016), the then Italian Minister of Foreign Affairs, Federica Mogherini, was appointed High Representative of the Union for Foreign Affairs and Security Policy. Capable and competent, she has played a delicate balancing role in an area where most member states are very jealous of their (shrinking) power and prerogatives. In the summer of 2017, after a long "European" career, both as Commissioner and Member of the European Parliament (MEP), Antonio Tajani (Forza Italia) was elected to the office of Speaker of the European Parliament (he was replaced by David Sassoli following the 2019 European elections). Last but not least, one must mention that Romano Prodi served as President of the European Commission from September 1999 to November 2004. Although, he was criticized in retrospect, Prodi's major achievement was the enlargement of the EU to ten new member states, all coming from East and Central Europe, which was fundamentally meant to stabilize their nascent democracies and to contribute to their economic growth.[4]

It is fair to say that for a long period of time there existed a virtuous circle in which the majority of Italian politicians – later, that is after 1976, joined by the Communists as well – were very much in favour of European institutions and a large majority of Italian voters shared and supported the same view, as exemplified by the outcome of the 1989 referendum. Then, a rift opened up within the political class when not only the Northern League, in its search for independence and even secession from Italy, but also Berlusconi began to criticize the EU, its regulations, its requests for fiscal discipline and its demands for compliance with the decisions that had been taken. Slowly, gradually, but significantly, the attitudes of quite a number of Italians, especially those voting for centre-right parties, changed. Of course, this negative evolution must also be attributed to Italian citizens' limited knowledge and scarce information concerning what the European institutions do and the consequences for the various member countries. But, on the whole, it is undeniable that the pro-European climate in Italy has undergone a profound transformation. In short, by 2018 Italians had become less "European" than the average citizen of the EU member states. Before dealing with survey data that will tell us part of the story, it is useful to look at two elements: the positions taken by the various parties and the way in which Italian governments and authorities have interacted with the EU and its policies.

Declining support for the European Union

Although initially it was not the most important element of its political platform,[5] the Northern League has constantly exhibited a highly sceptical view of the EU and, quite frequently, a negative evaluation of several of its policies. With the passing of time, those negative evaluations have prevailed, especially with reference to the euro, the alleged expropriation of national sovereignty and the presumed unwillingness of the EU to provide a solution to the "invasion" of Italy by migrants. Matteo Salvini, the new leader of what he has redefined the League, dropping "Northern", has gone so far as to embrace the sovereignist position taken by Marine Le Pen, the leader of the Front National, and some other right-wing parties in Europe. Salvini's strong and unremitting anti-EU political and electoral campaign has been rewarded by 9,175,208 voters (34.3 per cent). Not so paradoxically, many of the anti-euro and anti-EU stances taken by the League have often been independently shared by the newest Italian political protagonist: the Five Star Movement. Of course, the "objective" convergence between the League and the Five Star Movement is the consequence of their not insignificant dose of national populism and their willingness to exploit for electoral purposes dissatisfaction with the EU among some sectors of the public. In the recent past, the Five Star Movement has also indicated its intention to hold a referendum on Italian membership in the EU; this would be a consultative referendum, since the Italian Constitution forbids referendums on international treaties. Out of pure political expediency or simply because they have gone through a process of learning, the leaders of the Five Star Movement no longer seem inclined to question the euro, and they appear to have come to an overall, though critical, acceptance of the EU. Additional evidence of the political ambiguity surrounding the Movement's European stance comes from the appointment of some ministers (the Minister of Foreign Affairs being pro-European, but weak) and from the tense relationship between Italy and the EU. The 2019 situation is in flux, but I believe I am justified in stressing that, on the whole, the sovereignists have almost disappeared within the Movement's activists and parliamentarians, who by now have fundamentally accepted a pro-EU position.

Because of the types of socio-economic interests that, right from the very beginning, have supported him and have provided Forza Italia with quite a number of votes, and also because he has always been particularly inclined to raise objections to all sorts of rules and regulations and, if at all possible, to reject them, Berlusconi's dominant attitude towards the EU has been characterized by ambivalence, and with good reason. Within the electorate of Forza Italia, small farmers resent the EU's regulations, but small entrepreneurs enjoy the opportunities offered to them by the single market and by the euro; housewives may entertain a romantic opposition to the EU, but professionals know that the EU provides opportunities. In the European Parliament, Berlusconi's Forza Italia has joined the European Popular Party, but over the many years in which he was Prime Minister of Italy, Berlusconi never succeeded in playing a significant role in the European Council of heads of government. For him, more than for other Italian Prime Ministers, the overriding issue was essentially credibility – personal and political. Most of the other European heads of government simply did not believe that Berlusconi would keep his word and implement the decisions taken within the Council. The most devastating moment came on 23 October 2011, when, asked whether they believed that the Italian Prime Minister would do what the Council had decided, the French President Sarkozy smiled somewhat derisively and turned to Angela Merkel, who could not hide her own shy smile. Although in a way his Forza Italia has obtained very high recognition for one of his MEPs, Antonio Tajani, elected Speaker of the European Parliament in summer 2017, Berlusconi never entirely dismisses ideas inimical to a closer union and cherishes his own personal "friendship" with Vladimir Putin. Before and after the 2019 elections to the European Parliament, he has taken a stand against sanctions to be imposed on the Hungarian Prime Minister Orbán and has advocated an alliance of the Popular Party, the Conservatives and those he calls "enlightened" sovereignists against the Socialists, the Greens and the Liberal Democrats.

There is no doubt that, in the past, the most pro-European parties in Italy were those located in the centre of the political alignment: the Christian Democrats and the other centrist parties, especially the Republicans, the Liberals and the Social Democrats. Once the Socialists joined the centre-left government coalitions (1962), they too became increasingly in favour of the process of European political unification. Since 1992–94, all the minor parties have disappeared, which, of course, has somewhat weakened the pro-European inclination of the many Italians who voted for those parties. The European flag, so to speak, has remained in the hands of the former Christian Democrats, more with those who merged with the former Communists to give birth to the Democratic Party than with those siding with the centre-right. Since the former Communists also became good and committed Europeans, the PD automatically found itself to be the most pro-European Italian party. However, no attempt has been made by the Democrats to formulate their own idea of Europe. The programmes of the Schools of Politics run by the party very rarely (and then quite superficially) deal with the EU. None of the (few) intellectuals close to the party is famous for reflections on or analyses of the EU as it is and as it should become.[6] Finally, though weak and divided, the extreme left also harbours ambivalent feelings towards and many reservations about the EU as it is. Many leftists have shown a lot of sympathy for the Greek Prime Minister Alexis Tsipras and supported his electoral vehicle in the 2014 European elections. The different positions taken by Italian parties and their divisions have, of course, influenced public opinion towards a less favourable view of the EU. In Table 8.1,[7] I have combined some interesting data that provide an overall view of Italians having become significantly less "European" than the average European citizen.

A somewhat different picture, taken one year later (when it comes to Europe there is an inevitable volatility of public opinion), emerges from Table 8.2. On the one hand, the Italian respondents give higher ratings to the EU as a whole; on the other, they express their dislike of the Commission, which is the institution that looks after what member states do, do not do and do poorly – Italy often appearing on the defendant's bench.

Table 8.1   Italian and European feelings towards the EU, 2017 (percentage)

	Italy	Average EU
Interested in European affairs	45	56
Membership in the European Union is a good thing	35	57
Membership has produced benefits	44	60
Membership has contributed to economic growth	22	35

Source: Author's own compilation based on data provided by Eurobarometer.

Table 8.2   Ratings for the EU, Parliament and the Commission (selected countries)

Country	Union	Parliament	Commission
Poland	72	54	52
Spain	67	52	51
Germany	63	47	38
Netherlands	63	52	51
Sweden	62	53	49
France	62	49	48
Italy	58	48	41
Hungary	57	50	47
UK	48	35	32
Greece	37	30	26
Median	62	50	48

Source: Based on data published by the Pew Research Center, Spring 2018 Global Attitudes Survey (Questions 17d, 17h and 17i).

Table 8.3   The European Parliament: Italian and European evaluations, 2017 (percentage)

	Italy	Average EU
Do you feel informed on the European Parliament (very well, fairly well)	36	35
Do you think the European Parliament is reliable	40	40
Do you have a positive image of the European Parliament	31	24
Do you think the role played by the European Parliament is important	69	72
The European Parliament should have more important role	40	44

Source: Author's own compilation based on data provided by Eurobarometer.

Looking more specifically at the European Parliament, the opinions of Italians do not differ significantly from those of the average European citizen. If anything, it should be stressed that, though not well informed, Italians, together with a high percentage of other Europeans, consider the European Parliament very important and a substantial percentage of them would like to see its role become more important (Table 8.3).

Table 8.4 Most important European policies, 2017 (percentage)

	Italy	Average EU
Tackling poverty and social exclusion	31	51
Implementing an immigration policy in consultation with countries of origin	49	38
Combating terrorism while respecting individual freedoms	35	34
Formulating a security and defence policy	26	28
Coordinating economic budget and tax policies	30	27
Improving consumer and public health protection	26	25

Source: Author's own compilation based on data provided by Eurobarometer.

There are a few, but significant, differences between Italians and the average European citizen in the ranking order of the policies that the European Parliament ought to deal with (Table 8.4). Somewhat surprisingly, Italians have less confidence in the ability of the European Parliament to tackle poverty and social exclusion. Understandably, because of the overall impact of the phenomenon, Italians would like to see a greater involvement by the European Parliament in the complex issue of immigration. I would also stress that there is a significant difference between Italians and the average European when it comes to the issues of poverty and social exclusion. The data strongly suggest that Italians believe that both are better dealt with in the respective countries and/or that the European Parliament cannot do very much with reference to what are fundamentally domestic problems. Here, of course, one can find the roots of a lingering and emerging dose of sovereignism.

Among Italian citizens and policymakers, there is general agreement that Italy ought to try to get a better deal from Europe. Even though, of course, this is not declared openly, there is also some agreement on the fact that, because of the inefficiency of Italian bureaucracy and the vagaries of Italian politics, Italy's preferences do not get a satisfactory hearing in the EU. The facts speak for themselves. When a member state has not adopted an EU directive correctly or on time, or is applying single market rules in a less than appropriate way, the Commission may start "infringement proceedings". In 2012, Italy was the member state with the highest number of infringements (ninety-nine) due either to an ineffective Parliament unable to transpose several directives or to a defective government unable to spur Parliament to act. Then, the tide turned. Italy made almost unbelievable progress, reducing its number of infringements from sixty-seven (November 2014) to forty-one at the end of 2016, and also reducing significantly the response time to infringement procedures by 5.5 months, although it still requires 24.1 months to remedy its infringements. Moreover, starting in October 2018, the Five Star–League government has tried to make a point of challenging the negative evaluation of the Commission concerning its overall economic policies, implying no debt reduction but yet another increase in the state deficit.

The contemporary Italian political debate and the party controversies rotate around four major issues: the Maastricht criteria and the fiscal compact; the loss of sovereignty; Europe not being good to Italy and Italy being obliged to suffer; and, first and foremost, Italy claiming that it is left alone to face the intractable challenge of migration. The criticism of the fiscal compact – that is, the obligation for a country to have its national budget balanced, or, if not, to correct all significant deviations – is often extended back to the Maastricht criteria. In synthesis, those criteria were: price stability (inflation not more than 1.5 per cent higher than the average of the three best-performing countries); sound public finances (government deficit not exceeding 3 per cent of the gross national product); sustainable public finances (government debt no more than 60 per cent of the gross national product); and durability of convergence (long-term interest rates no more than 2 per cent above the rate of the three best-performing countries). These criteria were considered decisive for a country to join the euro from its inception. However, exceptions could be made for a limited period of time if a country had started a convergence trend. In any case, a "convergence" between the Italian formal commitment to abide by those criteria and, above all, German Chancellor Helmut Kohl's willingness to have Italy on board allowed Italy to join the euro. But it could not be denied that Italy was going to have a very difficult time respecting one of the criteria: the size of the government debt (see Box 8.2). Since then, not only has no downsizing of the debt started, but the trend has been upwards, especially

---

Box 8.2 Some economic indicators in 2018

Deficit: 2.9 per cent
Public debt: 132.2 per cent
Inflation: 1.1 per cent
Growth: 0.9%

from 2013 to 2016. There was a small decline in 2017, then debt went up again because of the policies of the Five Star–League government. It remains the second-largest debt in the EU, surpassed only by the Greek percentage, and has inevitably led the Commission to initiate an infringement procedure (see Figure 8.1).

Understandably, the Commission has repeatedly criticized Italy for not reducing its public debt and has repeatedly rejected Italian requests to be allowed to use more money for investments exceeding the 3 per cent ceiling of annual deficits. There are good reasons to believe that the Commission is very severe and strict with Italy not only with reference to economic criteria (in any case, Italy continues to be a laggard in economic terms), but also because Italian Prime Ministers and their Ministers of Finance have been unable to keep their promises. The overriding issue is Italian political credibility. Although in the 2013 electoral campaign "Europe" acquired remarkable relevance (Belluati and Serricchio 2013), it has never been the most salient topic in Italian political debate, not even at the time of national elections.[8] The 2019 electoral campaign for the renewal of the European Parliament was not at all "exceptional" in the sense that, in Italy, the dominant issues remained domestic, focusing on power relationships within the government and the performance of the new secretary of the Democratic Party. As in most European countries, the three most important issues in Italy are unemployment, security and education, accompanied recently – and dramatically surpassed in

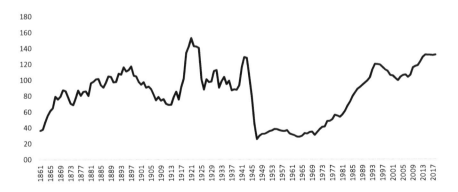

Figure 8.1   Evolution of the public debt to GDP in Italy, 1861–2017 (percentage)

Source: Author's own compilation based on data by Reinhart and Rogoff (2009), with personal updates.

the summer of 2018 – by the number of Italians who leave their country looking for jobs elsewhere. However, the dominant issue, not only for Italians but for the average European, with the notable exception of a few wealthy member states not easily reached by migrants, has proved to be immigration, as indicated by the data in Table 8.5.

Starting from 1 June 2018, the newly appointed Minister of the Interior Matteo Salvini has thrown all his political weight and ministerial power behind the issue of immigration (Caponio and Cappiali 2018). He has caught the feelings of a relative majority of Italians and, technically, he has become the "owner" of the issue. Now and for the conceivable future, he will be pursuing three highly important goals. First, Salvini wants to prove that he can oblige the EU to change its policy in a major way, something that previous Italian governments did not even attempt. Second, he was striving to shape, as he had declared openly, "a League of Leagues": that is, to gather together all the opponents to the EU and to the EU's poor handling of its two most significant problems (Table 8.6). Somewhat paradoxically, however, the other European sovereignists – the heads of the governments of Hungary, Poland, Slovakia, and, to some extent, Austria – have been of no help to him or Italy so far when it comes to the reallocation of migrants in their countries. Finally, Salvini believes that his determination will lead him to victory in the battle for leadership, not only within the Italian centre-right but also within the existing government coalition.

Table 8.5 Is migration a problem? (percentage)

	Yes	No
Greece	89	11
Spain	88	11
Hungary	80	17
Italy	80	17
Poland	68	28
France	48	52
UK	41	58
Germany	33	66
Netherlands	19	80
Sweden	18	81
Median	58	40

Source. Based on data collected by the Pew Research Center, Spring 2018 Global Attitudes Survey (Question 51).

Table 8.6   Rates of approval of the way in which the EU has dealt
with the economy and refugees (percentage)

Country	Economic issues	Refugees
Poland	58	23
Germany	52	27
Netherlands	52	37
Hungary	43	15
France	40	22
Sweden	39	13
Spain	38	26
UK	28	23
Italy	20	16
Greece	14	7
Median	40	23

Source: Based on data collected by the Pew Research Center, Spring 2018
Global Attitudes Survey (Questions 41a–c).

When it comes to what has been or must be done in order to explain the poor performance of Italy vis-à-vis the requests of the EU, almost all Italian politicians, but, of course, more frequently those with governmental power, resort to two rhetorical devices. I call the first device *alibi*. "We, the Italian government, are obliged to do or not to do this, for instance not to rescue a dying company or a bank resorting to state money, because otherwise the European Commission will punish us." This device receives a lot of attention from the Italian press and is rarely – almost never – submitted to serious scrutiny for lack of will and, often, of knowledge. The second device I call *scapegoat*. If anything goes wrong, especially in the field of social and economic policies, the Italian government will solemnly say that it is not its responsibility: "Those damaging policies have been imposed upon Italy by European directives. We would have done otherwise." Obviously, there are instances in which the rules and regulations of the EU are in fact responsible for affecting, for instance, Italian agriculture, especially with reference to quotas (famously the quotas for milk production). But the violation of those quotas was wilfully and deceptively carried out by Italian cattle farmers. Two consequences follow. All Italian governments regularly make an attempt to avoid accountability while the opposition ends up putting the blame both on what the government has done or has not done and on the EU for obliging Italians to behave in that way. Italian public opinion, shaped as it is by the mass media, whose coverage of EU activities and policies is infrequent and shallow, receives the overriding message that the EU, for reasons never convincingly explained, is too demanding and too severe with Italy. No surprise, then, if surveys reveal a decline in the percentage of Italians viewing the EU and its institutions in a less than favourable light. Nonetheless, as Table 8.7 shows, Italians are only slightly more negative and somewhat more critical than the majority of other Europeans in their assessments of the positive and negative traits of the EU.

Only one additional comment is absolutely necessary: one concerning the contribution to economic growth from membership of the EU. Probably because they have been influenced by the very difficult post-2008 situation, when the crisis started, only 41 per cent of Italians believe that the EU promotes prosperity, compared with an average of 55 per cent of other Europeans. In fact, taking a longer-term view, there is a general consensus, buttressed by a wealth of statistical data, among almost all economists that the EU has indeed significantly contributed to the economic growth of all the member states. However, this consensus is not shared by an important Professor of Economics at the University of Chicago, Luigi Zingales (2014), nor, as Table 8.7 indicates, by a majority of Italians (even though it runs counter to a wealth of reliable economic statistics).

Feelings

"Man does not live by bread alone" – nor can political communities grow and function satisfactorily if and when their members do not share a feeling of belonging. At the time of writing, immediately after the May 2019 European elections, the cleavage between the "Europeanists" and the "sovereignists" had reached its highest level of visibility and the complaint that membership of the EU has meant the loss of Italian sovereignty appeared to be shared by a very large section of Italian public opinion. Precise data on how many Italians would side with the Europeanists and how many with the sovereignists are not available;[9] however, the electoral success of the League and Fratelli d'Italia, which ran a campaign (with the slogan *In Europa per cambiare tutto* – In Europe to change everything) against the EU and the European Commission, suggests that the "sovereignists" may indeed have become a numerical majority among Italians.[10] This does not mean that attempts will follow for Italy to leave the EU; it is much more likely that the government led by Conte will utilize the number

Table 8.7 The EU: most positive and most negative traits

	Peace	Democratic values	Prosperity	Out of touch	Inefficiency	Intrusiveness
Greece	65	53	35	86	73	86
France	78	72	54	65	43	52
Italy	71	58	41	65	41	48
Netherlands	77	59	66	63	61	49
Hungary	59	60	56	62	39	42
UK	67	53	50	61	66	60
Spain	71	68	63	60	55	50
Sweden	85	69	63	59	68	41
Germany	82	71	48	49	52	52
Poland	80	67	70	42	33	68
Median	74	64	55	62	54	51

Source: Adapted from Pew Research Center, Spring 2018 Global Attitudes Survey (Questions 42a–f).

of these votes for bargaining purposes. The government will stress the point that Italy is too big to be relegated to the margins, so to speak, and definitely too big to be forced to leave, hence concessions will have to be made.

Although, of course, economic issues have their undeniable importance, belonging to a supranational organization also entails feelings and emotions. In 1882, the French historian Ernest Renan wrote that "a nation is a daily referendum". My interpretation of this statement is that most individuals stay together because they share similar feelings and renew them towards the same "object": the nation. Could one say the same for the EU? Probably not, but it is definitely important to know whether uniquely "European" feelings are being made. Table 8.8 offers a battery of Eurobarometer data that reveal the ambiguity of Italian feelings of attachment: one finds the city or town at the top, then the nation, and at the bottom less than half of Italians declare some attachment to the EU, well below the average for Europe.

Feelings of attachment to the EU are influenced by beliefs concerning the importance of certain elements in shaping European identity. Again, Table 8.9 indicates that there are a few, not totally negligible, differences between Italians and the average European. Especially noteworthy are the beliefs held by only 44 per cent of Italians that membership has produced benefits and by the even smaller 35 per cent that membership is a good thing.[11] Also, the differences concerning the values considered as being responsible for making a European identity (Table 8.10) are quite stark and somewhat disturbing, especially when one looks at two crucial elements: democracy and freedom and the euro.

When it comes to an analysis of responses to the question concerning the factors that would strengthen their feeling of being European citizens, one notices again that there are some, minor, differences between Italians and the average European, the former desiring a more active EU when dealing with emergencies (see Table 8.11).

Italy and the European Union: democracy and the quality of life

It is appropriate to conclude this chapter that has briefly analysed the relationships between Italy and the EU and the attitudes of Italians towards the EU with two considerations concerning participation, democracy and quality of life. At least in principle and in theory, the citizens of democratic countries are defined by the possibility they

Table 8.8   Feelings of attachment to the nation, the city and the EU (percentage)

	Italy	Average EU
Feeling attachment to their nation	89	91
Feeling attachment to their city/town	93	87
Feeling attachment to the EU	48	56

Source: Author's own compilation based on data provided by Eurobarometer.

Table 8.9   What is shared by Europeans (percentage)

	Italy	EU average
Interested in European affairs	45	56
Membership in the EU is a good thing	35	57
Membership has produced benefits	44	60
Membership has contributed to economic growth	22	35

Source: Author's own compilation based on data provided by Eurobarometer.

Table 8.10   Values shared by Europeans (percentage)

	Italy	EU average
What brings the citizens of EU member states together is more important than what separates them	61	74
The most important value of the European identity is: democracy/freedom	41	51
The most important value of the European identity is: the euro	41	48
The most important value of the European identity is: culture	31	30
The most important value of the European identity is: history	25	27

Source: Author's own compilation based on data provided by Eurobarometer.

have of actively participating in the decision-making process and of exercising some political influence. The data here reveal a striking contrast between the beliefs of Italian citizens and the average European citizen concerning their ability to be heard. The gap is quite large. Table 8.12 indicates that only one-third of Italians, compared with two-thirds of Europeans, believe that they have some political influence in their respective countries. When it comes to the EU, the

Table 8.11 Factors strengthening the EU (percentage)

	Italy	Average EU
Harmonization of a European social welfare system	41	45
European emergency response to natural disasters	33	28
Freedom of movement of retired people with their pension	26	26
European identity card	27	22

Source: Author's own compilation based on data provided by Eurobarometer.

Table 8.12 Do European citizens believe that they have an influence in their respective countries and on the European institutions? (percentage)

	Italy	Average EU
My voice counts in my country	36	63
My voice counts in the EU	26	53

Source: Author's own compilation based on data provided by Eurobarometer.

number of Europeans who believe that their voice counts is twice that of Italians, only a quarter of whom share that important belief. Without pursuing all the implications of these beliefs, I would like to stress only one special element. It is unsurprising that those Italians who believe that they do not have any influence on the EU will then support those parties and politicians who promise that they will return political sovereignty to the "nation", to the people, no matter that their voice will not count significantly in their own country either.

Inevitably, the European average hides many important differences among the member states. In all instances, it has been ascertained and is well known that the "old" West European democracies fare much better than the new Eastern European countries, whose democracy is recent and rarely functions in a satisfactory way for their citizens, and whose government, namely those of Hungary and Poland, are on the verge of being officially reprimanded and sanctioned for violating some of the defining democratic principles.

In the next chapter, I will analyse how democracy works in Italy. Here, in Table 8.13, we have a preview. In contrast to the average European citizen, who believes that his or her own democracy works much better than democracy in the EU, the Italians rate democracy in the EU slightly more favourably than democracy in their own country.

Table 8.13   Satisfaction with democracy and the quality of life (percentage)

	Italy	Average EU
Are you satisfied with the way democracy works in the EU	41	43
Are you satisfied with the way democracy works in your country	39	54
Was the quality of life better before (that is, in the preceding years)	72	55

Source: Author's own compilation based on data provided by Eurobarometer.

What is much more disturbing is the very high percentage of those who say that they had a better quality of life in the years before 2017. True, the long phase of economic recession has affected the majority of Europeans and a whopping three-quarters of Italians. While, of course, the causes of the economic problems are multiple and the blame ought to be put both on national policies and on European policies, once more the translation of this kind of dissatisfaction into political and electoral behaviour depends significantly on the ability of the parties. Anti-EU feelings have been courted, "organized" and channelled by parties of all shades of populism, which have all pointed their finger towards the institutions and policies of the EU, their ineffectiveness and their allegedly negative impact on the Italian economic system. In addition, because the propaganda of the pro-European parties has been far from incisive and convincing, populist parties have been believed and sizably rewarded by Italian voters.

Summing up, the relationship between Italy and the EU lends itself to several concluding remarks. First, the emergence of some Euroscepticism, cultivated especially by the centre-right but also by some sectors of the left, is not a very recent occurrence: it started in the 1990s. It has been accompanied and superseded by those who vociferously claim that it is necessary and possible fully (or largely) to recover the Italian national sovereignty that has been lost. The 2019 European elections have clearly indicated that there is a widespread anti-European sentiment in Italy that finds representation especially by and within Matteo Salvini's League. One cannot automatically draw the conclusion that Italians would like to abandon the euro or exit from the EU. However, the new situation suggests a future of tensions, conflicts and clashes between the Italian government and the European authorities. This situation will also entail a further diminished role for Italy in the EU and a negative impact on the Italian economy.

For a long time, the pro-European sentiment in Italy was accompanied by crucial decisions taken by the political authorities of the period: De Gasperi in 1949; the centrist coalition and its Minister of Foreign Affairs Gaetano Martino in 1957 (the Treaty of Rome establishing the Common Market); the Socialist secretary Bettino Craxi and the Single European Act in 1985; Prime Minister Romano Prodi and joining the euro in 1998. Throughout, one must underline the importance of the incessant and passionate prodding by Altiero Spinelli. Unfortunately, in the past ten years or so, too many Italian political leaders have preferred the easy game of criticizing the so-called European bureaucrats and technocrats instead of committing themselves to the transformation of the European Union as it is and of formulating their vision for the European Union to come. In spite of a lingering awareness that Italy's future lies within the EU and that a break from it will have many negative consequences, the overall popular sentiment has changed, producing a sort of psychological detachment from the European project. Although the Five Star–League government may not last for long, it seems unlikely that Italy will return to being as favourable and supportive of the EU and its institutions as it has been for more than forty years.

This chapter has analysed the complex relationships between Italy and the European institutions and their policies. It has also explored changing Italian attitudes towards the process of European political unification and has assessed evaluations of the working of the EU. There is an irrepressible connection between the dynamics of the Italian political system and the transformation of the EU. The next chapter will be devoted to an analysis of the factors that affect the quality of Italian democracy.

Notes

1 A former Communist expelled from the party because he vehemently opposed the Molotov–von Ribbentrop Pact of August 1939, Spinelli became the most important and relentless Italian federalist. In 1976 he was elected by the PCI to the House of Deputies as an Independent and in 1979 to the European Parliament. He was the author of a draft treaty, *For an Ever Closer Union*, approved by the European Parliament on 10 May 1984, providing the groundwork for the European Single Act (1985).

2 Informally, the Presidents of the European Commission and some of the Commissioners have been variously evaluated with reference to their performance, but, unfortunately, there is nothing comparable to what US historians have done for their Presidents, ranking them all with respect to the way in which

they have conducted themselves in office. For a good starting point, see Kassim (2012).

3 Draghi's most famous announcement is the one made in July 2012 that he would defend the euro "whatever it takes". In January 2015, Draghi's most important decision was to proceed to quantitative easing: that is, to have the European Central Bank buy bonds of some member states. Thus, he did indeed "save" the euro and the Eurozone and decisively contributed to the economic recovery of the EU.

4 It is quite unfair to criticize Prodi for "his" decision to proceed to the enlargement in the light of the illiberal path taken by the governments of Hungary and Poland and of the anti-refugee stand taken by the Visegráad group of countries: Hungary and Poland plus the Czech Republic and Slovakia. On the contrary, the enlargement was essentially made and justified in order to buttress and strengthen those nascent democratic political systems. Subsequently something went wrong.

5 The Northern League platform contained elements that appealed to different sectors of the electorate. It is difficult to rank them in order of importance, but they included: North versus South; northern regions versus the (centralized and bureaucratic) state; regionalism; federalism; and independence (Bull and Gilbert 2001). Although it may also be defined as populist and rightwing, these elements were not a major part of its identity. The anti-European, "sovereignist" turn is quite recent, reflecting the new leader's, Matteo Salvini's, political preferences.

6 In fact, there does not exist one single Italian intellectual of some stature comparable for his commitment to the political unification of Europe to, to mention just a few names, Raymond Aron, Ralph Dahrendorf, Bronisław Geremek or Jürgen Habermas.

7 All the data come from the reliable surveys run by Eurobarometer in 2017.

8 For instance, no chapter is devoted to European issues in the volume edited by Bellucci and Segatti (2010); surprisingly, for a long time, these issues were not considered relevant in shaping voting options.

9 Some degree of Euroscepticism has made its appearance (see Bellucci and Serricchio 2016).

10 To the votes obtained by Salvini's Lega (9,175,208 or 34.26 per cent) and by Fratelli d'Italia (1,726,189 or 6.44 per cent), one must add those received by two Neo-Fascist organizations – Casa Pound (89,142 or 0.33 per cent) and Forza Nuova (41,077 or 0.15 per cent) – and by the most certainly anti-EU Partito Comunista (235,542 or 0.88 per cent). More or less wide streaks of creeping sovereignism exist within Berlusconi's Forza Italia and within another small leftist party, La Sinistra (469,943 or 1.75 per cent).

11 These data show an irresistible tendency to change. In a survey conducted for the Italian daily *Corriere della Sera* by the reliable Nando Pagnoncelli (27 April 2019, p. 1, 11), 45 per cent of Italians declared that belonging to the EU is a positive thing. Only 24 per cent said that it is negative and 24 per cent answered neither positive nor negative. Of course, there were significant differences deriving from

party preferences. Those voting for the PD were the most appreciative, while those voting for the League (29 per cent positive and 30 per cent negative) and those voting for the Five Star Movement (34 per cent positive and 27 per cent negative) were the least appreciative.

References

Belluati, M. and Serricchio, F. (2013). Quale e quanta Europa in campagna elettorale e nel voto degli italiani. In ITANES (ed.) *Voto amaro: Disincanto e crisi economica nelle elezioni del 2013* (pp. 181–192). Bologna: Il Mulino.

Bellucci, P. and Segatti, P. (eds) (2010). *Votare in Italia: 1968–2008.* Bologna: Il Mulino.

Bellucci, P. and Serricchio F. (2016). Europeismo, euroscetticismo e crisi economica. In D. Pasquinucci and L. Verzichelli (eds) *Contro l'Europa? I diversi scetticismi verso l'integrazione europea* (pp. 215–232). Bologna: Il Mulino.

Bull, A. C. and Gilbert, M. (2001). *The Lega Nord and the Northern Question in Italian Politics.* London: Palgrave.

Caponio, T. and Cappiali, T. M. (2018). Italian Migration Policies in Times of Crisis: The Policy Gap Reconsidered. In *South European Society and Politics,* 23 (1), pp. 115–132.

Kassim, H. (2012). The Presidents and the Presidency of the European Commission. In E. Jones, A. Menon and S. Weatherhill (eds) *The Oxford Handbook of the European Union* (pp. 219–232). Oxford: Oxford University Press.

Moravcsik, A. (1998). *The Choice for Europe: Social Purpose and State Power from Messina to Maastricht.* Ithaca: Cornell University Press.

Reinhart, C. M. and Rogoff, K. S. (2009). *This Time Is Different: Eight Centuries of Financial Folly.* Princeton: Princeton University Press.

Viola, D. (ed.) (2016). *Routledge Handbook of European Elections.* London and New York: Routledge.

Zingales, L. (2014). *Europa o no. Sogno da realizzare o incubo da cui uscire?* Milan: Rizzoli.

The quality of democracy 9

This chapter is devoted to an evaluation of the quality of Italian democracy. I rely on a variety of available data showing that, as expected, there are several weaknesses in the Italian political system and the performance of its governments. In order to provide a more convincing picture, I attempt to offer a comparative view. It is easy to see that Italians are dissatisfied with the working of their democracy. On their part, politicians have been seeking electoral and institutional reforms, but, so far, these have been ineffective. However, I argue that there is no crisis of democracy in Italy and no real challenge to it, but there are many problems within Italian democracy.

Which quality?

The quality of democracy is in the eyes of the beholder(s). Most of the beholders – Italians and non-Italians, citizens and commentators – believe that the quality of Italian democracy is modest, and not satisfactory. Most Italians share this belief, often in a mute, resigned way. Only occasionally are there explosions of protest, and these do not last long. So far, nobody has said that Italy should get rid of its democratic system and go beyond it. However, when they are given the opportunity, Italian citizens translate their dissatisfaction into something tangible. In the March 2018 elections, quite a number of Italian voters supported the two political actors that are the most critical of the state of Italian democracy: the Five Star Movement and the League. In the past, Italian political parties have been the backbone of Italian democracy, in one way or another. Their decline and even their disappearance have certainly had a negative effect on the quality of Italian democracy. Those, especially on the left, who are dissatisfied with the performance of political parties usually support and extol the activities of social-collective movements. Rarely have these movements become a vehicle for the mobilization of sectors of society intending specifically to improve the quality of democracy. Their goals have always been more limited, their targets more specific. Unfortunately, there is no exhaustive record of the many social movements that have made their appearance in post-war Italy, of their activities or of their achievements. Nonetheless, on the basis of several scattered studies, I feel justified in stating that, most of the time, Italian social movements have been single-issue (Ruzza 2017) and only partially successful.

Although dissatisfaction is always a more or less powerful motivation of criticism, it is seldom quickly translated into action. For a long time in the past, the opinion held mainly, but not exclusively, by Italian left-wing voters was that the quality of Italian democracy was poor. More recently, a majority of centre-right voters has probably been more inclined to volunteer a negative evaluation. In a way, one can say that the Five Star Movement has emerged as the beneficiary of both left- and right-wing dissatisfaction. Obviously, no serious analyst can rely on impressions only. Beholders may see something, but they may also overlook something else that is more important. But here is the major point of contention. Have the scholars reached an agreement on what one should take into consideration and possibly measure in order to come to a shared and acceptable evaluation of the quality of democracy in contemporary political systems?

Having read quite a number of articles and books devoted to the identification of what is considered to be the quality of democracy (Altman and Pérez-Liñán 2002; Ringen 2011; Morlino, Piana and Raniolo 2013), I have reached two preliminary conclusions. The first is that there is no generalized agreement among scholars on which criteria to use, but that some specific criteria should definitely appear in any attempt to evaluate the quality of democracy. The second conclusion is that all attempts to measure the quality of any democracy should be characterized by parsimony and elegance: that is, they should rely on a few manageable variables that are connected to each other in a very simple way and that will capable of leading to assessments and explanations as widely shared as possible. Therefore, I will try to find a few precise criteria, explain their relevance and apply them to an analysis and assessment of the quality of contemporary Italian democracy.

Two indispensable criteria: rule of law and political corruption

My starting point is that when and where there is no political order (Huntington 1968; Fukuyama 2014), the quality of that regime, be it democratic or not, is doomed to be very poor. Indeed, where life is "poor, nasty, brutish and short", as Thomas Hobbes described it, the overall quality of the regime is bound to be very bad and miserable. The existence of political order, how it has been obtained and how it is maintained are fundamental preconditions for whatever evaluation we would like to formulate. Of course, one ought to be aware that the "type" of political order imposed on Warsaw by Napoleon's generals through repression and massacre is not the one that characterizes democracies. The political order that has been achieved in democratic regimes is totally different from the one existing in military-ruled countries. The democratic political order is fundamentally based on the recognition of the citizens' rights and their freedom, where heads are not cut off but are counted and people are allowed to express their views.

Conventionally, when speaking of democracies, political order is defined as *rule of law*. Even though often contested, the existence of the rule of law characterizes all democracies, past, present and future. All processes of democratization revolve around the success of the democratizers to facilitate the emergence of the rule of law and to consolidate it. The first and most important "law" that must "rule" is, without question, the Constitution. Democratizing political systems have to draft a Constitution that is acceptable to and accepted by all the actors, or at least by the most prominent ones, those capable of mobilizing a substantial amount of political, economic, social, cultural and military resources. Paraphrasing Giuseppe Di Palma (1990), the Constitution must become, be recognized as and remain "the only game in town" (again, at least for all the major political, economic and social protagonists and for the voters at large). For the past forty years or so, at least partially, this has *not* been fully the case in Italy. The 1948 Constitution has been frequently called into question and criticized, especially by the centre-right. Many attempts have been made to introduce significant changes into the Italian Constitution, some of them potentially leading to disequilibria. A not so subtle process of delegitimization has been at work. Recently, even some foreign observers have joined the now rather crowded Italian choir criticizing some post-World War Two Constitutions (more precisely, those in Italy, Portugal and Spain) for being "Socialist". The most insidious attempt to make disjointed and destabilizing changes – made by Matteo Renzi, the secretary of the Democratic Party, and his centre-left government – was defeated in a popular referendum held on 4 December 2016. Unfortunately, the outcome of the referendum is still questioned by the losers, which means that, if a new opportunity arises, they will try again to "reform" the Constitution.[1] In any case, at the time of writing, some controversial reforms, especially concerning parliamentarians and the legislative process, have already been launched by the yellow–green government.

Be that as it may, it seems that foreign scholars and commentators in particular have not fully grasped the many political implications of a partially or fully delegitimized Italian Constitution. Some Italians have and are working precisely towards that goal. Although the task has been beyond the interest and, perhaps, the capabilities of any single individual scholar so far, a comparative exploration of the degree of acceptance of the Constitution in several democratic regimes would significantly contribute to an overall assessment of the quality of their democracies. Still, in the absence of this type of study, I am confident in stating that, minor changes, mainly amendments, aside, all the Constitutions of the Western political systems have remained essentially what they were at the time of their drafting and approval. Particularly noteworthy is the German case: the 1949 *Grundgesetz* was easily transformed into the official Constitution of unified Germany after 1990. The most remarkable exception is France, whose 1946 Constitution gave birth to the Fourth Republic. It was replaced by the 1958 Gaullist Constitution that inaugurated the Fifth Republic[2] and that has been only slightly amended since then.

There is a second level at which the rule of law plays an important role in the quality of a democracy. The majority of scholars have practically no doubts about this: democratic states are supposed to protect the life and the property of their subjects. In some cases, nation states were created precisely in order to pursue these two paramount goals. With regard to the protection of the lives of its citizens, Table 9.1 shows that Italy fares comparatively well. It has one of the lowest homicide rates among Western countries as well as within the EU.

Interestingly, Italy also has a prison population rate that is significantly lower than those in the majority of European states (Table 9.1). However, it is well known, as several Italian activists argue, that living conditions in Italian prisons are awful and deplorable. What these data do not convey to us is the power of organized crime (Paoli 2014, 2015; Varese 2017), especially in four southern regions: the Mafia in Sicily; 'Ndrangheta in Calabria; Camorra in Campania; and, to a much lesser extent, Sacra Corona Unita in Apulia. The law cannot

Table 9.1   Intentional homicides and prison populations in European
countries, 2016

	Intentional homicides (per 100,000 inhabitants)	Prison population (per 100,000 inhabitants)
Austria	0.6	100.1
Belgium	1.9	97.8
Bulgaria	1.5	102.8
Croatia	1.0	76.6
Cyprus	1.7	66.8
Czech Republic	0.7	205.5
Denmark	1.0	58.2
Estonia	3.0	216.2
Finland	1.5	57.4
France	1.4	101.4
Germany	1.0	77.9
Greece	0.8	89.1
Hungary	2.1	178.3
Iceland	0.6	38.6
Ireland	0.8	79.9
Italy	0.7	90.1
Latvia	3.4	218.7
Lithuania	5.6	243.9
Luxembourg	0.9	122.7
Malta	1.0	129.9
Netherlands	0.6	63.3
Norway	0.5	79.5
Poland	0.7	188.6
Portugal	0.6	136.6
Romania	1.3	140.8
Slovakia	0.9	183.5
Slovenia	0.7	65.6
Spain	0.6	130.5
Sweden	1.1	58.4
Switzerland	0.6	78.7
United Kingdom	1.1	122.2

Source: Author's own compilation based on data provided by Eurostat.

be said to rule in situations in which organized crime has acquired
a fair amount of political domination over the inhabitants, their socio-
economic activities and even their lives, which is what has happened
in some, not minor, regions. This situation is reflected in the rankings
offered in Figure 9.1. It is difficult to say how exactly and how

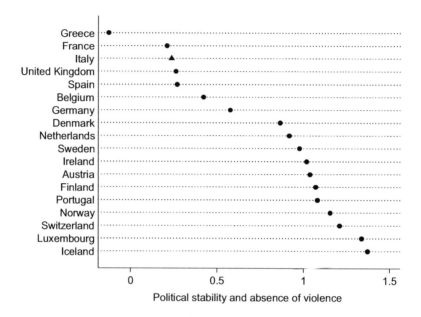

Figure 9.1 Political stability and absence of violence in eighteen West European democracies, 2017

Note: Estimate of governance measured on a scale from approximately −2.5 to 2.5. Higher values correspond to better governance.

Source: Author's own compilation based on data provided by World Bank (http://info.worldbank.org/governance/wgi/index.aspx#home).

negatively criminal violence impacts on the quality of Italian democracy. To start with, one may want – indeed ought – to stress that the four regions mentioned above are among the least developed and less prosperous of all Italian regions. In fact, Calabria is found at the bottom of all conceivable indicators: income, education, health and employment. Moreover, the level of foreign investment in these regions, compared with other less developed southern European regions of Portugal and Spain, suggests that the existence of organized crime in Italy is what discourages potential investors. Finally, in the regions where organized crime is very powerful, politics and politicians are exposed to blackmail and corrupt practices, too often condoned by the parties to which those who are indicted (and convicted) belong.[3]

Often, those who denounce the existence of organized crime and fight against it complain that much of the problem derives from "the absence of the state", as if there were no bureaucracy, no police and no judiciary in the southern regions. This explanation must be challenged. There are even too many public employees in southern regions, often recruited on clientelist grounds, but never enough to reduce youth unemployment. There are many tribunals and judges. There are quite a number of police and military garrisons. It is not the number of state representatives and civil servants that is lacking in the South. It is the humus, the soil in which public employees, police and judges are working and interacting with their surroundings that makes the difference. From time to time there have been investigations that have found instances of collusion between some public servants and organized crime, that have discovered that there are more than few cases of connivance between them, and that, of course, some notable and noble exceptions aside, local politicians powerfully contribute to the persistence and to the reproduction of the conditions that feed organized crime.[4]

The third level, although this is not a ranking of order of importance, where the rule of law is negatively affected is represented by the degree of corruption. Political corruption runs deep, albeit with some differences, through all the parties, the bureaucracy, political activities and, inevitably, many areas and associations of civil society. Of course, the goal pursued by resorting to political corruption is to affect the decision-making processes at which public policies are formulated, can be bought, and will be subjugated to the preferences of selected private interests (della Porta and Vannucci 1999). Let me start with some rhetorical, but undeniable, statements. Corruption corrupts. Political corruption corrupts everything. In a society in which it becomes known that any and all decisions made by politicians and bureaucrats can be influenced and oriented from beginning to end by some sort of exchange, usually revolving around money and other resources, most, if not all, of those who can afford the cost may be willing at some point to enter the circle of corruption. Hence, corruption is bound to corrupt all newcomers. While not much can be said of corruption in transactions among individuals unless they affect other individuals, if it is known that the political sphere is a realm of corruption, quite a number of non-political actors will be inclined to condone corrupt exchanges at the social level. In practice, political corruption will affect the entire system: how licences are granted; how permits are issued; how exemptions are obtained; how parties are financed; how electoral campaigns are run; how government decisions are taken; how trials end. If and when corrupt politicians gain leadership positions within their party, ousting them may require an all-out struggle. In order to retain their office, corrupt politicians will continue and even increase their activity in corrupt exchanges. In Italy, the cost to the socio-economic system as well as to the state budget is very high. To a large extent it has been translated into a higher level of public debt. Italy's position in all comparative rankings of political corruption can be read as an indictment of the entire political class (although, of course, to those who wielded more political power must be attributed more responsibility, and vice versa), but this should not spare civil society.

In the early 1990s, the much vaunted (rightly so) investigation *Mani Pulite* (Clean Hands) discovered that political corruption had affected almost all parties and had seen the conscious participation of quite a number of private entrepreneurs and public managers. It had become "systemic corruption". Contrary to many a report, *Mani Pulite* succeeded in obtaining the conviction of quite a number of politicians, bureaucrats and entrepreneurs. Thus, that investigation was definitely not a failure (Rhodes 2015). Indeed, quite a number of members of the Italian political class, at the local as well as the national level, have been found guilty of some form of political corruption.[5] Although some

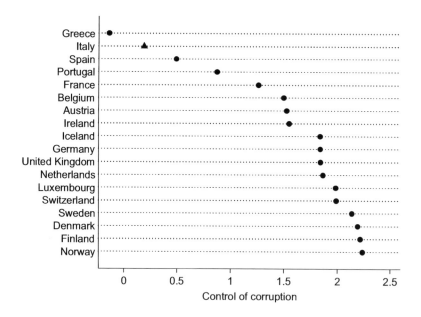

Figure 9.2 Control of corruption in eighteen West European democracies, 2017

Note: Estimate of governance measured on a scale from approximately −2.5 to 2.5. Higher values correspond to better governance.

Source: Author's own compilation based on data provided by World Bank (http://info.worldbank.org/governance/wgi/index.aspx#home).

Italians would question the validity of the Transparency International corruption ranking, because it is based on the *perceptions* of actors doing business in Italy, what is remarkable is that those "perceptions" have changed very little over time. Italy has always been ranked between the high forties and the sixties (in 2017 Italy's rank was fifty-four, one hundred being the least corrupted), an embarrassing position. Political corruption is linked to public ethics and, as Hine (2015) has convincingly argued, it is responsible for creating a situation of distrust among Italians towards the state and democracy; both are considered unable to defeat the corrupt actors and responsible for their proliferation and impact. The high levels of political corruption are a profound wound to the rule of law. Figure 9.2 adds to the various considerations I have offered the fact that Italy is almost totally unable to shape or implement instruments meant to put corruption under control.

Institutions and their performance

The quality of democracy also has to be defined and measured with reference to the institutions: not so much to their structures – that is, parliamentary, presidential, semi-presidential or directorial (the latter applying to Switzerland and, some would add, the EU today) – but to their functioning and performance.[6] In Chapter 5, I tried to convince readers that the instability of Italian governments was always less of a problem that many would be willing to recognize – and still is even today. I stick to my words, but I cannot neglect the fact that many scholars and most Italian citizens would definitely prefer stable governments – governments that remain in office, unaffected by minor crises – to unstable ones, and that they definitely dislike frequent changes of government and early elections. In what way and how much these governmental changes may be detrimental to the quality of democracy remains to be seen. However, it cannot be denied that governmental stability is often an important factor that allows, even encourages, economic operators in all fields to conceive and organize their activities over a longer span of time. No doubt the possibility of producing forecasts has not been provided by unstable Italian governments, even when led by the same Prime Minister and staffed by many of the same ministers. A case could be made – and indeed I have made it – that the Italian experience has been characterized both by the instability of governments and by the "exaggerated" stability in office of the same parties and their political elites. Hence, in the past, the major problem with Italian governments presented itself in different forms: lack of alternation, no circulation of the political class, policy stagnation, inability to react to exogenous conditions and events. However, though welcome, the post-1994 waves of alternations have led only to a partial renewal of the political elites and to rather few significant changes in public policies. In any case, though welcome in the Italian case, alternation in itself would be very misleading as a criterion to be used in order to evaluate the quality of a democracy. Alternation seems to say more about the volatility of voters' preferences and about the amount of electoral and political competition among the parties (Valbruzzi 2016) than about the quality of democracy.

Many and frequent alternations do not necessarily improve the quality of a democracy. On the other hand, a lack of alternation means that many of the same politicians and the same parties occupy important offices, that networks between politicians and bureaucrats make their appearance and become strong, and that encounters and negotiations take place between the same power holders and social and economic operators. Briefly, the conditions are set in which some actors know that they can take advantage of their powerful positions and some realize that they have no other option but to accept a deal if they want to obtain the information, the decisions or the resources they need. The lack of alternation is a precondition of systemic corruption. At least, this was the case in Italy for as long as the Christian Democrats and the centrist parties felt secure in their government coalitions, especially between 1989 and 1992.

In many ways, the quality of democracy is connected to the quality of politics in all political systems and, more precisely, to the amount of power (*kratos*) that the people (*demos*) can exercise. Here, notwithstanding the critical remarks by Sartori (1987: 34–5), I believe it is appropriate to make reference to President Abraham Lincoln's definition of democracy – "government by the people, government of the people, government for the people" – which brings into the picture several elements. Electoral turnout and its impact on those who are elected; other instruments through which the people are allowed to influence the processes of decision making and the decision makers themselves; the consequences of government activities on the production of political, social and economic goods – these are all important elements in order to reach a convincing evaluation of the quality of democracy.

Although they have never been especially interested in politics or well informed about political issues, Italians have regularly voted in very high numbers from 1946 until recent times. For a certain period voting was compulsory, but sanctions for non-voting were rarely applied and entailed only minor administrative consequences. Since non-voting is a very complex phenomenon (*Paradoxa* 2013; for an illuminating interpretation, see Ragsdale and Rusk 2017), even though it appears that it has not yet reached dramatic dimensions in Italy, it would be preferable not to use it as a measure of the quality of Italian democracy. Paradoxically, those who decide to make use of turnout as a measure would probably be obliged to stress the conclusion that Italian democracy was of a very high quality in the 1950s and 1960s when turnout remained constantly above 90 per cent. Figure 9.3 shows the quite impressive trend of turnout decline. One may consider high turnout in a positive light, but then one ought to want to know more about the conditions that led to such huge numbers of voters going to the polls. Also, one should be politically and "democratically" preoccupied both by sudden declines and by sudden surges in the electoral participation rate. We know that in Italy in the past the high turnout was the product of three factors: (i) the existence of well-organized and deeply entrenched class and confessional mass parties; (ii) the high level of socio-political hostility between the Christian Democrats and the Socialist-Communist left, which was conducive to a head-on confrontation in the Cold War period; and (iii) the vote being compulsory up until 1993 – even though the sanctions were mild and rarely applied, their very existence may have produced

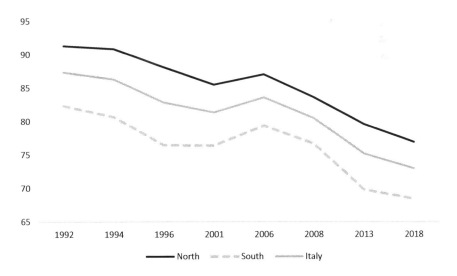

Figure 9.3 Turnout in Italian general elections by area, 1992–2018 (percentage)

Source: Author's own compilation based on data provided by the Ministry of the Interior (https://elezionistorico.interno.gov.it/index.php).

a mass conformity effect. All three factors have now disappeared and it will be impossible to revive them.

Following the disappearance of the Communist Party and the Christian Democrats, for a time it was the antagonizing presence of Silvio Berlusconi that contributed to keeping the level of political conflict and mobilization quite high. Thereafter, what by now seems to be an irreversible, though slow, process of turnout decline started at the beginning of the new millennium and has gradually continued unabated. Moreover, in Italy non-voting no longer carries any social stigma. On the contrary, there are many who declare themselves proud non-voters. There are several social explanations for non-voting. It is possible to identify three groups or types of non-voters (see *Paradoxa* 2013): those who cannot vote for some reason, those who do not want to vote, and those who are or feel that they are outside electoral-political networks.[7]

The first group is rather mixed since it comprises old people unable to go to the polls and those Italians who do not find themselves in their electoral district when voting is held (there is no postal ballot in Italy and no voting by proxy), including students abroad, tourists and entrepreneurs. Of course, this group of non-voters is bound to grow because of demographic and social trends. These trends also affect the third group, which is made up of individuals, more women than men, who are no longer active, who have no associational ties any longer and who live alone. Citizens who are single by choice or by their life circumstances are also less inclined to go to the polls. By far the most interesting group is made up of those who not only criticize Italian politics (and there are many good reasons to do so) but also reject it and refuse to cast a vote because their goal is to delegitimize politics and all politicians. Interestingly, several surveys found that a number of potential non-voters nonetheless went to the polls in February 2013 to cast their vote for the explicitly anti-political Five Star Movement. In the end, however, one cannot escape an unpalatable conclusion. For an albeit slowly growing number of Italians, non-voting is the thing to do because voting does not make any difference. According to them, non-voting is more than just legitimate political behaviour. It is the only way they believe they can express their rejection of party elites who do not care about what they say, they do or they need (see data and analyses in ITANES 2013, 2018), while at the same time venting their frustration for being fundamentally deprived of political power. Hence, while not a measure of the quality of democracy, non-voting is, within limits, suggestive of the existence of drawbacks in the way politics works in Italy, no differently from in several other countries.

Voice and accountability

The tripartite differentiation "loyalty–voice–exit", intelligently devised by Albert O. Hirschman (1970), provides a very useful tool to analyse how much power Italian citizens can exercise and in what way they can channel their support/dissatisfaction/opposition. *Loyalty* covers diffuse support for the political system and the Constitution, as well as specific support[8] for subsequent governments. It can be measured, for instance, through evaluations concerning the functioning of democracy (discussed later). When dealing with political systems, *exit* may be interpreted as the refusal to participate in any political activities whatsoever – voting, for instance. As we have seen, non-voting has increased with the passing of time, but it has not reached particularly disturbing heights. What is of major interest when evaluating the quality of a democracy is the citizens' possibility of expressing their opinions and preferences as well as the likelihood that their *voice* will be heard and taken into account.[9] Figure 9.4 offers a comparative assessment of the relationship between the citizens' voice and its impact on office holders' accountability, an assessment that is clearly neither flattering nor positive for Italy.

The "voice" of the citizens that can be heard most easily is pronounced in their vote. How much impact, in terms of transmission of opinions and preferences, the vote has depends on the features and mechanisms of the electoral law. Since 2006, because of the electoral reform enacted by the centre-right majority of Berlusconi (whose negative impact on the quality of Italian democracy is admirably assessed by Newell (2019)), there has been a significant shift of power from the voters to party and faction leaders. As I have already indicated, all Italian voters have been allowed to do is to draw a cross on the symbol of their favourite party or list or candidate.[10] They cannot have any influence at all on the election of parliamentarians because all lists are closed. Therefore, in practice, all parliamentarians are – and have been – appointed by party and faction leaders. No wonder that the most often heard complaint of Italian citizens is that nobody represents them. Between 1946 and 1987, Italian voters had at their disposal between three and four preference votes (depending on the size of the constituency). In 1992 they had one preference vote. In the three national elections in 1994, 1996 and 2001, three-quarters of the constituencies were single-member. In 2006, 2008 and 2013, the lists were closed and PR was used plus a majority bonus for the winning coalition, which meant that approximately 15 or 20 per cent of parliamentarians had practically no relationship with the voters. In 2018 it was

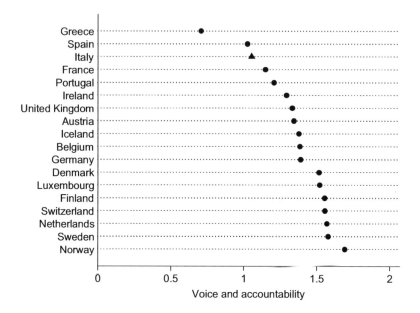

Figure 9.4   Voice and accountability in eighteen West European democracies, 2017

Note: Estimate of governance measured on a scale from approximately −2.5 to 2.5. Higher values correspond to better governance.

Source: Author's own compilation based on data provided by World Bank (http://info. worldbank.org/governance/wgi/index.aspx#home).

even worse (see Chapter 2). When no relationship is established between parliamentarians and voters, it becomes impossible to have and to enforce any kind of accountability. Moreover, the absence of any residency requirement means that powerful politicians have decided to be candidates in safe constituencies and that powerful parliamentarians choose the constituencies where they have more chance of winning the seat. They have no incentive to be accountable to the voters who elected them since they may not be re-selected a second time in that specific constituency. Electoral accountability has a poor and nasty life in Italy. It affects the entire political accountability loop in a crucially negative way.

The power of the people – that is, directly exercised by the people – has found its expression through two traditional instruments and, more recently, a third ensemble of mechanisms and procedures. The two instruments are the referendum and the recall. The ensemble is offered by the practices of participatory and/or deliberative democracy (for an excellent reconstruction of the ideas leading to this type of democracy, see Floridia 2017). The recall does not exist in the Italian Constitution nor in the electoral rules at any level. However, the introduction of the recall is one of the requests of the Five Star Movement in their march away from parliamentary democracy towards what they call direct democracy. No details are provided. As for deliberative democracy, some bits and pieces, especially in the drafting of shared budgets, have made their appearance at the local level, but not enough to allow scholars and practitioners to draw some general considerations or lessons. On the whole, there is fundamentally no public debate devoted to deliberative democracy.

Following Switzerland and Australia (as well as California, if one equates propositions with referendums), Italy has been the parliamentary democracy where there has been the most frequent resort to popular referendums following approval in 1970 of the law that defines their procedures. There are two types of referendum in Italy. One type is utilized when constitutional reforms are submitted to the voters. A plurality is sufficient to reject or to ratify reforms approved by an absolute majority of Italian parliamentarians (the most recent instance, a true watershed, took place on 4 December 2016). The other type of referendum applies to all existing laws, which can be repealed in full or in part provided that at least 50 per cent plus one of the registered voters go to the polls. Italian referendums perform two highly democratic tasks. On the one hand, they are instruments through which the people exercise the power to choose among clear alternatives: to keep an existing law or to repeal it. On the other hand, referendums are a sort of sword of Damocles serving the purpose of threatening power holders and lawmakers for what they may want to do or have done.

There can be little doubt that, on the whole, Italian voters have fully appreciated the possibility of resorting to the referendum to repeal laws approved by Parliament (the best comparative analysis remains Uleri 2003; see also Qvortrup 2018). Indeed, because of the existence of this specific type of referendum, all parliamentarians quickly became aware that they were going to be considered accountable for the legislation they had drafted and approved. Since May 1974, sixty-seven referendums have been held in Italy. Thirty-nine have seen the participation of more than half of the Italian voters; twenty-eight failed because the participation rate was below 50 per cent. The voters succeeded in repealing twenty-three laws and rejected the request to repeal the law in sixteen cases. Table 9.2 provides a wealth of information on the number of referendums, turnout and rate of success.

Table 9.2 Frequency of popular referendums in Italy, 1946–2018

	Number	Average turnout (%)	No. majority in favour: yes vote	No. majority against: no vote	Average yes (%)	Average no (%)
Quorum achieved	39	67.6	23	16	60.8	39.2
Quorum not achieved	28	31.1	27	1	78.7	21.3
Total	67	52.4	50	17	68.3	31.7

Although Italian politicians, as well as the media, often complain that there have been too many referendums, it is fair to say that the Italian referendum has tended to play a positive, even progressive, role in the Italian political system. Nevertheless, when it comes to political accountability, one cannot deny that frequently all the politicians have attempted to dodge their accountability for the laws they have sponsored and approved or for their unwillingness and/or inability to resolve existing laws that are no longer adequate. In order to avoid the "judgment of the people", many politicians have cunningly resorted to encouraging Italian voters to abstain[11] in order to invalidate the referendum: a very bad practice. It is debatable whether non-voting in a referendum might be considered fully legitimate according to Article 48 of the Constitution, which states that voting is a "civic duty". In practice, non-voting has been a meaningful and influential behaviour, in sixteen cases successfully leading to the survival of a specific law. But non-voting has also meant that the politicians who drafted or were supporting a law have been able to evade accountability at no cost just by encouraging the voters not to go to the polls and/or seconding those voters' already existing inclination to abstain.[12] Adding the flight from referendum accountability to the quasi-impossible electoral accountability leads to a situation in which Italian citizens and voters are more than justified when they declare that their elected representatives could not care less about their opinions or needs.

The 50 per cent turnout requirement has been repeatedly criticized because it is too easy to manipulate. In fact, the effort required from the opponents of a specific referendum is not Herculean. They have to convince 30–35 per cent of the voters to add their abstentions to those 20–25 per cent of voters who already habitually no longer go to the polls. The turnout requirement was finally tackled in the 2016 governmental package of constitutional reforms. The proposal was that, whenever the promoters of the referendum proved able to collect 800,000 signatures (a rather high threshold), the required turnout would drop to 50 per cent plus one of those who had voted in the previous national elections. Although not central to the constitutional reform package, this change fell together with all the other more controversial reforms.

Both elections and referendums are meant to allow citizens to pass judgment on what those in the government and those in the opposition have done, have not done or have done poorly. According to Powell (2000), elections are instruments of accountability. Electoral accountability in the Italian case appears to be close to zero for parliamentarians. "Appointed" by their party and faction leaders, all parliamentarians are fully aware that their re-selection will not depend on how satisfactorily they serve the needs and represent the preferences of the voters of their constituency;[13] rather, it will be the consequence of an evaluation based on unknown, less than transparent and expedient criteria made on their behaviour by party and faction leaders. Again, I must stress that a close relationship between voters and parliamentarians is practically impossible to establish and to make work, especially because the existing Rosato electoral law allows candidates to stand in one single-member district plus up to five constituencies. In fact, Italian Parliamentarians have *zero* electoral accountability; this also explains their wide freedom of action in moving from one parliamentary group to another, reviving the old, but never cherished nor appreciated by voters, practice of *trasformismo* (Valbruzzi 2015). Since party and faction leaders do not want in the least to be deprived of the power to choose and appoint "their" parliamentarians, accountability has not figured at all in any motivation concerning how to formulate electoral laws. To conclude, on the basis of how elections are run and how referendums work in Italy, and of how much power Italian voters *really* hold and can bring to bear on their parliamentary representatives and the issues, it is fair to state that the overall lack of political accountability is probably the most important factor negatively affecting the quality of Italian democracy.

The third element in Lincoln's definition of democracy, "government for the people", is extremely significant. In the Marxian terminology, it signals the transition from formal democracy to substantial democracy, from a democracy based on rules and procedures to a democracy capable of providing goods for citizens. I would go even further: the conceptual and practical transition takes place from liberal democracy to social democracy. Fundamentally, when Lincoln said that the government is "for the people" he had in mind a democracy capable not just of making decisions without granting any specific or undue advantage to some citizens, groups or associations, but equipped to perform "for the people", willing to successfully operate for the welfare of citizens. On this matter, contemporary scholars are quite fortunate because, thanks to the United Nations, an excellent set of indicators is available to provide for a convincing evaluation of the performance of all political regimes, and hence also of the quality of their democracy. The Human Development Index (HDI) does exactly this (see Figure 9.5). Combining indicators regarding life expectancy, level of education and per capita income, the HDI offers the possibility of comparing the performance of many countries over a long period of time. On the whole, Italy's score, though not brilliant in comparison with many West

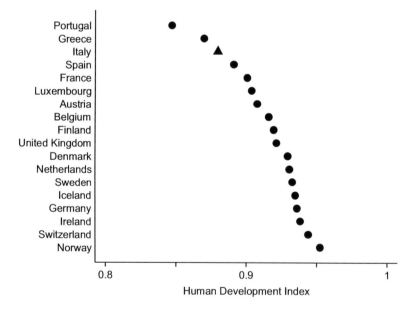

Figure 9.5   Human Development Index in eighteen West European democracies, 2018

Note: The Human Development Index (HDI) is a summary measure of average achievement in key dimensions of human development: a long and healthy life, being knowledgeable and having a decent standard of living. The HDI is the geometric mean of normalized indices for each of the three dimensions. Higher values correspond to better performance.

Source: Author's own compilation based on data provided by the United Nations (http://hdr.undp.org/en/content/human-development-index-hdi).

European democracies, is respectable. In 1975, Italy was ranked twentieth (with a score of 0.845); in 2016, twenty-sixth (0.887). The highest scores belonged to Norway, at 0.949, followed by Australia and Switzerland at 0.939. This ranking can be taken to confirm that unstable Italian governments but stable policies have generally performed satisfactorily in the fields of health, education and income.

Overall performance

In a way, the HDI measures in a convincing way the performance of various regimes over time. But even though democracy is, indeed, "government for the people", no people is necessarily fully satisfied with the provision of coveted goods. Emotions and feelings must come into play when evaluating the quality of a democracy. I started this chapter by saying that, in view of the difficulties scholars have in arriving at a shared and convincing definition of the quality of democracy, it will be the task of the beholders, those who look more or less closely at their democracy, to do so. We are fortunate to have data collected by Eurobarometer since 1973. Figure 9.6 indicates that, most

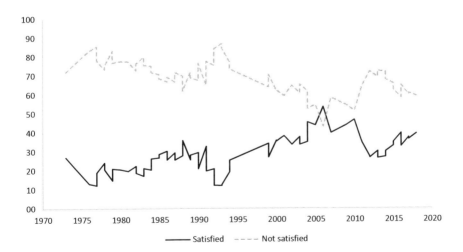

Figure 9.6 Satisfaction with the working of Italian democracy, 1973–2018 (percentage)

Note: Satisfied = Very satisfied + Fairly satisfied; Not satisfied = Not very satisfied + Not at all satisfied.

Source: Author's own compilation based on data provided by Eurobarometer.

of the time, a considerable majority of Italians have declared that they are more dissatisfied than satisfied with the working of their democracy. Only in 2006 did the satisfied exceed the dissatisfied. I venture to say that perhaps this was because the centre-left coalition led by Prodi had defeated the incumbent Berlusconi. By 2018, the gap between the dissatisfied and the satisfied was about 20 percentage points or slightly more. This was largely translated into significant numbers of votes for the Five Star Movement and the League.

In Table 9.3 one can find comparative percentages derived from the answers to the questions "How would you judge the current situation in your country?" and "Are you satisfied with the way democracy works in the European Union?" Italy fares very poorly. Indeed, the performance of the country is evaluated in a negative way by a massive 74 per cent of Italians.

Understandably, there have been several variations over time, appropriately reflecting the changing evaluations by Italian citizens due in part to real changes in the government of the country. Also, I tend to believe that with the passing of time many Italian citizens have become better informed on the functioning of other European democracies, especially those with which they consider it appropriate to compare their own country. However, it is impossible to tell whether Italian citizens have become more demanding or more resigned to the way their democracy works during this period. The numbers who gradually but increasingly abstain from voting suggest

Table 9.3 Citizens' evaluations of their own country's situation and of democracy in the EU, 2017 (percentage)

	Your country		European Union	
	Bad/very bad	Good/very good	Fairly/very satisfied	Not very/not at all satisfied
Italy	74	24	41	47
France	58	39	45	45
Spain	57	22	48	43
United Kingdom	48	46	40	45
Germany	18	81	50	44
Sweden	16	84	52	40
EU average	48	50	48	42

Source: Author's own compilation based on data provided by Eurobarometer.

that some resignation bordering on alienation may be at work. Or perhaps there is another explanation that finds its justification in the data collected and analysed by Eurostat: the fact that, in 2018, more than two-thirds of Italians stated that they were satisfied with the life they led (68 per cent satisfied versus 31 per cent dissatisfied). However, in comparative perspective, Italian citizens are well below the average European (83 per cent satisfied versus 17 per cent dissatisfied) as well as the Spanish (83 per cent versus 17 per cent), the French (85 per cent versus 15 per cent), the British and Germans (both 93 per cent versus 7 per cent) and the Swedes (94 per cent versus 6 per cent). I believe that, among other things, it is appropriate to infer from these percentages that politics matters. If the quality of politics is poor, it negatively affects citizens' lives.

Returning to the factors influencing the quality of a democracy, Table 9.4 offers relevant data regarding political rights and civil liberties. In comparative perspective, the overall score for Italy is less than satisfactory, but, on the other hand, it is not totally disconcerting. In Italy there still prevails an inclination on the part of civil servants of

Table 9.4   Political rights and civil liberties in the countries of the EU

	Political rights	*Civil liberties*	*Overall score*
Finland	40	60	100
Norway	40	60	100
Sweden	40	60	100
Netherlands	40	59	99
Luxembourg	38	60	98
Denmark	40	57	97
Portugal	39	58	97
Ireland	39	57	96
Switzerland	39	57	96
Belgium	39	56	95
Iceland	37	58	95
Austria	37	57	94
Germany	39	55	94
Spain	38	56	94
United Kingdom	40	54	94
France	38	52	90
Italy	36	53	89
Greece	35	50	85

Source: Author's own compilation based on data provided by Freedom House (https://free domhouse.org/).

all types to deal with Italian citizens in a rather cavalier and haughty manner; it is as if what citizens believe is their due, civil servants consider an act of kindness on their part, almost a "gift". This kind of attitude – which, of course, is never exhibited towards the upper classes or powerful members of Italian society – significantly contributes to the diffusion and permanence of anti-political beliefs and sentiments among the public at large, and these feelings are easily extended to criticisms of democracy as such.

Not only are the Freedom House data fundamentally reliable, they also encourage comparisons over time and among various democratic countries.[14] The 2018 report locates Italy in a good position among the countries defined "free". Political rights and civil liberties receive the highest score, but somewhat surprisingly Italy obtains an aggregate score of 89 (100 being the maximum attained). In any case, this is a truly satisfactory result, which, nevertheless, most observers of Italian politics would consider somewhat too flattering when compared with the status of contemporary Italian democracy.

It is not the end

To improve the quality of Italian democracy, or at least to prevent its further degeneration, some politicians and scholars have engaged in the difficult task of formulating electoral and institutional reforms.[15] I will leave aside here the amount of expediency that has motivated several politicians and the degree of narcissism exhibited by too many scholars. I am fully convinced that a better electoral law could be found, one that would be capable of positively influencing the behaviour of the political class, increasing its credibility in chastising civil society while accepting full responsibility for what it does, and encouraging its willingness to work for the future by taking risks in formulating and implementing innovative policies that will result in improvements to Italian democracy, but I do not see it happening any time soon. It remains a daunting, but not impossible, task. Whether the energies, the knowledge or the capabilities needed to produce major transformations exist in Italy at this point in time is a difficult question to answer.[16] Tentatively, my educated guess would be that the signals of a positive transformation are unlikely to appear on the horizon in the foreseeable future.

In conclusion, Italian democracy is obviously not on the verge of collapse, no matter who governs. But, most certainly, who governs makes a difference to the quality of life and the quality of democracy.

Nor is Italian democracy on the road towards positive transformations or significant improvements. All things considered, Italian democracy does not thrive, but it is not true to say that it simply survives. Experiencing many difficulties and having to overcome several obstacles, enjoying good periods and suffering through bad phases, Italian democracy continues to perform, though less than satisfactorily and below the expectations of a composite majority of its citizens, as well as below its and their potentialities. It is a democracy of modest quality. One may formulate something that is more than just a hypothesis: the overall performance of the Italian democratic political system is negatively affected not only by the behaviour of its political class, but also by the actions of a significant number of citizens who do not fulfil their duties and of too many associations that still follow the principles of amoral corporatism. There is no crisis of democracy in Italy, but there are many problems and shortcomings affecting the way in which politics and democracy work. None of them will be easily overcome.[17]

Notes

1 Needless to say, the losers who refuse to accept electoral results are responsible for persistent conflicts and tensions that negatively affect the quality of a democracy. On this central issue, see the important study by Anderson, Blais, Bowler et al. (2005).

2 I have often argued the case for the transformation of the Italian parliamentary democracy, the most similar regime to the French Fourth Republic (1946–58), into a semi-presidential Republic similar to the one designed by the French Fifth Republic (Pasquino 2010). Although most certainly not enjoying widespread support, this proposal remains alive.

3 The overall evaluation can be found at www.istat.it/it/files/2016/12/Indica tori-del-benessere.pdf.

4 A major trial in July 2018 came to the conclusion that, in the early 1990s, top state representatives and some influential politicians decided to negotiate with Sicilian Mafia bosses. Perhaps the best works on the Mafia are the many novels by the Sicilian writer Leonardo Sciascia (1921–89), for instance *The Day of the Owl*, and, for the Camorra, the best-selling book by the Neapolitan Roberto Saviano (2006), from which an excellent movie *Gomorra* was made. Since the publication of his book, Saviano has been obliged to live under escort.

5 In August 2013, the former Prime Minister Silvio Berlusconi was convicted of financial fraud. The former President of the Region of Sicily, Salvatore Cuffaro, served four years (2011–15) after having been found

guilty of having ties with the Mafia. Forza Italia Senator Marcello Dell'Utri has been sentenced to twelve years for having favoured Mafia activities. The former President of the Veneto Region, and a minister several times, Giancarlo Galan, has been convicted of political corruption. The same applies to the former President of the Lombardy Region and Senator Roberto Formigoni. Forza Italia undersecretary Nicola Cosentino has been convicted of fraud and ties with the Camorra in Campania. Forza Italia Senator Denis Verdini has been convicted of fraud and of the bankruptcy of a bank of which he was the president.

6 Of course, one could achieve a fruitful comparative analysis within the field of parliamentary democracies, as I have attempted to do (Pasquino 2007; see also Magone 2015).

7 Here I adopt and adapt the categories elaborated by Verba, Schlozman and Brady (1995) and utilized to explain (the absence of) political participation in the USA.

8 The distinction between diffuse and specific support was formulated by Easton (1965). It neatly captures the substance and meaning of important variations in public opinion.

9 Then, of course, but only then, one may also want to know whether the citizens' voice has had an impact on the decisions taken by the power holders.

10 As already explained in Chapter 2, the Rosato law used for the March 2018 elections automatically translates the vote given to a candidate to the coalition supporting that candidate, and vice versa, deliberately making the voters' voice quite weak.

11 This is a complex story that must be told and remembered. Prime Minister Craxi, in 1985, was the first to entertain the idea of inviting voters not to go to the polls, but in the end he decided not to do so and won the watershed referendum on the indexation system. Then, in 1991, non-voting was the message sent not only by Craxi but by all the leaders of the *pentapartito* coalition plus the Neo-Fascist Gianfranco Fini and the leader of the Northern League, Umberto Bossi. The call was rejected by 62.5 per cent of voters for the referendum on the single preference vote. All the referendums in 1993 enjoyed a significant turnout, but then all subsequent referendums on electoral issues failed. Another referendum that failed was the one to repeal the law on "assisted reproduction", which was making it extremely difficult. In June 2005, Cardinal Camillo Ruini, president of the Conference of Italian Bishops, joined by the centre-right, openly campaigned for non-voting. Only 25 per cent of Italians went to the polls (I did) because the issue was both very controversial and very complex.

12 The poorly drafted and highly controversial law on medically assisted reproduction contained many clauses inimical to women's health. Piece by piece, it has been almost completely dismantled by the Constitutional Court.

13 The comparison between the behaviour of US Congressmen and UK Members of Parliament, analysed by Cain, Ferejohn and Fiorina (1987), with what occurs in Italy in terms of political accountability is especially telling.

14 Unfortunately, Lijphart (2012: Appendix) does not utilize the wealth of data he has collected to come to an overall ranking of the thirty-six countries he analyses, and in which Italy is included but misclassified among the consensual democracies.

15 Curiously, while Lijphart (2012) gives a highly positive evaluation of so-called "consensus" democracies, which in truth ought to be called "proportional", Italy having been one of them from 1946 to 1992 and from 2006 to the present, quite a number of Italian politicians, the mass media and the majority of political commentators and pundits advocate the construction of a bipolar, majoritarian democracy.

16 Perhaps, it is high time not only to ask whether the quality of democracy can be improved by institutional and constitutional reforms, but also to ask by which principle those reforms should be inspired and according to which criteria they should be evaluated. Or are constitutional reforms just a game Italian politicians have played, aiming at the manipulation of public opinion for their own political success and personal prestige? The outcome of the December 2016 referendum suggests that the most recent manipulative effort has been resoundingly rejected, but such attempts are bound to resurface sooner or later. My preferences are argued in Pasquino (2015).

17 I have come to a conclusion similar to the one reached in his excellent study by Capussela (2018). Admittedly, I have fewer illusions on the (near) future.

References

Altman, D. and Pérez-Liñán, A. (2002). Assessing the Quality of Democracy: Freedom, Competitiveness and Participation in Eighteen Latin American Countries. *Democratization* 9 (2), pp. 85–100.

Anderson, C. J., Blais, A., Bowler, S., Donovan, T. and Listhaug, O. (2005). *Losers' Consent: Elections and Democratic Legitimacy*. Oxford: Oxford University Press.

Cain, B., Ferejohn, J. and Fiorina, M. (1987). *The Personal Vote: Constituency Service and Electoral Independence*. Cambridge: Harvard University Press.

Capussela, A. L. (2018). *The Political Economy of Italy's Decline*. Oxford: Oxford University Press.

della Porta, D. and Vannucci, A. (1999). *Corrupt Exchanges: Actors, Resources, and Mechanisms of Political Corruption*. London: Routledge.

Di Palma, G. (1990). *To Craft Democracies. An Essay on Democratic Transitions*. Berkeley and Los Angeles: University of California Press.

Easton, D. (1965). *A Systems Analysis of Political Life*. New York, London and Sydney: John Wiley and Sons.

Fabbri, M. and Diani, M. (2015). Social movement campaigns from global justice activism to the Movimento Cinque Stelle. In A. Mammone, E. Giap Parini and G. A. Veltri (eds) *The Routledge Handbook of Contemporary Italy* (pp. 225–236). London: Routledge.

Floridia, A. (2017). *From Participation to Deliberation: A Critical Genealogy of Deliberative Democracy*. Colchester: European Consortium for Political Research Press.

Fukuyama, F. (2014). *Political Order and Political Decay: From the Industrial Revolution to the Globalization of Democracy*. New York: Farrar, Straus & Giroux.

Hine, D. (2015). Public Ethics and Political Corruption in Italy. In E. Jones and G. Pasquino (eds) *The Oxford Handbook of Italian Politics* (pp. 608–620). Oxford: Oxford University Press.

Hirschman, A. O. (1970). *Exit, Voice, Loyalty: Responses to Decline in Firms, Organizations and States*. Cambridge: Harvard University Press.

Huntington, S. P. (1968). *Political Order in Changing Societies*. New Haven and London: Yale University Press.

ITANES. (2013). *Voto amaro: Disincanto e crisi economica nelle elezioni del 2013*. Bologna: Il Mulino.

ITANES. (2018). *Vox populi: Il voto ad alta voce del 2018*. Bologna: Il Mulino.

Lijphart, A. (2012). *Patterns of Democracy: Government Forms and Performance in Thirty-Six Countries*. New Haven and London: Yale University Press.

Magone, J. M. (ed.) (2015). *Routledge Handbook of European Politics*. London and New York: Routledge.

Morlino, L., Piana, D. and Raniolo, F. (eds) (2013). *La qualità della democrazia in Italia*. Bologna: Il Mulino.

Newell, J. L. (2019) *Silvio Berlusconi: A Study in Failure*. Manchester: Manchester University Press.

Paoli, L. (ed.) (2014). *Oxford Handbook of Organized Crime*. Oxford: Oxford University Press.

Paoli, L. (2015). Mafia, Camorra, and 'Ndrangheta. In E. Jones and G. Pasquino (eds) *The Oxford Handbook of Italian Politics* (pp. 668–681). Oxford: Oxford University Press.

Aux urnes, citoyens! (2013). *Paradoxa*. VII (1), January/March.

Pasquino, G. (2007). *Sistemi politici comparati*. Bologna: Bononia University Press.

Pasquino, G. (2010). Una Repubblica da imitare? In G. Pasquino and S. Ventura (eds) *Una splendida cinquantenne: la Quinta Repubblica francese* (pp. 249–281). Bologna: Il Mulino.

Pasquino, G. (2015). *Cittadini senza scettro: Le riforme sbagliate*. Milan: Egea-UniBocconi.

Powell, G. B., Jr. (2000). *Elections as Instruments of Democracy: Majoritarian and Proportional Visions*. New Haven and London: Yale University Press.

Qvortrup, M. (2018). *Government by Referendum*. Manchester: Manchester University Press.

Ragsdale, L. and Rusk, J. G. (2017). *The American Non-Voter*. Oxford: Oxford University Press.

Rhodes, M. (2015). Tangentopoli – More than 20 Years On. In E. Jones and G. Pasquino (eds) *The Oxford Handbook of Italian Politics* (pp. 309–324). Oxford: Oxford University Press.

Ringen, S. (2011). The Measurement of Democracy: Towards a New Paradigm. *Society* 48 (1), pp. 12–16.

Ruzza, C. (2017) Social Movements and Italian Civil Society in Times of Crisis. In A. Grasse, M. Grimm and J. Labitzke (eds) *Italien zwischen Krise und Aufbruch: Reformen und Reformversuche der Regierung Renzi* (pp. 207–227). Wiesbaden: Springer.

Sartori, G. (1987). *The Theory of Democracy Revisited*. Chatham: Chatham House Publishers.

Saviano, R. (2006). *Gomorra: Viaggio nell'impero economico e nel sogno di dominio della camorra*. Milan: Mondadori.

Uleri, P. (2003). *Referendum e democrazia: Una prospettiva comparata*. Bologna: Il Mulino.

Valbruzzi, M. (2015). Trasformismo. In E. Jones and G. Pasquino (eds) *The Oxford Handbook of Italian Politics* (pp. 26–40). Oxford: Oxford University Press.

Valbruzzi, M. (2016). L'alternanza e la qualità della democrazia. In A. Panebianco (ed.) *Una certa idea di scienza politica: Saggi in onore di Gianfranco Pasquino* (pp. 57–82). Bologna: Il Mulino.

Varese, F. (2017). *Vita di mafia: Amore, morte e denaro nel cuore del crimine organizzato*. Turin: Einaudi.

Verba, S., Schlozman, L. and Brady, H. E. (1995). *Voice and Equality: Civic Voluntarism and American Politics*. Cambridge: Harvard University Press.

Index